P9-CDP-000

GREEN AND BLACK ARROW CANARY

741.5 GRE
Bedard, Tony.
Green Arrow and Black
Canary :   road to the altar /

Road to the Altar

PALM BEACH COUNTY
LIBRARY SYSTEM
3650 .... RD.
DISCARD
WEST PALM BEACH, FLORIDA 33406

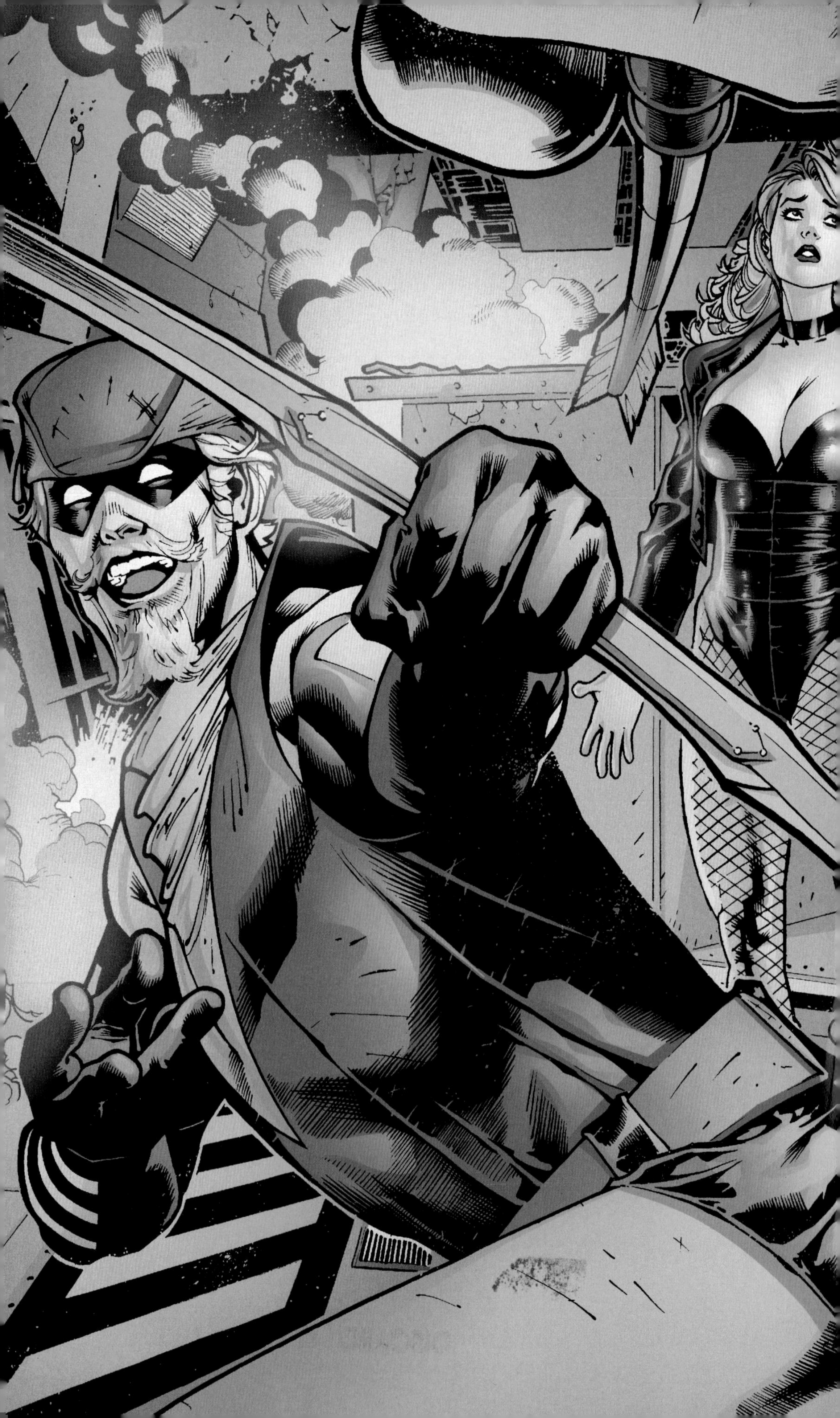

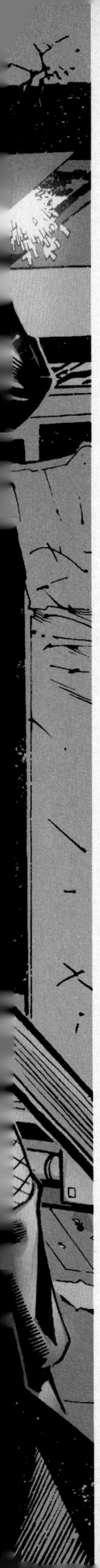

Green Arrow and Black Canary

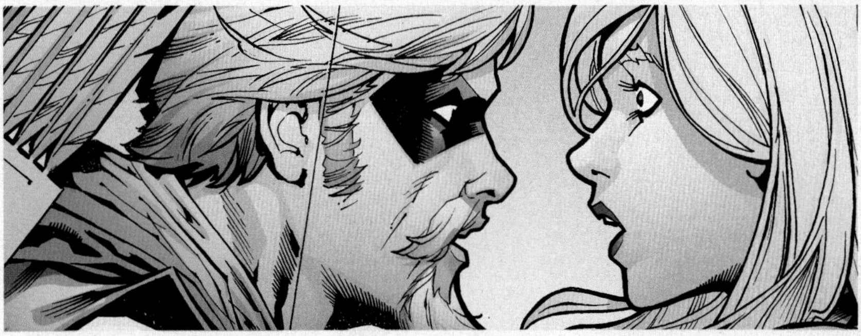

Road to the Altar

Tony Bedard
J. Torres
Writers

Paulo Siqueira
Lee Ferguson
Tom Derenick
Nicola Scott
Christine Norrie
Joe Prado
Pencillers

Amilton Santos
Karl Story
Rodney Ramos
Doug Hazlewood
Christine Norrie
Joe Prado
Inkers

Mike Norton
Additional Layouts

I.L.L.
Tanya & Richard Horie
Hi-Fi Designs
Colorists

Pat Brosseau
Travis Lanham
Jared K. Fletcher
Letterers

Paulo Siqueira & Amilton Santos with David Baron
Stephane Roux
Original Cover Artists

"Proposal" sequence by
Judd Winick, Scott McDaniel & Andy Owens

Dan DiDio Senior VP-Executive Editor

Mike Carlin Jann Jones Editors-original series

Tom Palmer Jr. Associate Editor-original series

Elisabeth V. Gehrlein Adam Schlagman Assistant Editors-original series

Anton Kawasaki Editor-collected edition

Robbin Brosterman Senior Art Director

Paul Levitz President & Publisher

Georg Brewer VP-Design & DC Direct Creative

Richard Bruning Senior VP-Creative Director

Patrick Caldon Executive VP-Finance & Operations

Chris Caramalis VP-Finance

John Cunningham VP-Marketing

Terri Cunningham VP-Managing Editor

Alison Gill VP-Manufacturing

David Hyde VP-Publicity

Hank Kanalz VP-General Manager, WildStorm

Jim Lee Editorial Director-WildStorm

Paula Lowitt Senior VP-Business & Legal Affairs

MaryEllen McLaughlin VP-Advertising & Custom Publishing

John Nee Senior VP-Business Development

Gregory Noveck Senior VP-Creative Affairs

Sue Pohja VP-Book Trade Sales

Steve Rotterdam Senior VP- Sales & Marketing

Cheryl Rubin Senior VP-Brand Management

Jeff Trojan VP-Business Development, DC Direct

Bob Wayne VP-Sales

GREEN ARROW/BLACK CANARY: ROAD TO THE ALTAR

Published by DC Comics. Cover and compilation Copyright © 2008 DC Comics. All Rights Reserved.

Originally published in single magazine form as: GREEN ARROW #75, BIRDS OF PREY #109, BLACK CANARY #1-4, BLACK CANARY WEDDING SPECIAL #1 Copyright © 2007 DC Comics. All Rights Reserved. All characters, their distinctive likenesses and related elements featured in this publication are trademarks of DC Comics. The stories, characters and incidents featured in this publication are entirely fictional. DC Comics does not read or accept unsolicited submissions of ideas, stories or artwork.

DC Comics, 1700 Broadway, New York, NY 10019
A Warner Bros. Entertainment Company
Printed in Canada. First Printing.
ISBN: 978-1-4012-1863-8

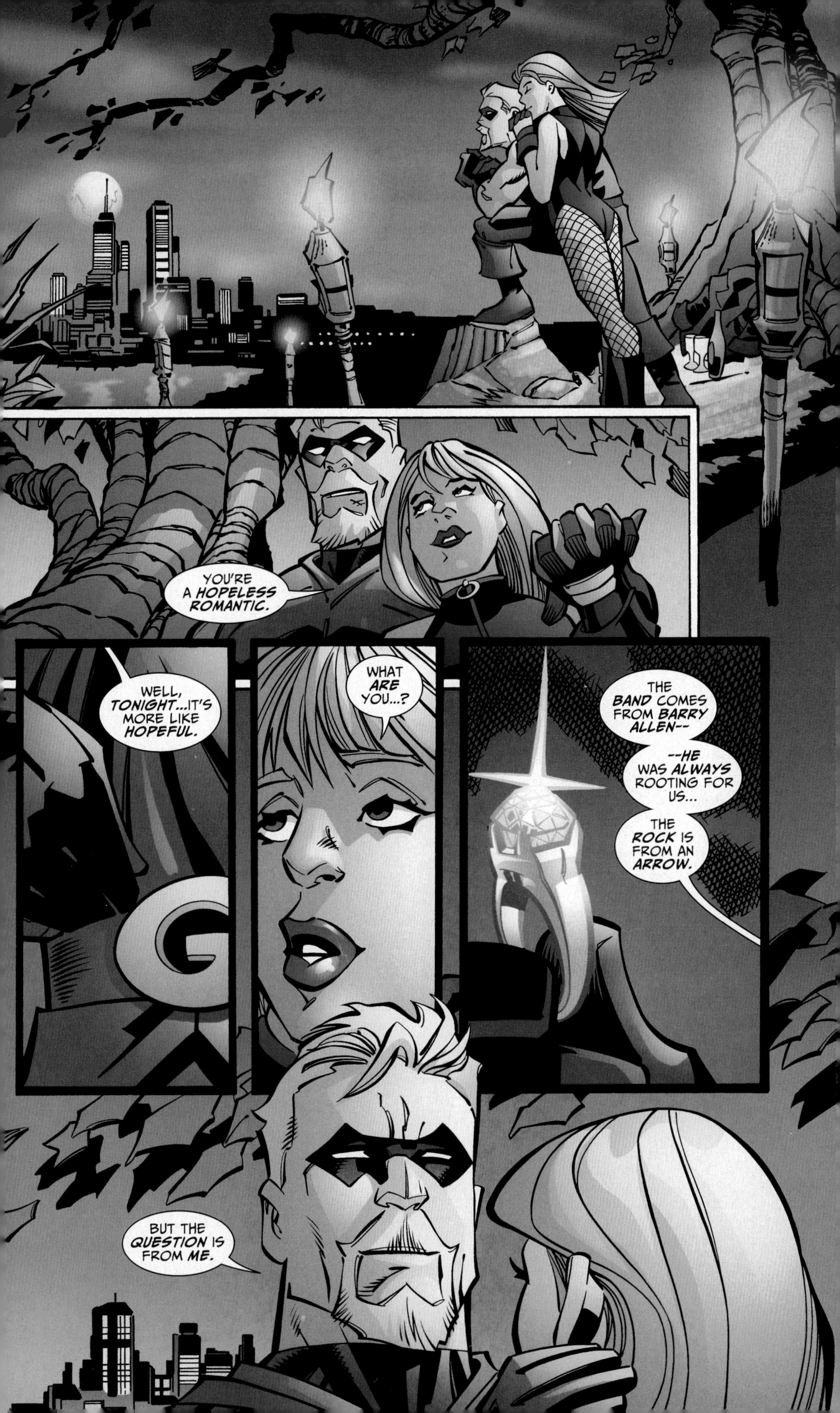
YOU'RE A HOPELESS ROMANTIC.
WELL, TONIGHT...IT'S MORE LIKE HOPEFUL.
WHAT ARE YOU...?
THE BAND COMES FROM BARRY ALLEN--
--HE WAS ALWAYS ROOTING FOR US...
THE ROCK IS FROM AN ARROW.
BUT THE QUESTION IS FROM ME.

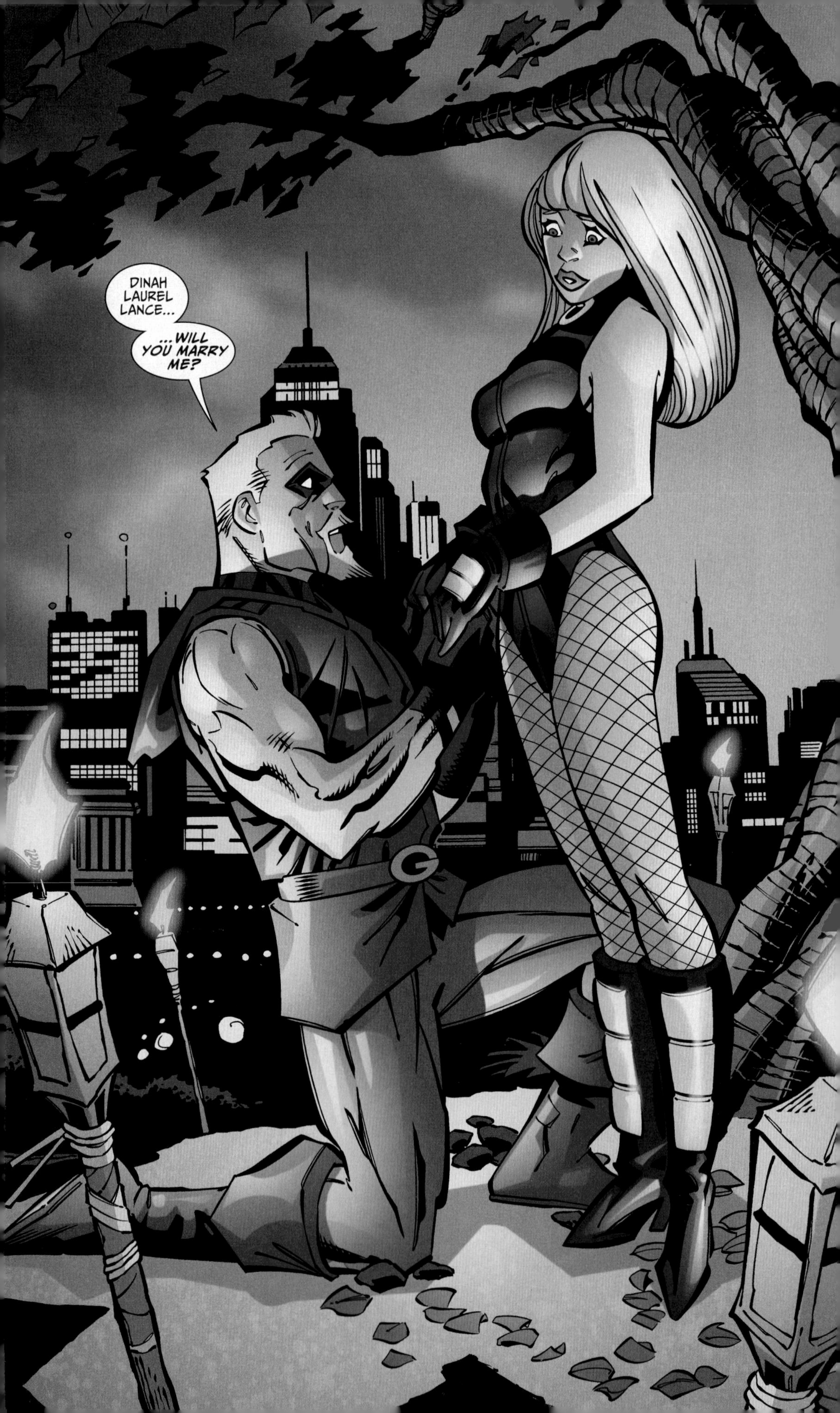
DINAH LAUREL LANCE...
...WILL YOU MARRY ME?

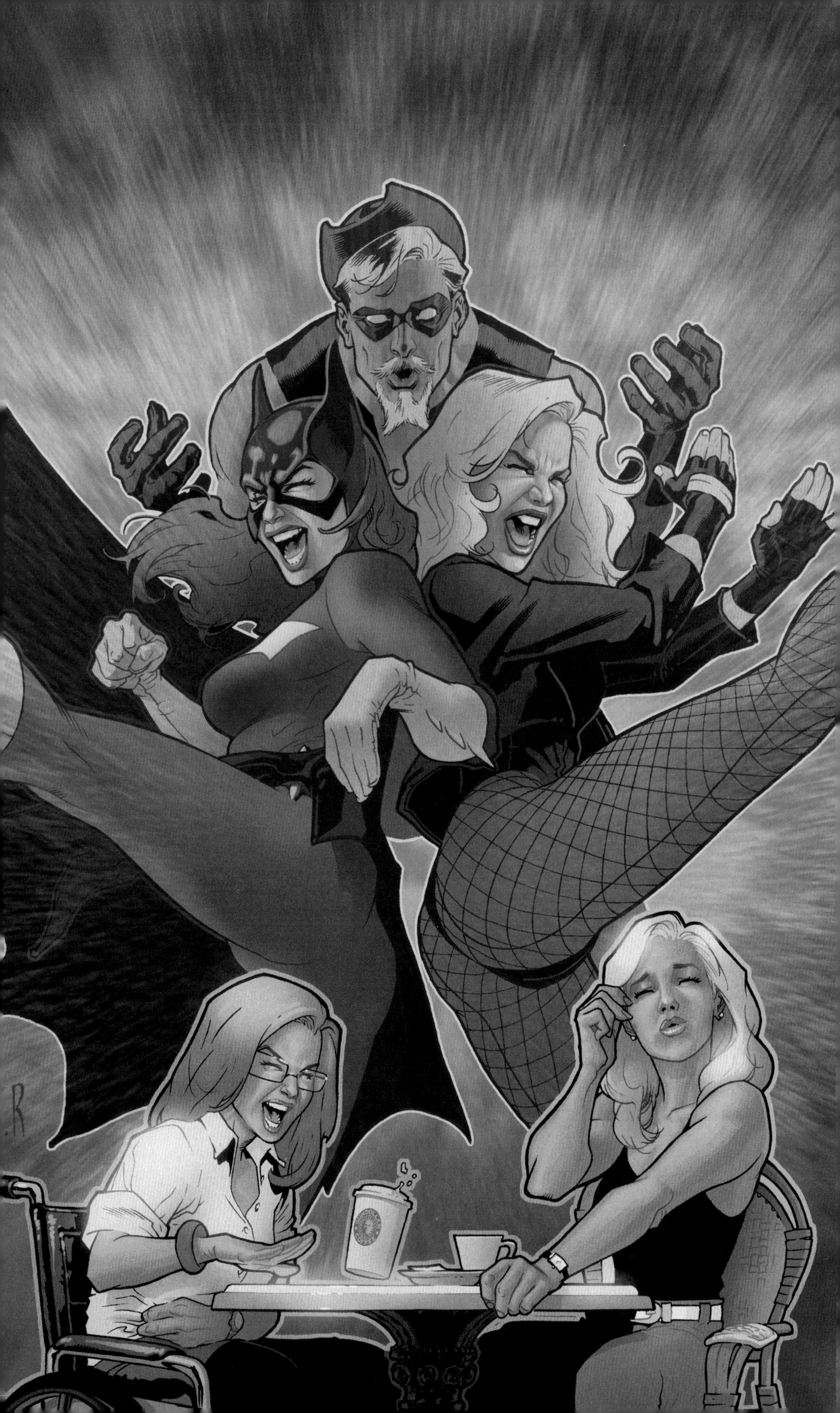

BIRDS OF PREY #109

TONY BEDARD
WRITER

NICOLA SCOTT
PENCILLER

DOUG HAZLEWOOD
INKER

HI-FI DESIGNS
COLORIST

TRAVIS LANHAM
LETTERER

STEPHANE ROUX
COVER

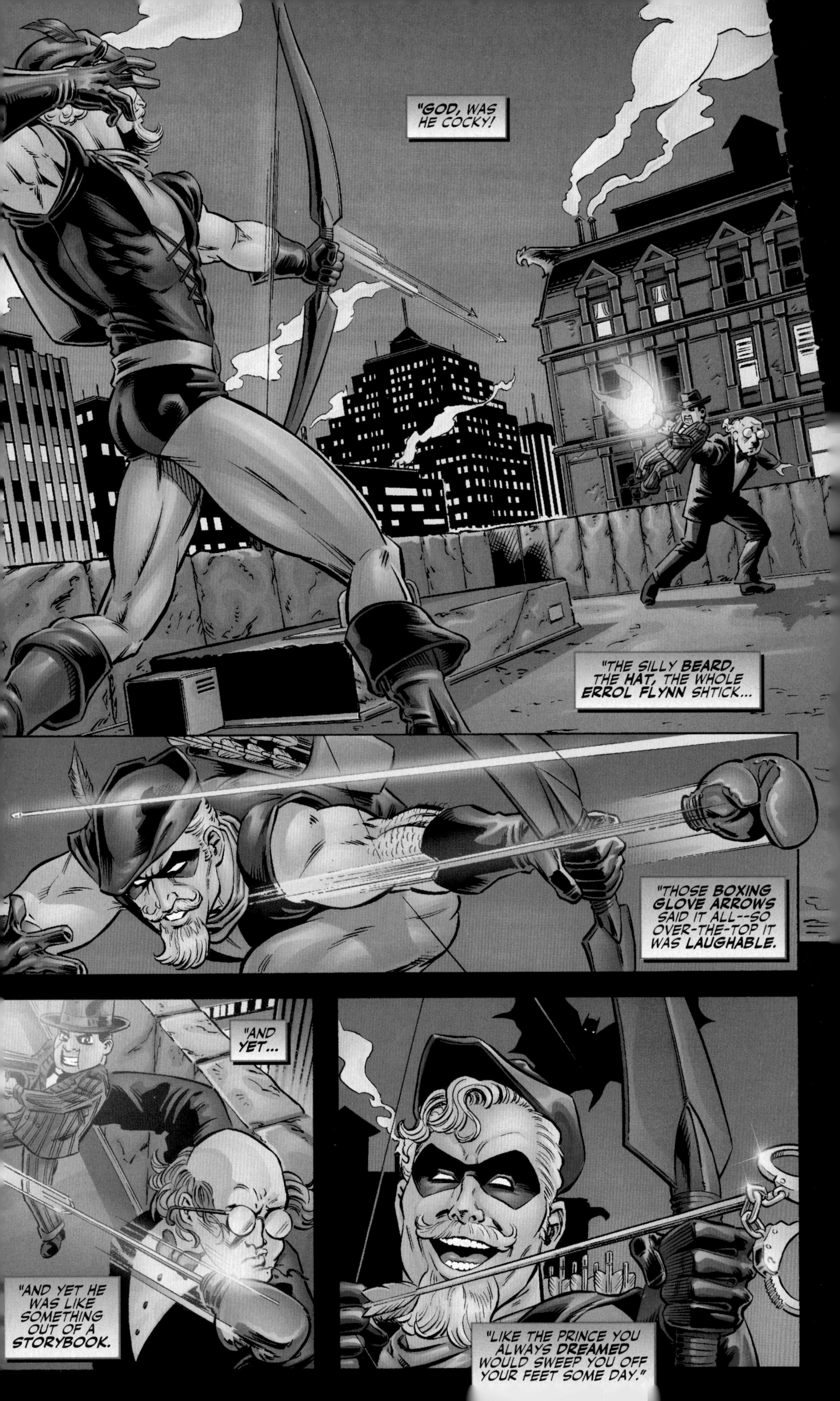
"GOD, WAS HE COCKY!
"THE SILLY BEARD, THE HAT, THE WHOLE ERROL FLYNN SHTICK...
"THOSE BOXING GLOVE ARROWS SAID IT ALL--SO OVER-THE-TOP IT WAS LAUGHABLE.
"AND YET...
"AND YET HE WAS LIKE SOMETHING OUT OF A STORYBOOK.
"LIKE THE PRINCE YOU ALWAYS DREAMED WOULD SWEEP YOU OFF YOUR FEET SOME DAY."

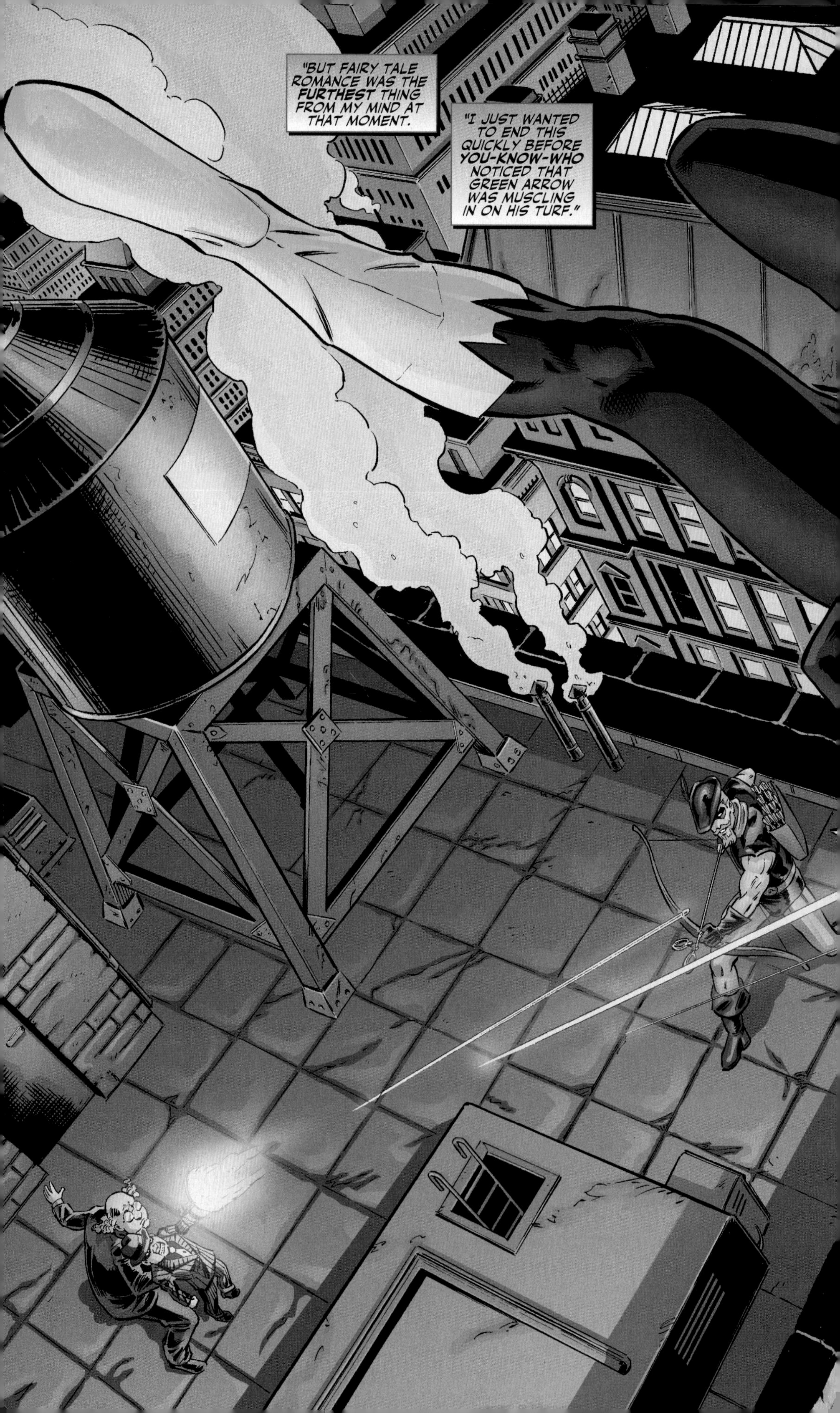
"BUT FAIRY TALE ROMANCE WAS THE FURTHEST THING FROM MY MIND AT THAT MOMENT.
"I JUST WANTED TO END THIS QUICKLY BEFORE YOU-KNOW-WHO NOTICED THAT GREEN ARROW WAS MUSCLING IN ON HIS TURF."

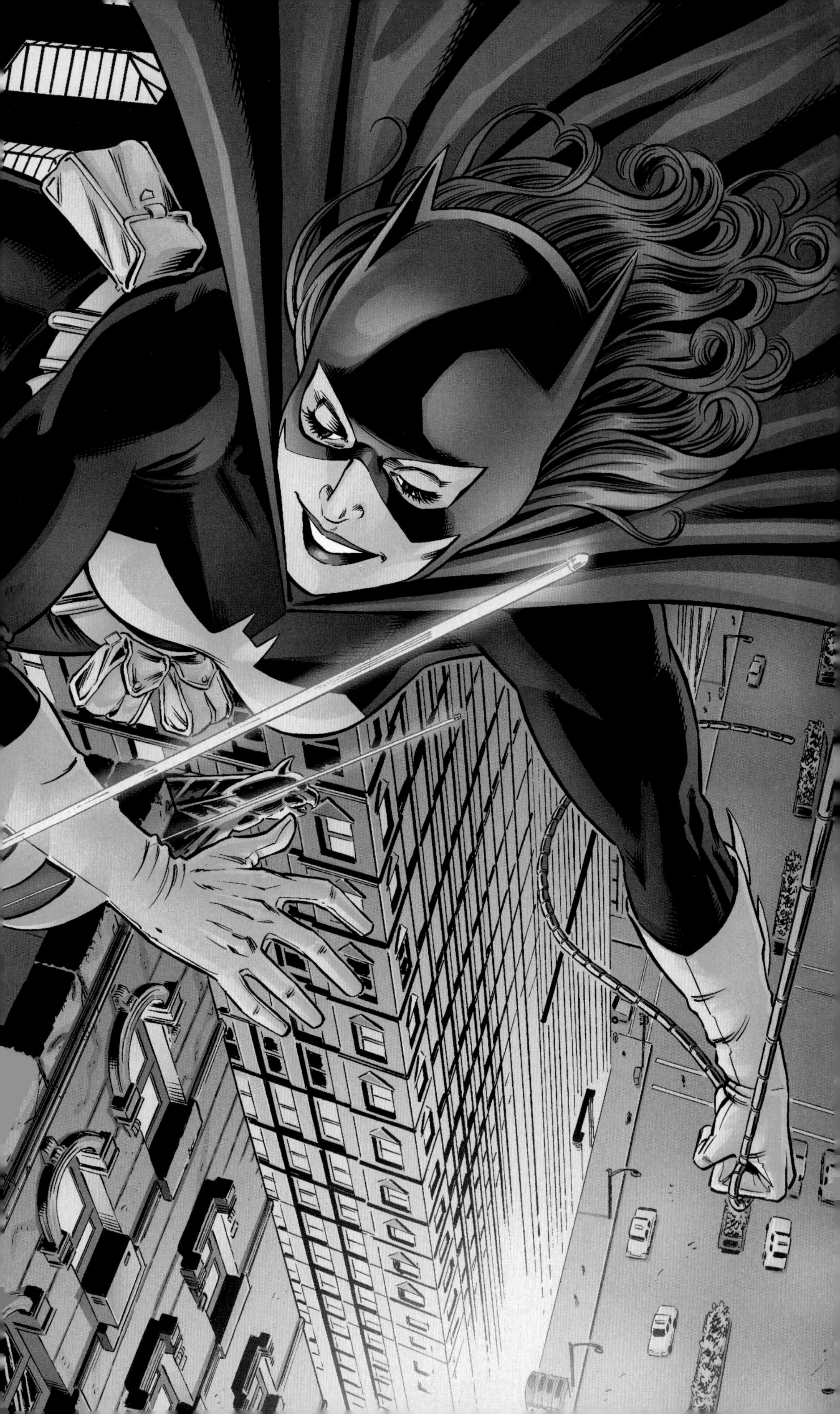

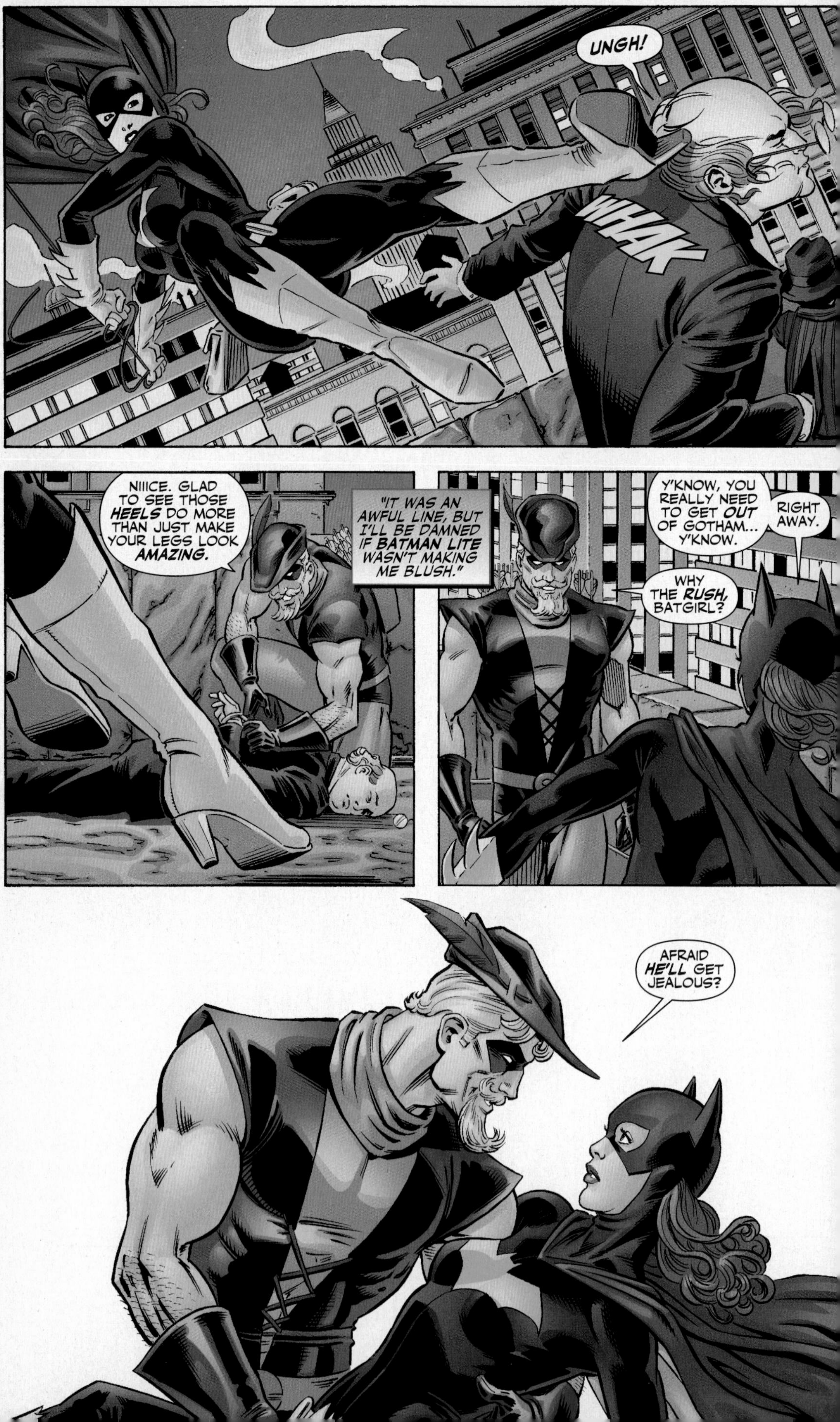
UNGH!
WHAK
NIIICE. GLAD TO SEE THOSE HEELS DO MORE THAN JUST MAKE YOUR LEGS LOOK AMAZING.
"IT WAS AN AWFUL LINE, BUT I'LL BE DAMNED IF BATMAN LITE WASN'T MAKING ME BLUSH."
Y'KNOW, YOU REALLY NEED TO GET OUT OF GOTHAM... Y'KNOW.
RIGHT AWAY.
WHY THE RUSH, BATGIRL?
AFRAID HE'LL GET JEALOUS?

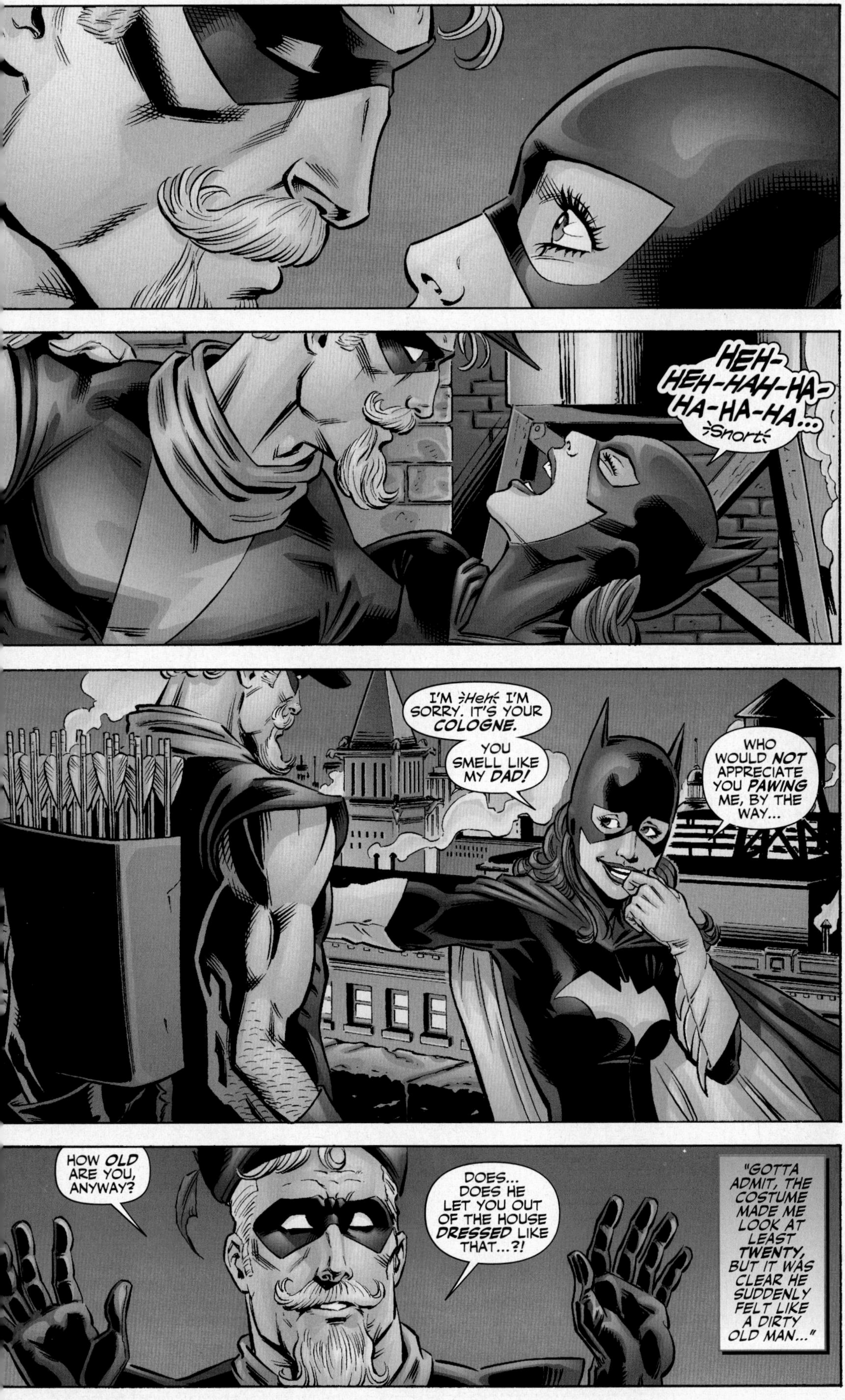
HEH-HEH-HAH-HA-HA-HA-HA... ⋟Snort⋞
I'M ⋟Heh⋞ I'M SORRY. IT'S YOUR COLOGNE.
YOU SMELL LIKE MY DAD!
WHO WOULD NOT APPRECIATE YOU PAWING ME, BY THE WAY...
HOW OLD ARE YOU, ANYWAY?
DOES... DOES HE LET YOU OUT OF THE HOUSE DRESSED LIKE THAT...?!
"GOTTA ADMIT, THE COSTUME MADE ME LOOK AT LEAST TWENTY, BUT IT WAS CLEAR HE SUDDENLY FELT LIKE A DIRTY OLD MAN..."

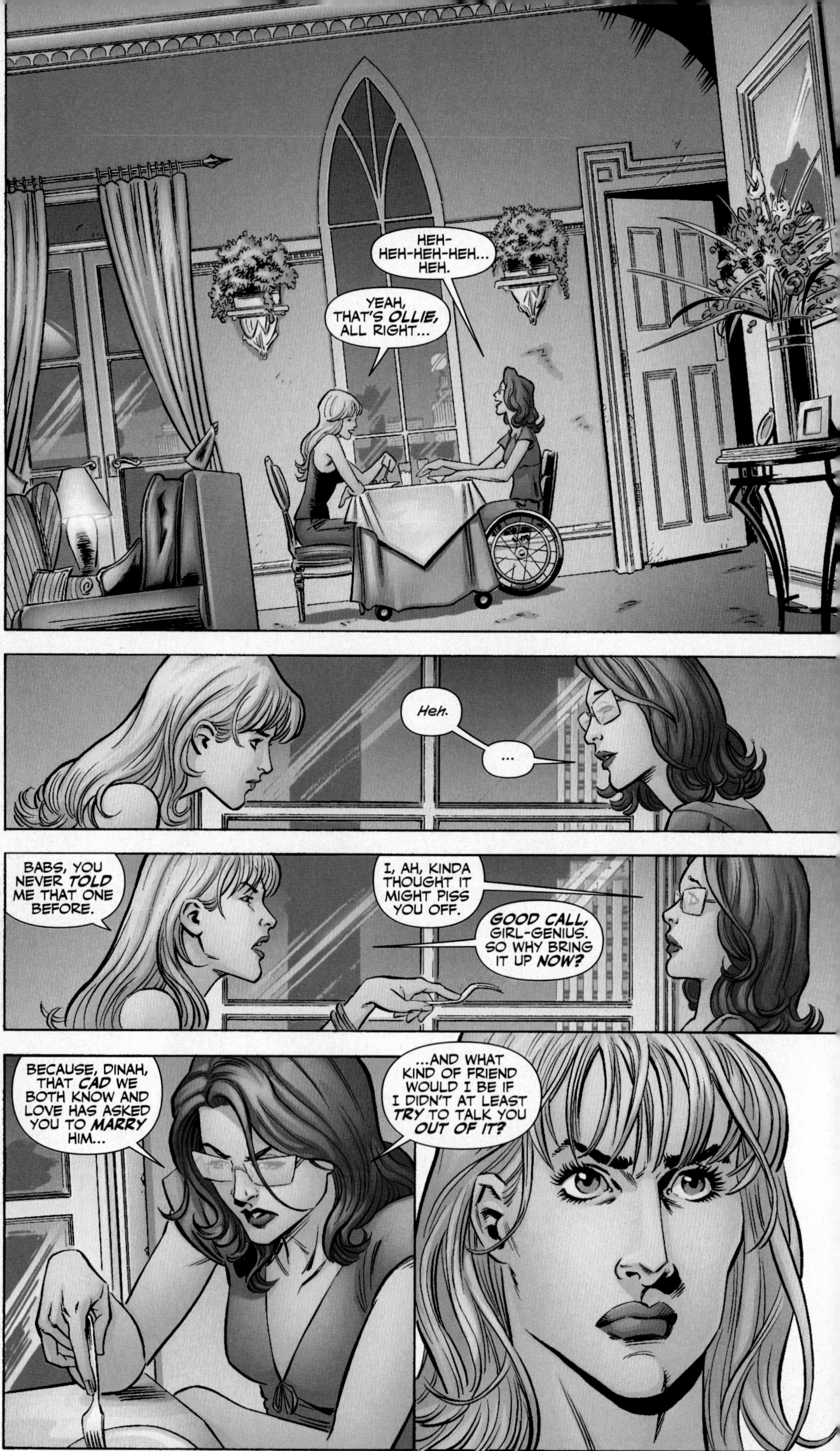
HEH-
HEH-HEH-HEH... HEH.
YEAH, THAT'S OLLIE, ALL RIGHT...
Heh.
...
BABS, YOU NEVER TOLD ME THAT ONE BEFORE.
I, AH, KINDA THOUGHT IT MIGHT PISS YOU OFF.
GOOD CALL, GIRL-GENIUS. SO WHY BRING IT UP NOW?
BECAUSE, DINAH, THAT CAD WE BOTH KNOW AND LOVE HAS ASKED YOU TO MARRY HIM...
...AND WHAT KIND OF FRIEND WOULD I BE IF I DIDN'T AT LEAST TRY TO TALK YOU OUT OF IT?

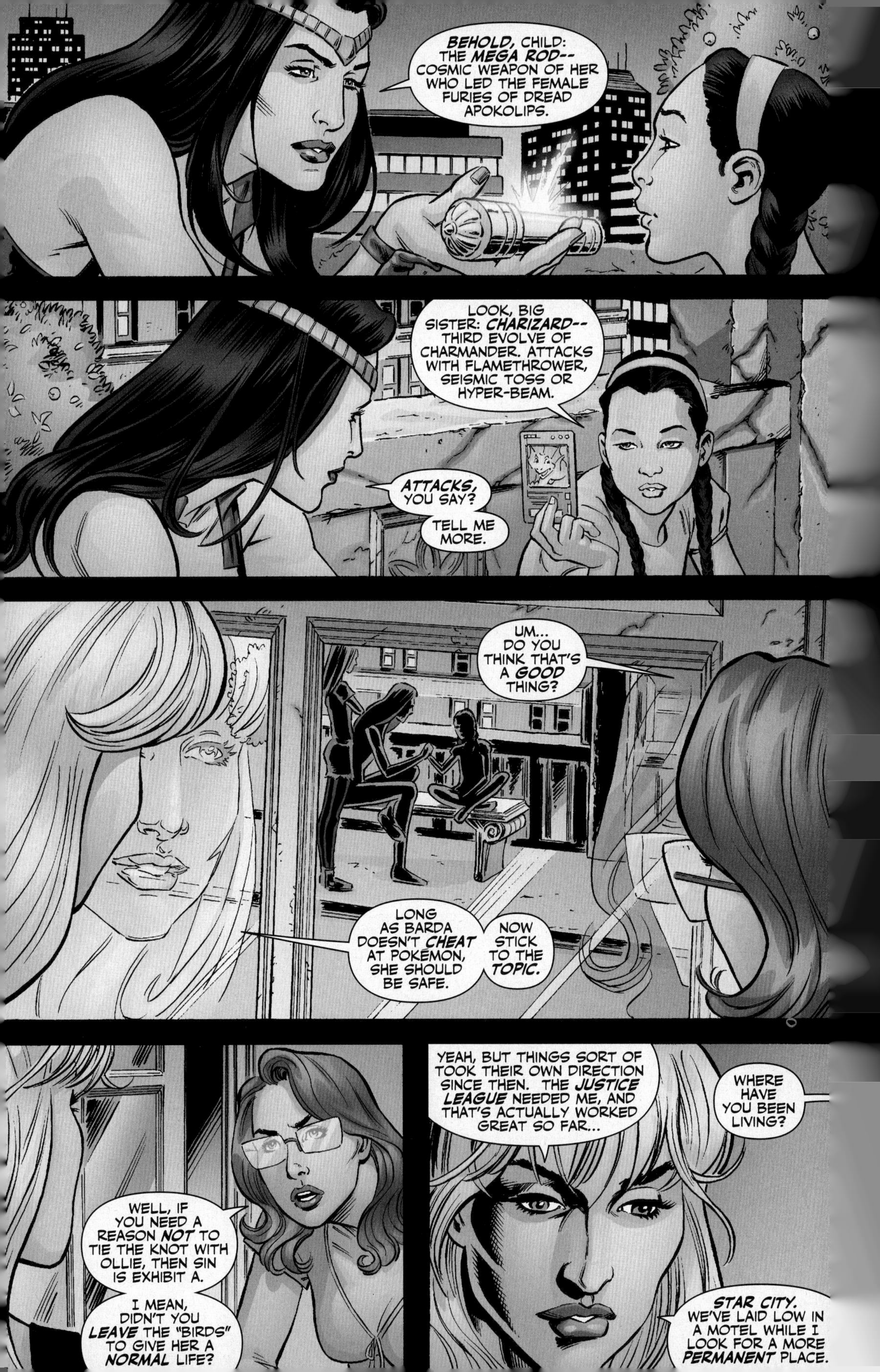
BEHOLD, CHILD: THE MEGA ROD-- COSMIC WEAPON OF HER WHO LED THE FEMALE FURIES OF DREAD APOKOLIPS.
LOOK, BIG SISTER: CHARIZARD-- THIRD EVOLVE OF CHARMANDER. ATTACKS WITH FLAMETHROWER, SEISMIC TOSS OR HYPER-BEAM.
ATTACKS, YOU SAY?
TELL ME MORE.
UM... DO YOU THINK THAT'S A GOOD THING?
LONG AS BARDA DOESN'T CHEAT AT POKEMON, SHE SHOULD BE SAFE.
NOW STICK TO THE TOPIC.
WELL, IF YOU NEED A REASON NOT TO TIE THE KNOT WITH OLLIE, THEN SIN IS EXHIBIT A.
I MEAN, DIDN'T YOU LEAVE THE "BIRDS" TO GIVE HER A NORMAL LIFE?
YEAH, BUT THINGS SORT OF TOOK THEIR OWN DIRECTION SINCE THEN. THE JUSTICE LEAGUE NEEDED ME, AND THAT'S ACTUALLY WORKED GREAT SO FAR...
WHERE HAVE YOU BEEN LIVING?
STAR CITY. WE'VE LAID LOW IN A MOTEL WHILE I LOOK FOR A MORE PERMANENT PLACE.

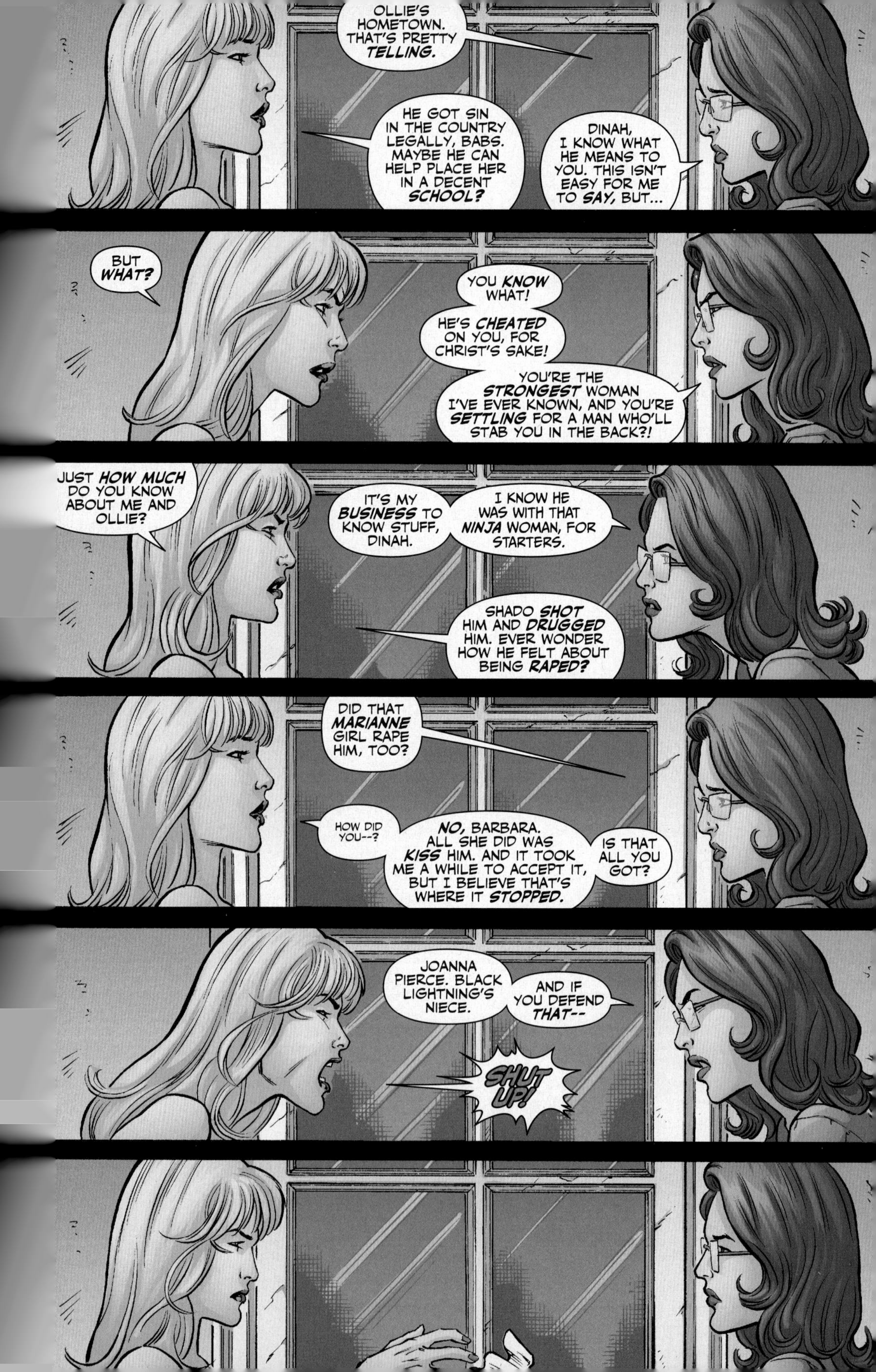
OLLIE'S HOMETOWN. THAT'S PRETTY TELLING.
HE GOT SIN IN THE COUNTRY LEGALLY, BABS. MAYBE HE CAN HELP PLACE HER IN A DECENT SCHOOL?
DINAH, I KNOW WHAT HE MEANS TO YOU. THIS ISN'T EASY FOR ME TO SAY, BUT...
BUT WHAT?
YOU KNOW WHAT!
HE'S CHEATED ON YOU, FOR CHRIST'S SAKE!
YOU'RE THE STRONGEST WOMAN I'VE EVER KNOWN, AND YOU'RE SETTLING FOR A MAN WHO'LL STAB YOU IN THE BACK?!
JUST HOW MUCH DO YOU KNOW ABOUT ME AND OLLIE?
IT'S MY BUSINESS TO KNOW STUFF, DINAH.
I KNOW HE WAS WITH THAT NINJA WOMAN, FOR STARTERS.
SHADO SHOT HIM AND DRUGGED HIM. EVER WONDER HOW HE FELT ABOUT BEING RAPED?
DID THAT MARIANNE GIRL RAPE HIM, TOO?
HOW DID YOU--?
NO, BARBARA. ALL SHE DID WAS KISS HIM. AND IT TOOK ME A WHILE TO ACCEPT IT, BUT I BELIEVE THAT'S WHERE IT STOPPED.
IS THAT ALL YOU GOT?
JOANNA PIERCE. BLACK LIGHTNING'S NIECE.
AND IF YOU DEFEND THAT--
SHUT UP!

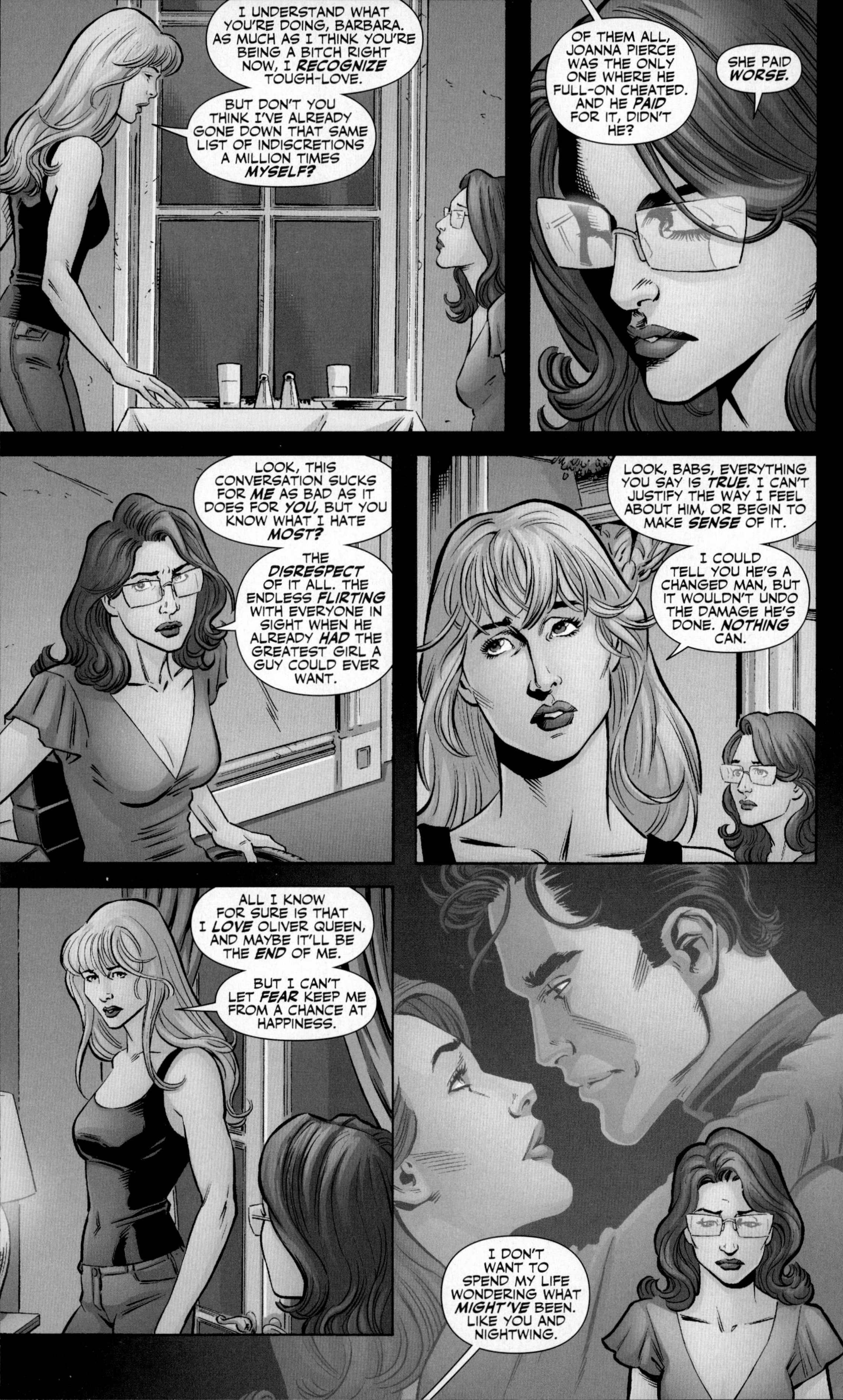
I UNDERSTAND WHAT YOU'RE DOING, BARBARA. AS MUCH AS I THINK YOU'RE BEING A BITCH RIGHT NOW, I RECOGNIZE TOUGH-LOVE.
BUT DON'T YOU THINK I'VE ALREADY GONE DOWN THAT SAME LIST OF INDISCRETIONS A MILLION TIMES MYSELF?
OF THEM ALL, JOANNA PIERCE WAS THE ONLY ONE WHERE HE FULL-ON CHEATED. AND HE PAID FOR IT, DIDN'T HE?
SHE PAID WORSE.
LOOK, THIS CONVERSATION SUCKS FOR ME AS BAD AS IT DOES FOR YOU, BUT YOU KNOW WHAT I HATE MOST?
THE DISRESPECT OF IT ALL. THE ENDLESS FLIRTING WITH EVERYONE IN SIGHT WHEN HE ALREADY HAD THE GREATEST GIRL A GUY COULD EVER WANT.
LOOK, BABS, EVERYTHING YOU SAY IS TRUE. I CAN'T JUSTIFY THE WAY I FEEL ABOUT HIM, OR BEGIN TO MAKE SENSE OF IT.
I COULD TELL YOU HE'S A CHANGED MAN, BUT IT WOULDN'T UNDO THE DAMAGE HE'S DONE. NOTHING CAN.
ALL I KNOW FOR SURE IS THAT I LOVE OLIVER QUEEN, AND MAYBE IT'LL BE THE END OF ME.
BUT I CAN'T LET FEAR KEEP ME FROM A CHANCE AT HAPPINESS.
I DON'T WANT TO SPEND MY LIFE WONDERING WHAT MIGHT'VE BEEN. LIKE YOU AND NIGHTWING.

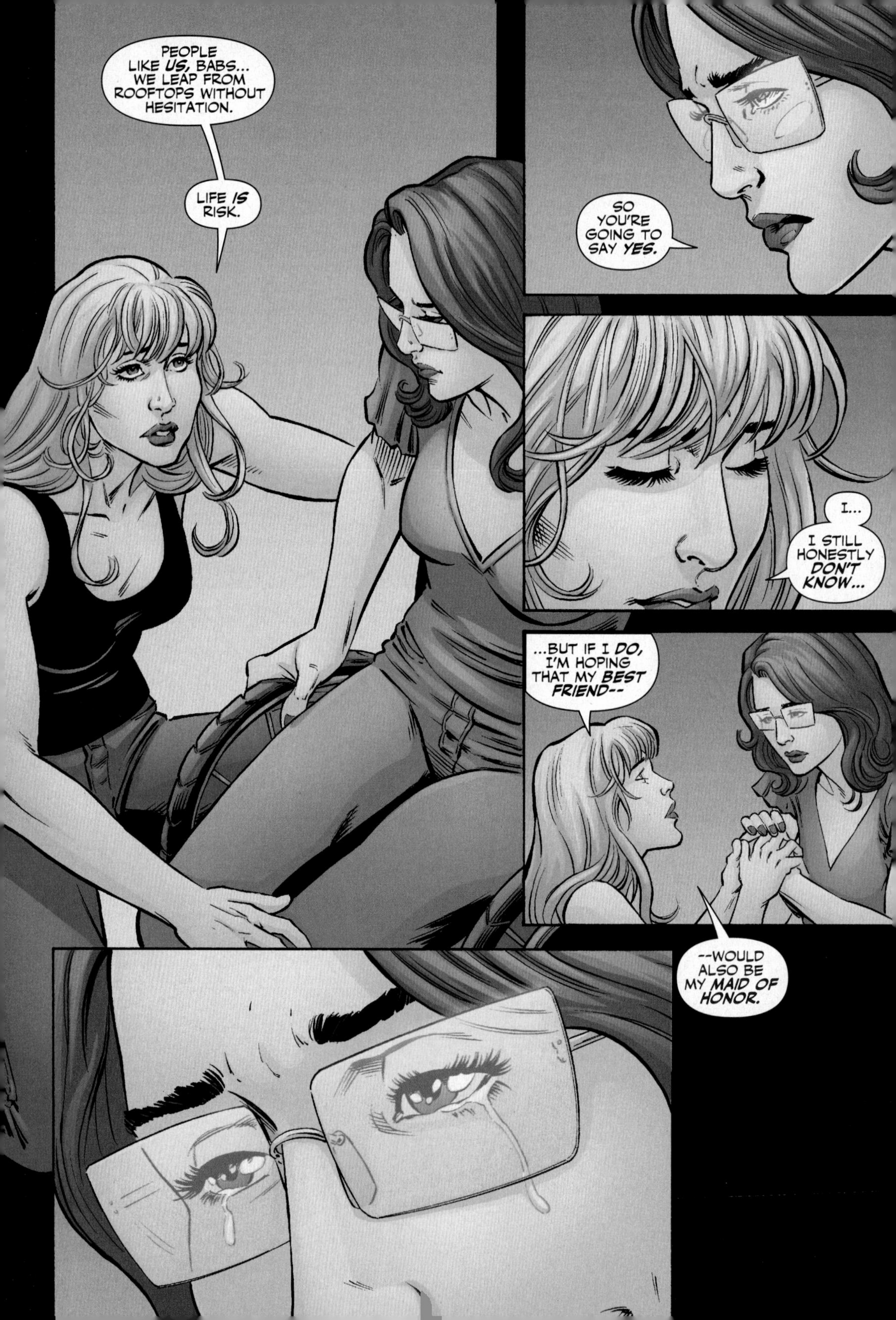
PEOPLE LIKE US, BABS... WE LEAP FROM ROOFTOPS WITHOUT HESITATION.
LIFE IS RISK.
SO YOU'RE GOING TO SAY YES.
I...
I STILL HONESTLY DON'T KNOW...
...BUT IF I DO, I'M HOPING THAT MY BEST FRIEND--
--WOULD ALSO BE MY MAID OF HONOR.

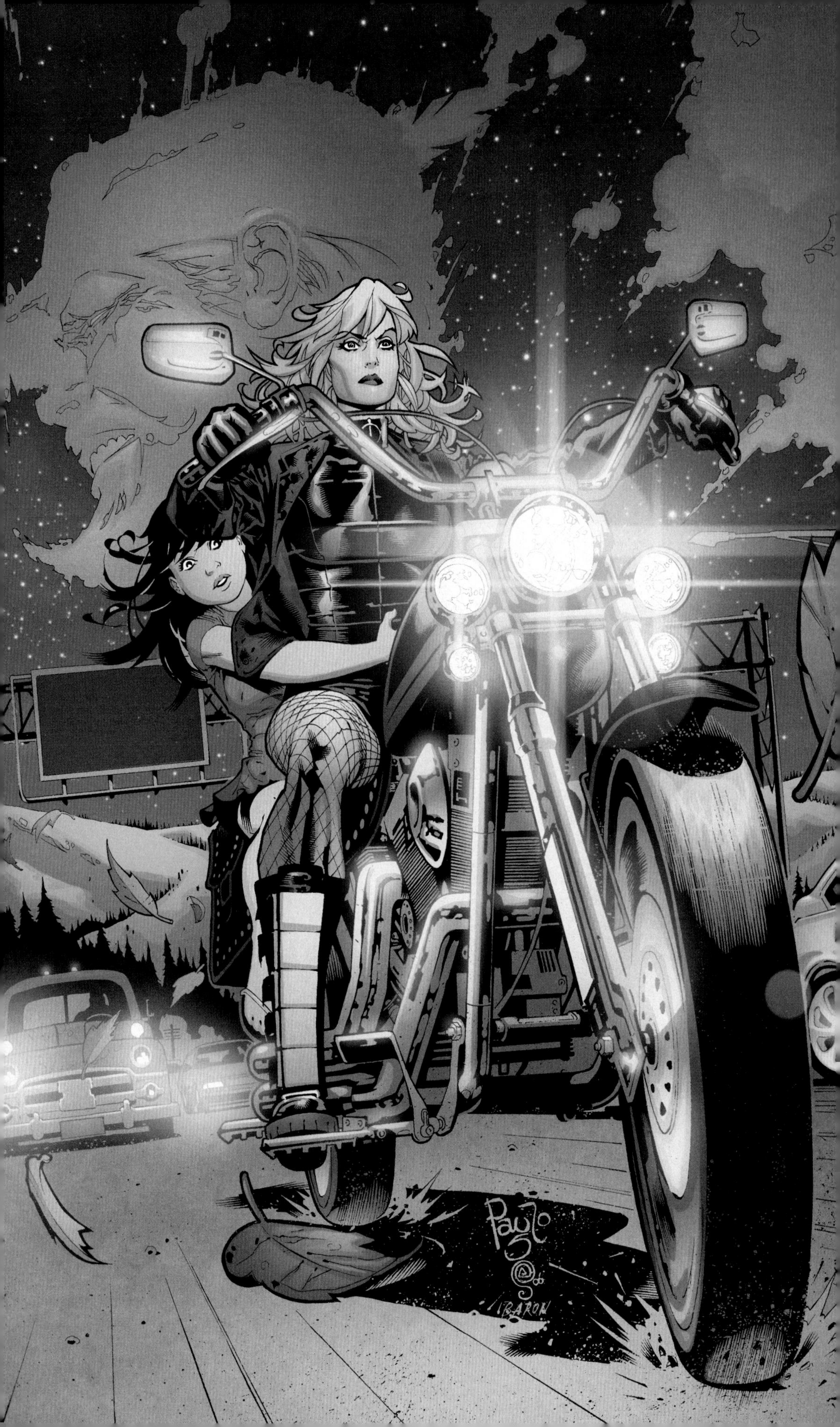

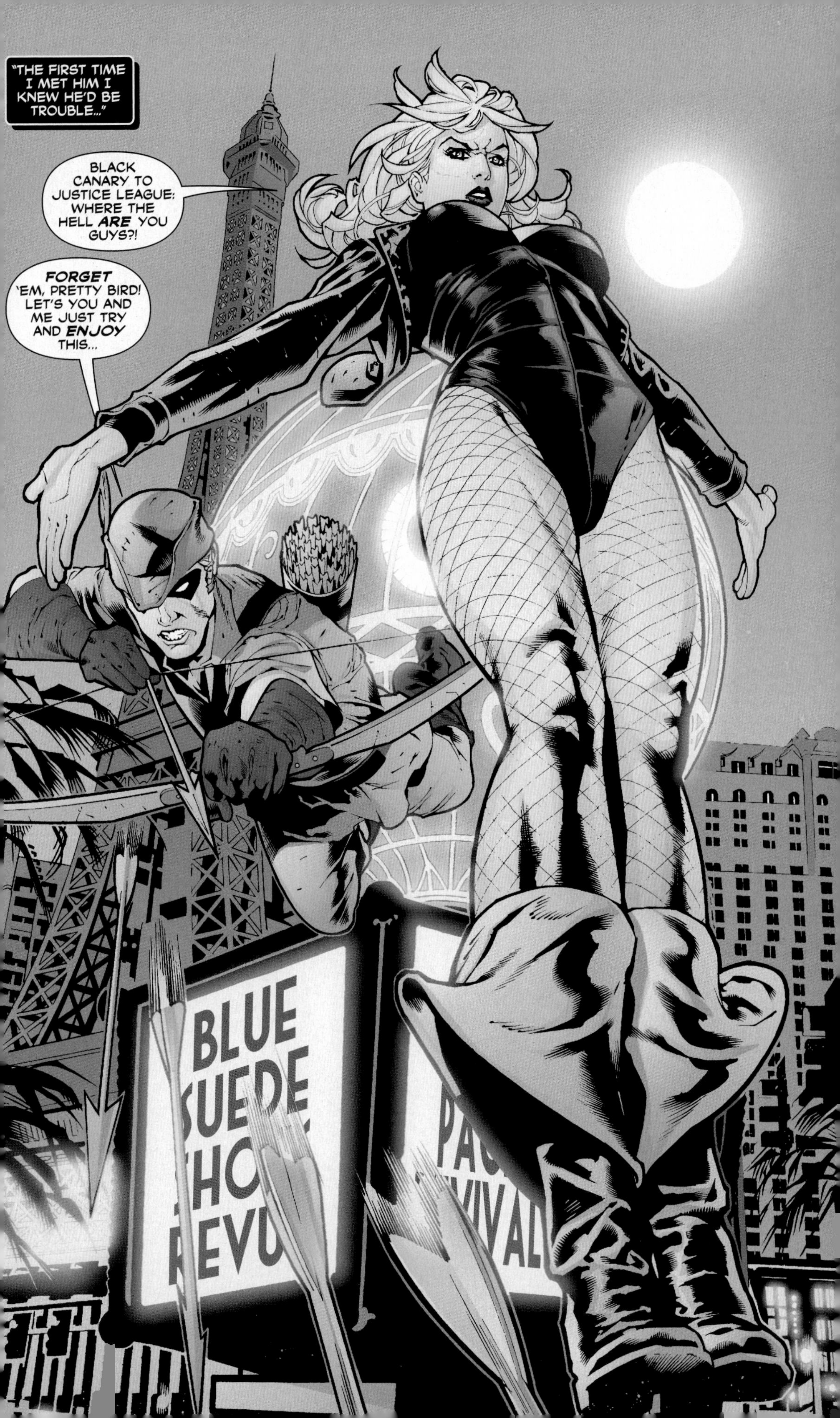
"THE FIRST TIME I MET HIM I KNEW HE'D BE TROUBLE..."
BLACK CANARY TO JUSTICE LEAGUE: WHERE THE HELL ARE YOU GUYS?!
FORGET 'EM, PRETTY BIRD! LET'S YOU AND ME JUST TRY AND ENJOY THIS...
BLUE SUEDE SHO REVU
PA VIVAL

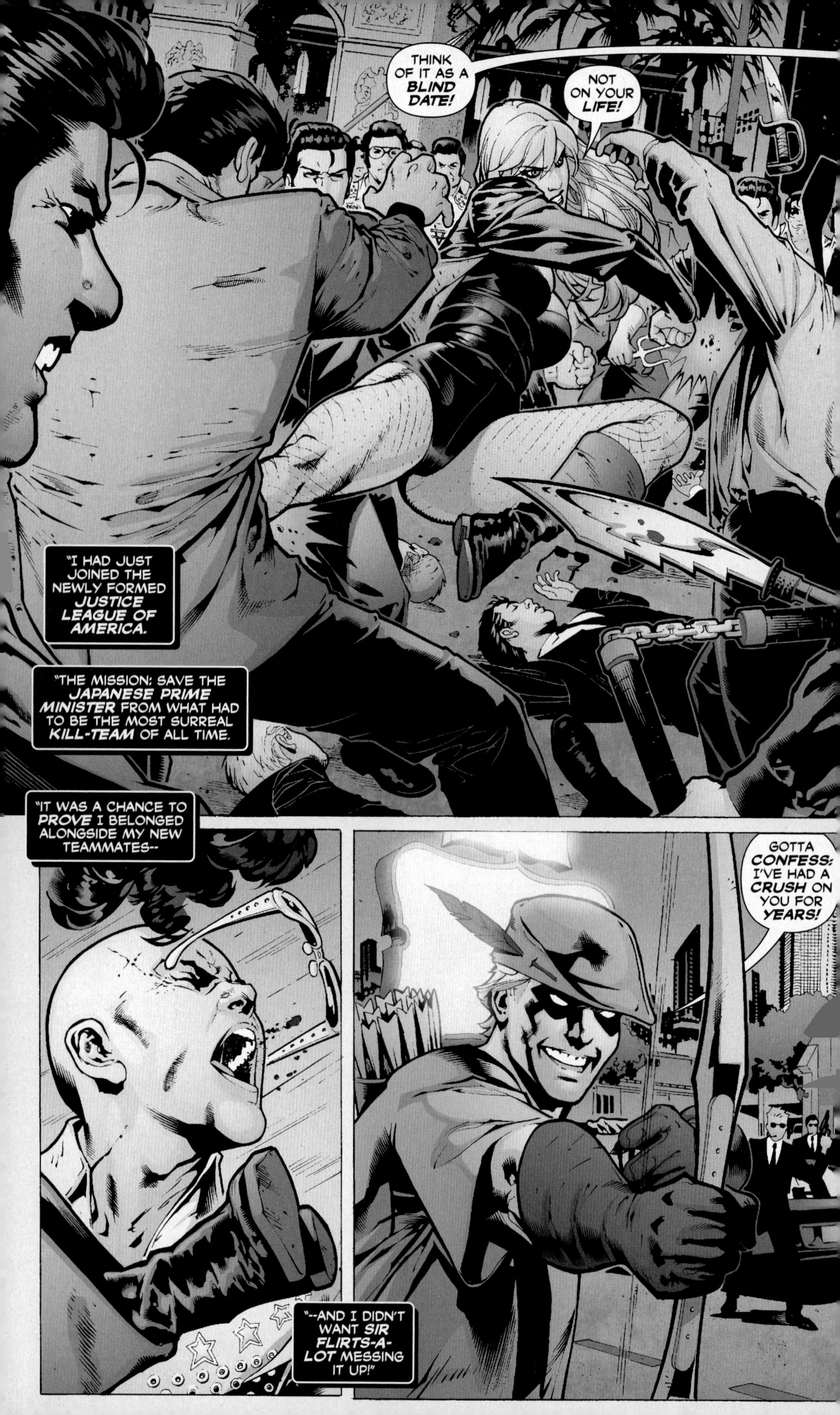
THINK OF IT AS A BLIND DATE!
NOT ON YOUR LIFE!
"I HAD JUST JOINED THE NEWLY FORMED JUSTICE LEAGUE OF AMERICA.
"THE MISSION: SAVE THE JAPANESE PRIME MINISTER FROM WHAT HAD TO BE THE MOST SURREAL KILL-TEAM OF ALL TIME.
"IT WAS A CHANCE TO PROVE I BELONGED ALONGSIDE MY NEW TEAMMATES--
GOTTA CONFESS: I'VE HAD A CRUSH ON YOU FOR YEARS!
"--AND I DIDN'T WANT SIR FLIRTS-A-LOT MESSING IT UP!"

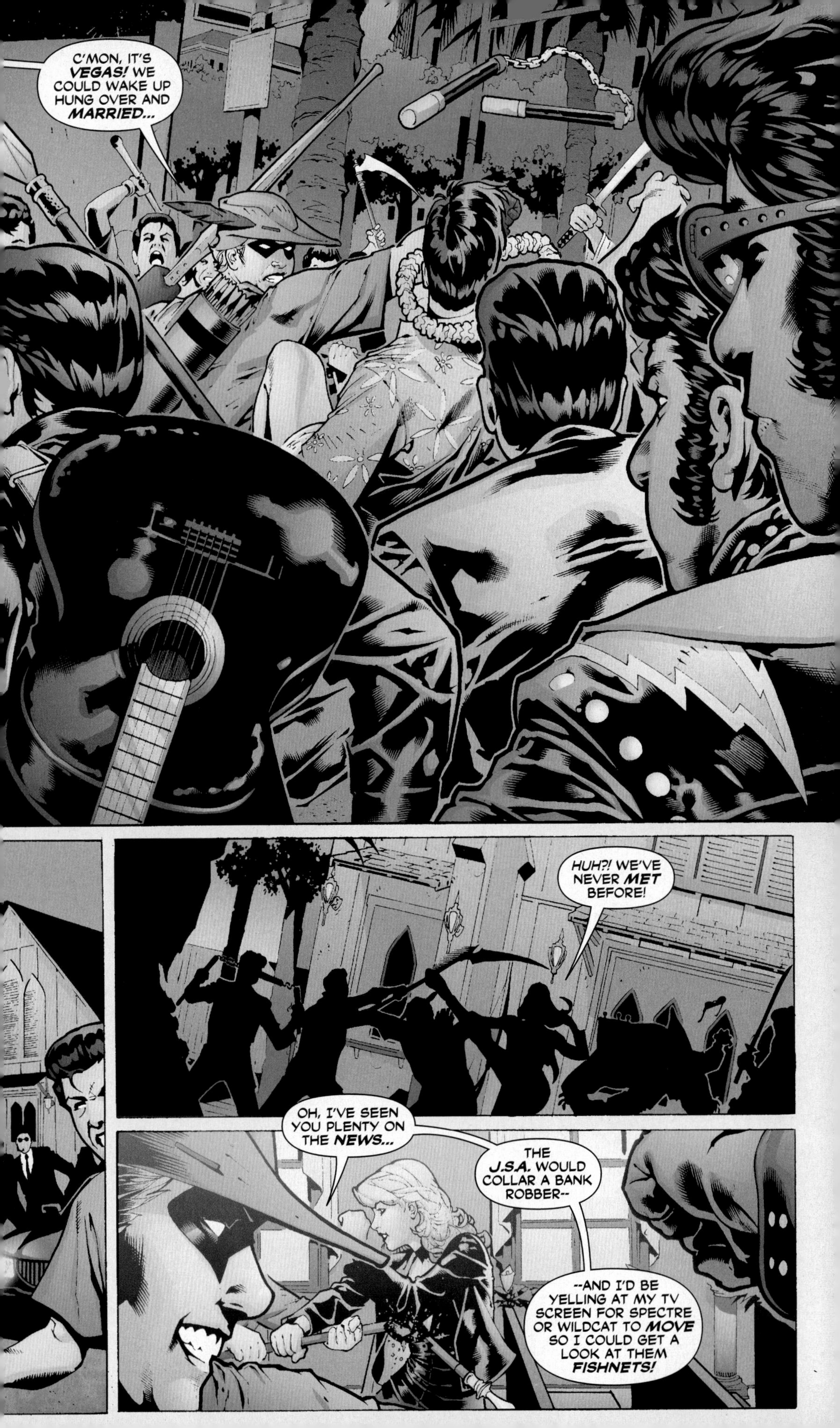
C'MON, IT'S VEGAS! WE COULD WAKE UP HUNG OVER AND MARRIED...
HUH?! WE'VE NEVER MET BEFORE!
OH, I'VE SEEN YOU PLENTY ON THE NEWS...
THE J.S.A. WOULD COLLAR A BANK ROBBER--
--AND I'D BE YELLING AT MY TV SCREEN FOR SPECTRE OR WILDCAT TO MOVE SO I COULD GET A LOOK AT THEM FISHNETS!

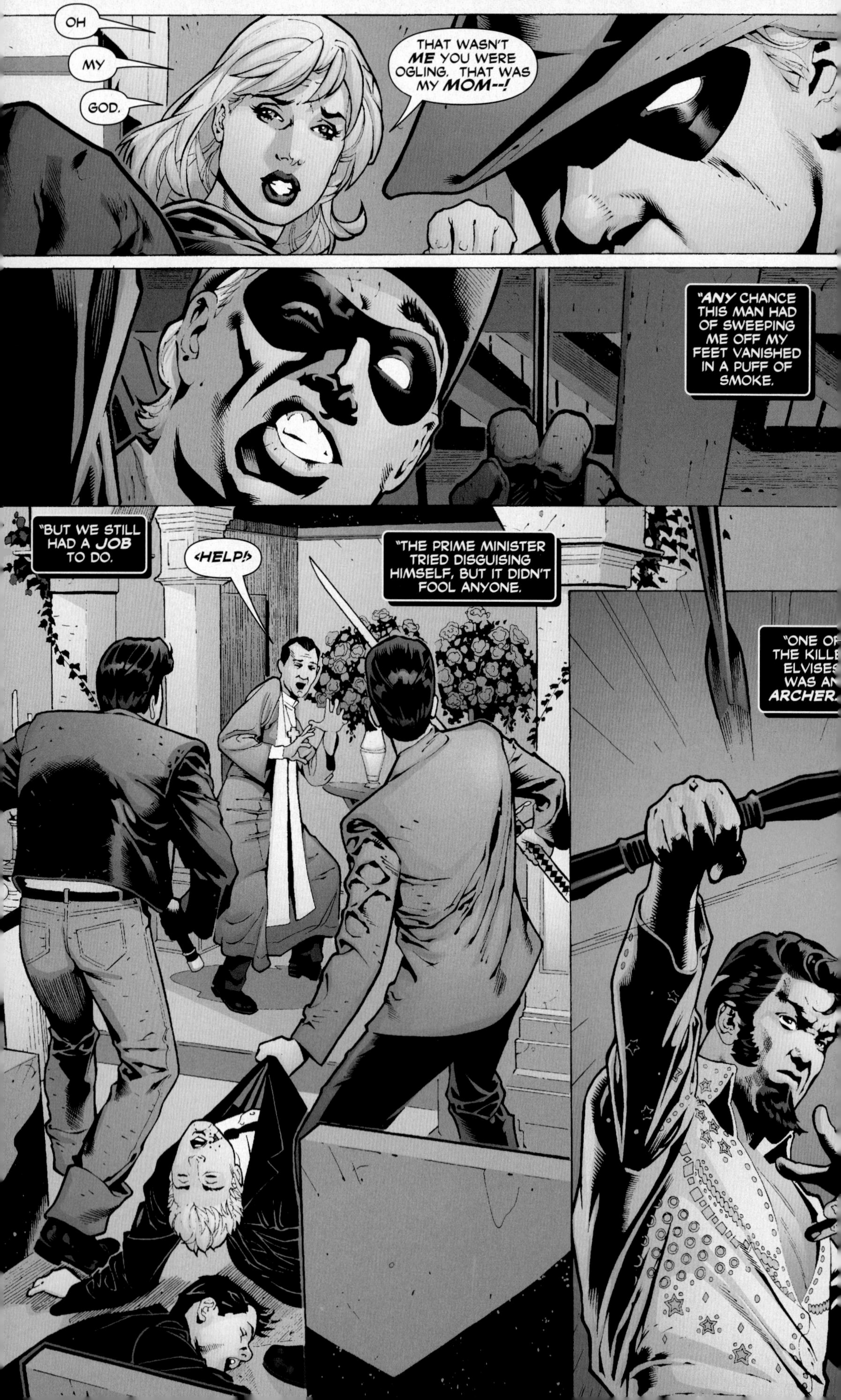
OH
MY
GOD.
THAT WASN'T ME YOU WERE OGLING. THAT WAS MY MOM--!
"ANY CHANCE THIS MAN HAD OF SWEEPING ME OFF MY FEET VANISHED IN A PUFF OF SMOKE.
"BUT WE STILL HAD A JOB TO DO.
<HELP!>
"THE PRIME MINISTER TRIED DISGUISING HIMSELF, BUT IT DIDN'T FOOL ANYONE.

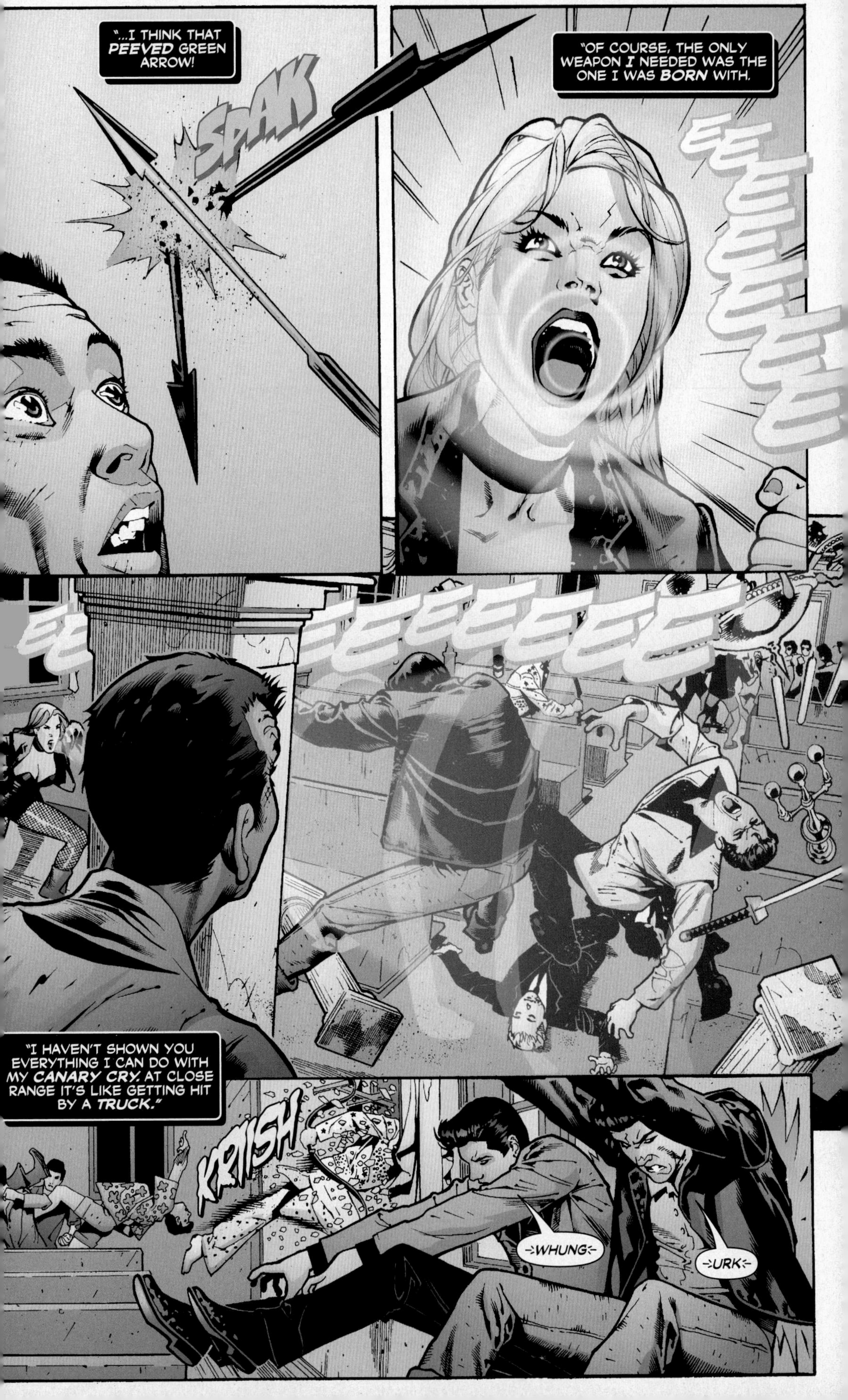
"...I THINK THAT PEEVED GREEN ARROW!
SPAK
"OF COURSE, THE ONLY WEAPON I NEEDED WAS THE ONE I WAS BORN WITH.
"I HAVEN'T SHOWN YOU EVERYTHING I CAN DO WITH MY CANARY CRY. AT CLOSE RANGE IT'S LIKE GETTING HIT BY A TRUCK."
KRASH
WHUNG
URK

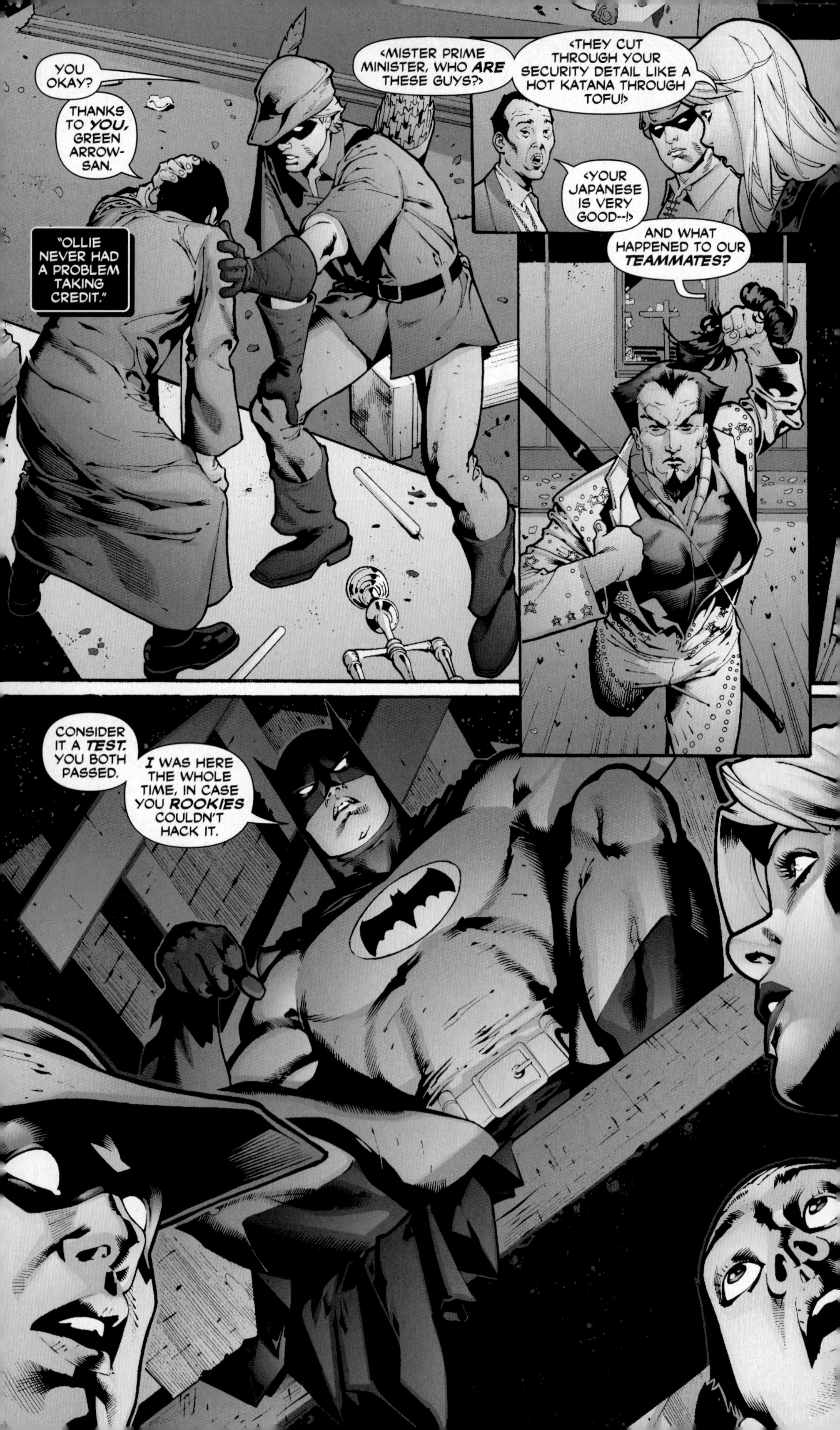
YOU OKAY?
THANKS TO *YOU,* GREEN ARROW-SAN.
"OLLIE NEVER HAD A PROBLEM TAKING CREDIT."
<MISTER PRIME MINISTER, WHO *ARE* THESE GUYS?>
<THEY CUT THROUGH YOUR SECURITY DETAIL LIKE A HOT KATANA THROUGH TOFU!>
<YOUR JAPANESE IS VERY GOOD--!>
AND WHAT HAPPENED TO OUR *TEAMMATES?*
CONSIDER IT A *TEST.* YOU BOTH PASSED.
I WAS HERE THE WHOLE TIME, IN CASE YOU *ROOKIES* COULDN'T HACK IT.

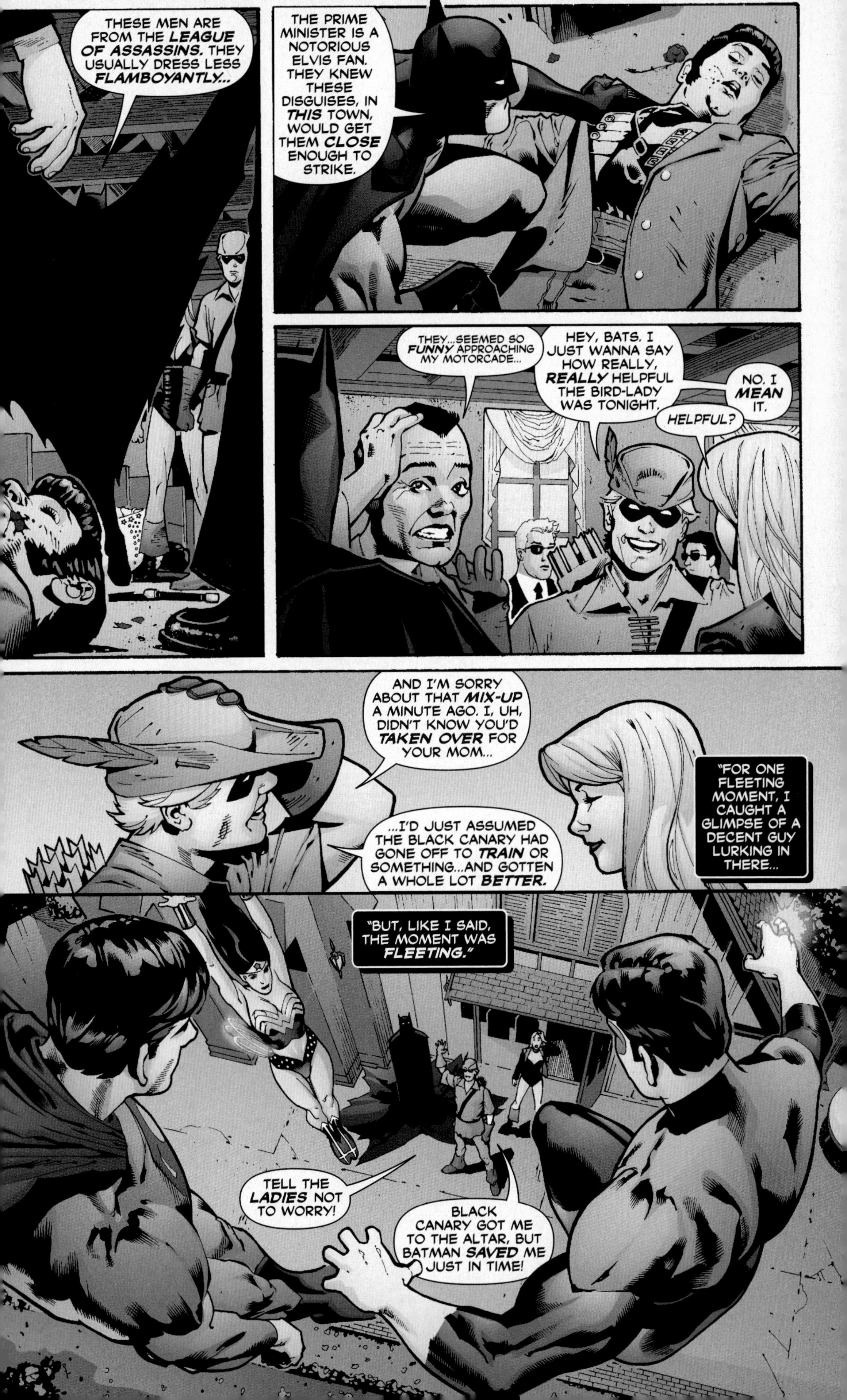
THESE MEN ARE FROM THE LEAGUE OF ASSASSINS. THEY USUALLY DRESS LESS FLAMBOYANTLY...
THE PRIME MINISTER IS A NOTORIOUS ELVIS FAN. THEY KNEW THESE DISGUISES, IN THIS TOWN, WOULD GET THEM CLOSE ENOUGH TO STRIKE.
THEY...SEEMED SO FUNNY APPROACHING MY MOTORCADE...
HEY, BATS. I JUST WANNA SAY HOW REALLY, REALLY HELPFUL THE BIRD-LADY WAS TONIGHT.
HELPFUL?
NO. I MEAN IT.
AND I'M SORRY ABOUT THAT MIX-UP A MINUTE AGO. I, UH, DIDN'T KNOW YOU'D TAKEN OVER FOR YOUR MOM...
...I'D JUST ASSUMED THE BLACK CANARY HAD GONE OFF TO TRAIN OR SOMETHING...AND GOTTEN A WHOLE LOT BETTER.
"FOR ONE FLEETING MOMENT, I CAUGHT A GLIMPSE OF A DECENT GUY LURKING IN THERE...
"BUT, LIKE I SAID, THE MOMENT WAS FLEETING."
TELL THE LADIES NOT TO WORRY!
BLACK CANARY GOT ME TO THE ALTAR, BUT BATMAN SAVED ME JUST IN TIME!

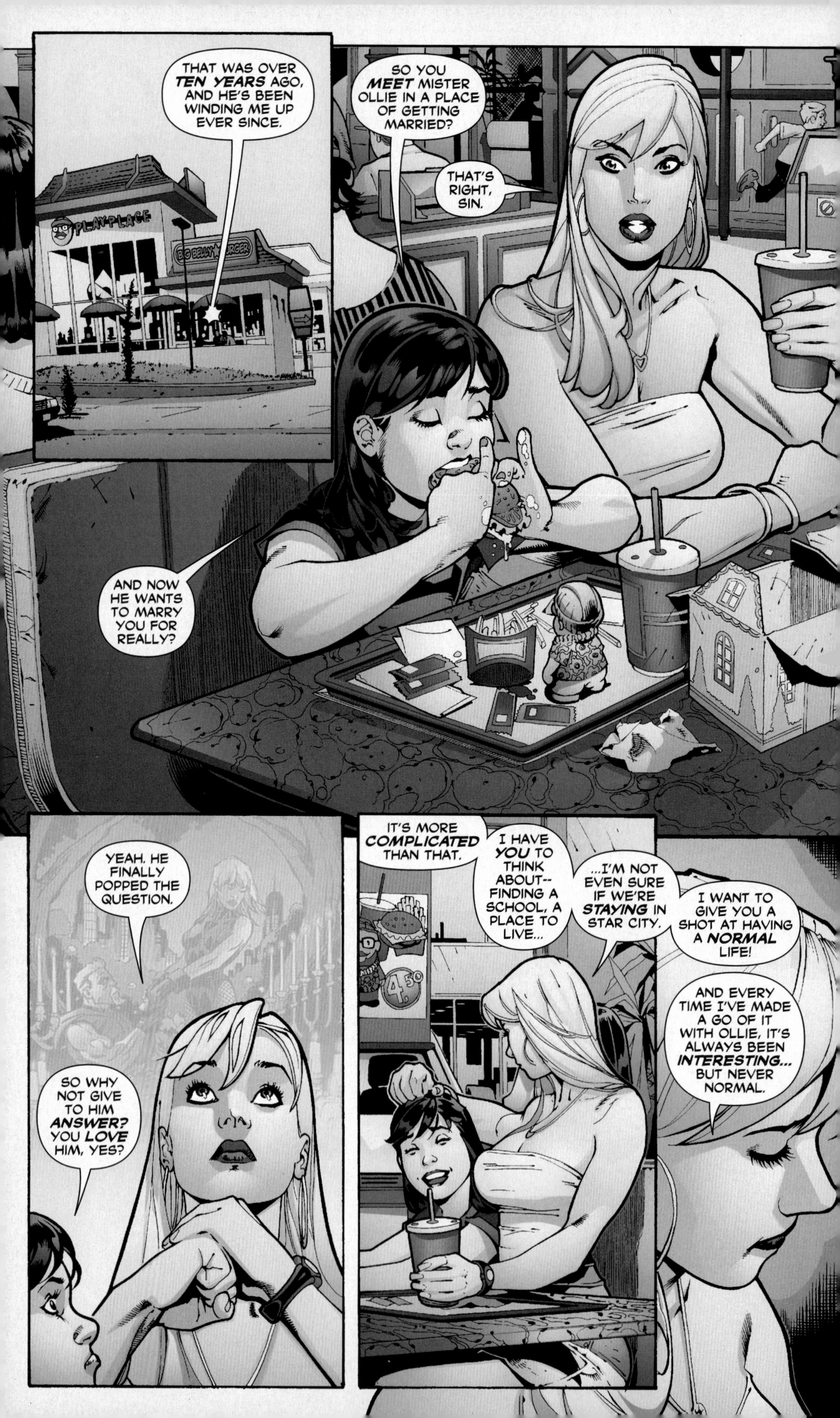
THAT WAS OVER TEN YEARS AGO, AND HE'S BEEN WINDING ME UP EVER SINCE.
PLAY-PLACE
BIG BELLY BURGER
SO YOU MEET MISTER OLLIE IN A PLACE OF GETTING MARRIED?
THAT'S RIGHT, SIN.
AND NOW HE WANTS TO MARRY YOU FOR REALLY?
YEAH. HE FINALLY POPPED THE QUESTION.
SO WHY NOT GIVE TO HIM ANSWER? YOU LOVE HIM, YES?
IT'S MORE COMPLICATED THAN THAT.
I HAVE YOU TO THINK ABOUT-- FINDING A SCHOOL, A PLACE TO LIVE...
...I'M NOT EVEN SURE IF WE'RE STAYING IN STAR CITY.
I WANT TO GIVE YOU A SHOT AT HAVING A NORMAL LIFE!
AND EVERY TIME I'VE MADE A GO OF IT WITH OLLIE, IT'S ALWAYS BEEN INTERESTING... BUT NEVER NORMAL.

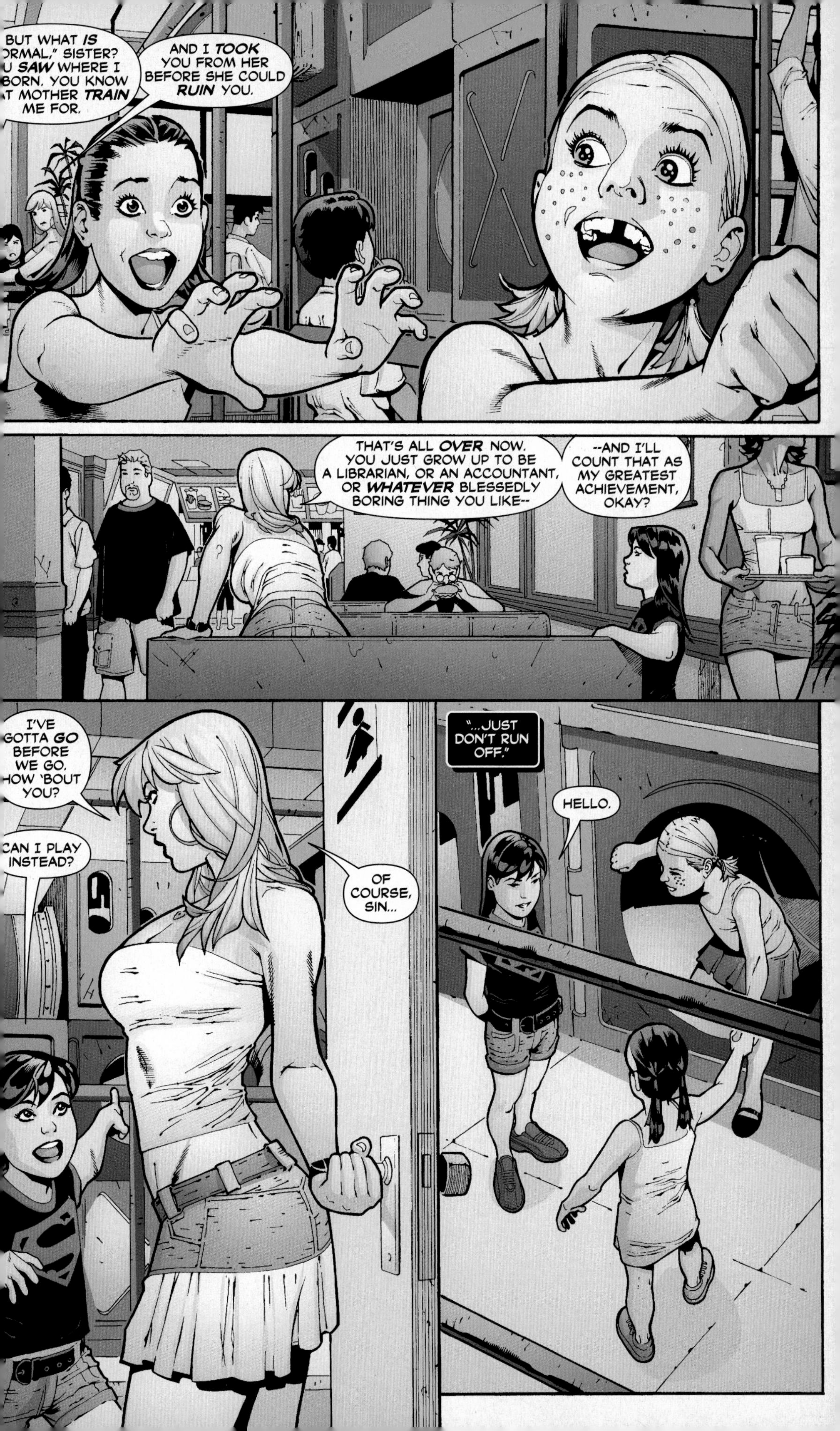
BUT WHAT *IS* ...ORMAL," SISTER? ...U *SAW* WHERE I ...BORN. YOU KNOW ...T MOTHER *TRAIN* ME FOR.
AND I *TOOK* YOU FROM HER BEFORE SHE COULD *RUIN* YOU.
THAT'S ALL *OVER* NOW. YOU JUST GROW UP TO BE A LIBRARIAN, OR AN ACCOUNTANT, OR *WHATEVER* BLESSEDLY BORING THING YOU LIKE--
--AND I'LL COUNT THAT AS MY GREATEST ACHIEVEMENT, OKAY?
I'VE ...OTTA *GO* BEFORE WE GO. ...OW 'BOUT YOU?
...CAN I PLAY INSTEAD?
OF COURSE, SIN...
"...JUST DON'T RUN OFF."
HELLO.

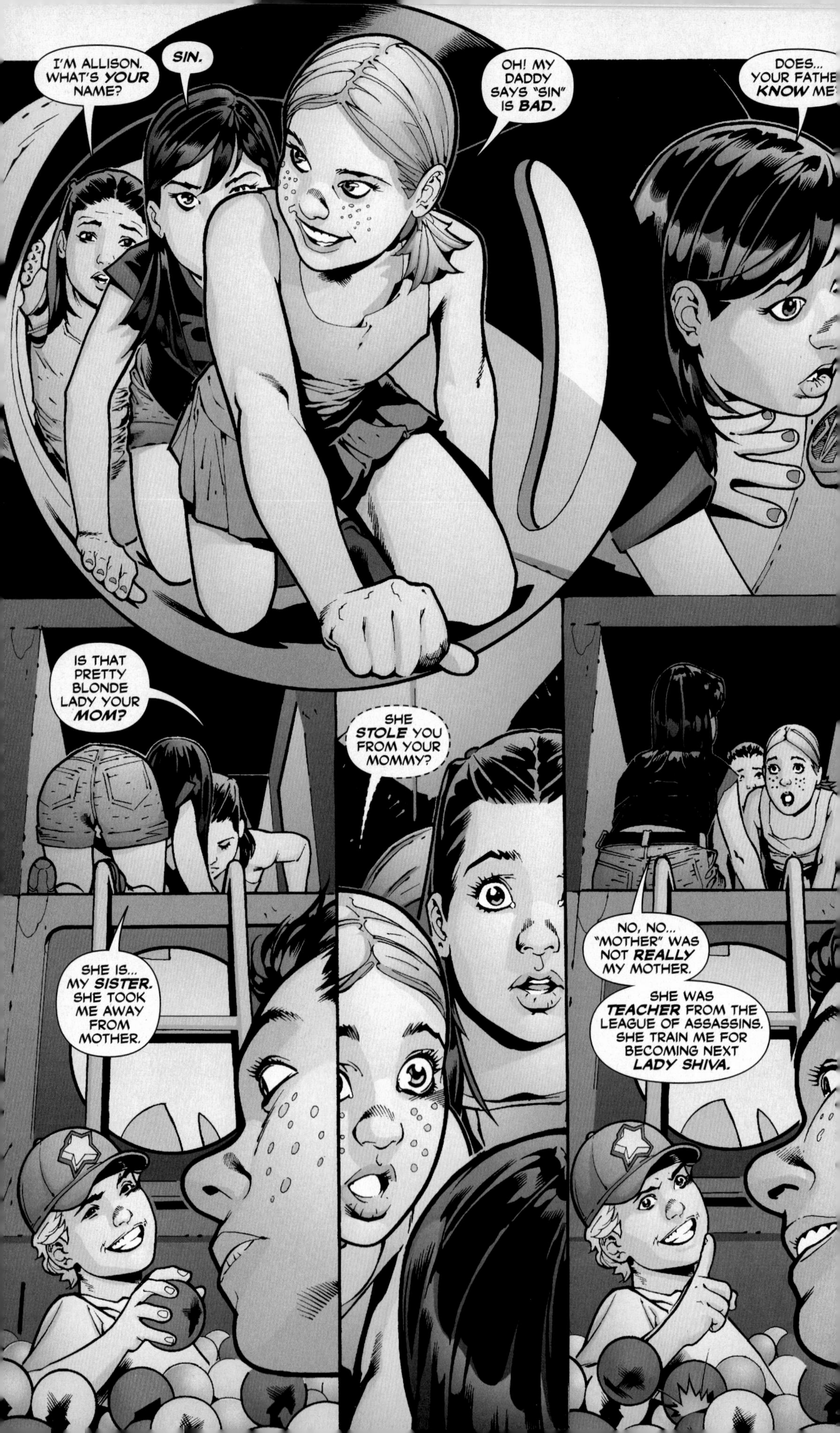
I'M ALLISON. WHAT'S YOUR NAME?
SIN.
OH! MY DADDY SAYS "SIN" IS BAD.
DOES... YOUR FATHE KNOW ME
IS THAT PRETTY BLONDE LADY YOUR MOM?
SHE IS... MY SISTER. SHE TOOK ME AWAY FROM MOTHER.
SHE STOLE YOU FROM YOUR MOMMY?
NO, NO... "MOTHER" WAS NOT REALLY MY MOTHER.
SHE WAS TEACHER FROM THE LEAGUE OF ASSASSINS. SHE TRAIN ME FOR BECOMING NEXT LADY SHIVA.

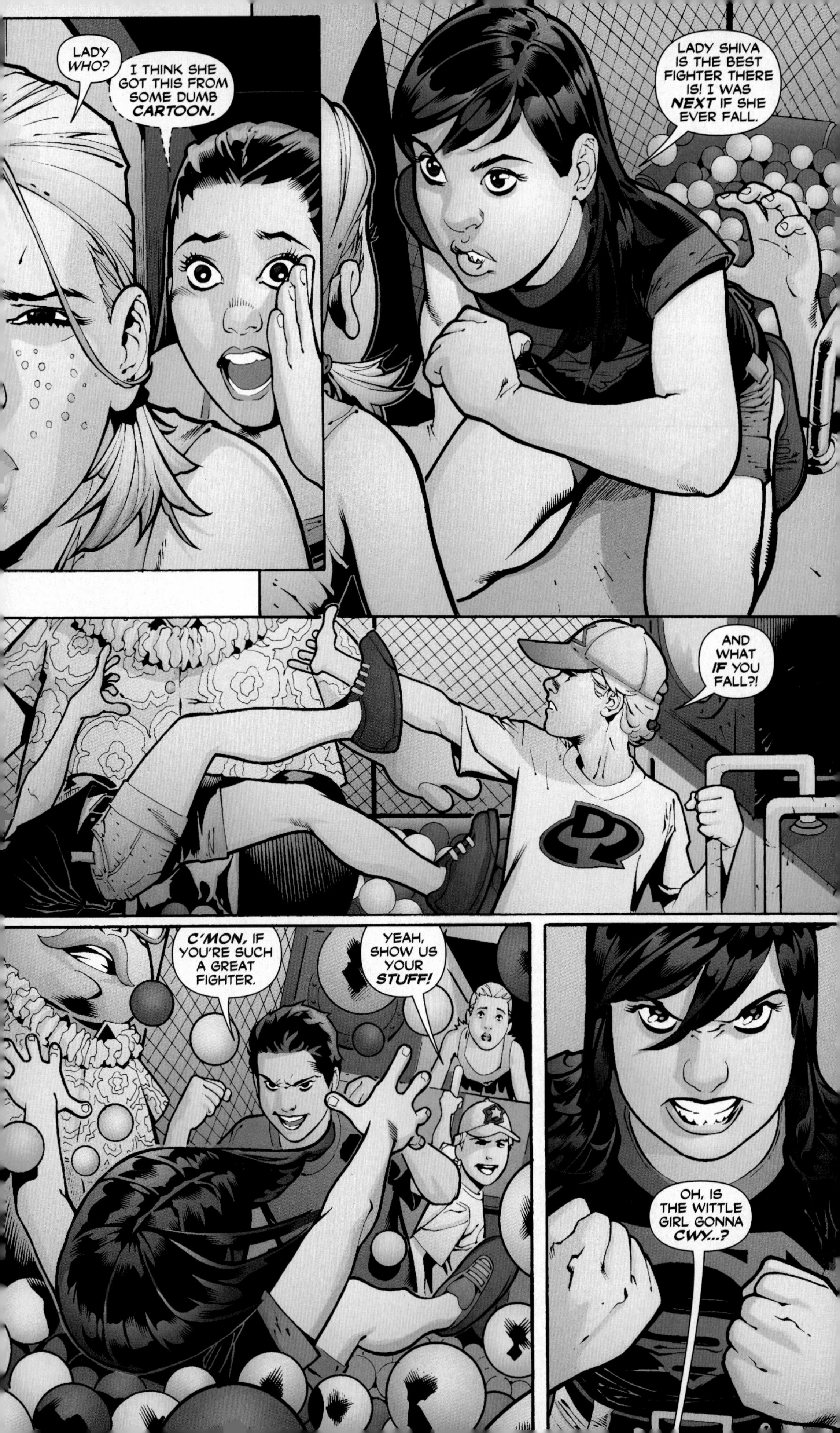
LADY WHO?
I THINK SHE GOT THIS FROM SOME DUMB CARTOON.
LADY SHIVA IS THE BEST FIGHTER THERE IS! I WAS NEXT IF SHE EVER FALL.
AND WHAT IF YOU FALL?!
C'MON, IF YOU'RE SUCH A GREAT FIGHTER.
YEAH, SHOW US YOUR STUFF!
OH, IS THE WITTLE GIRL GONNA CWY...?

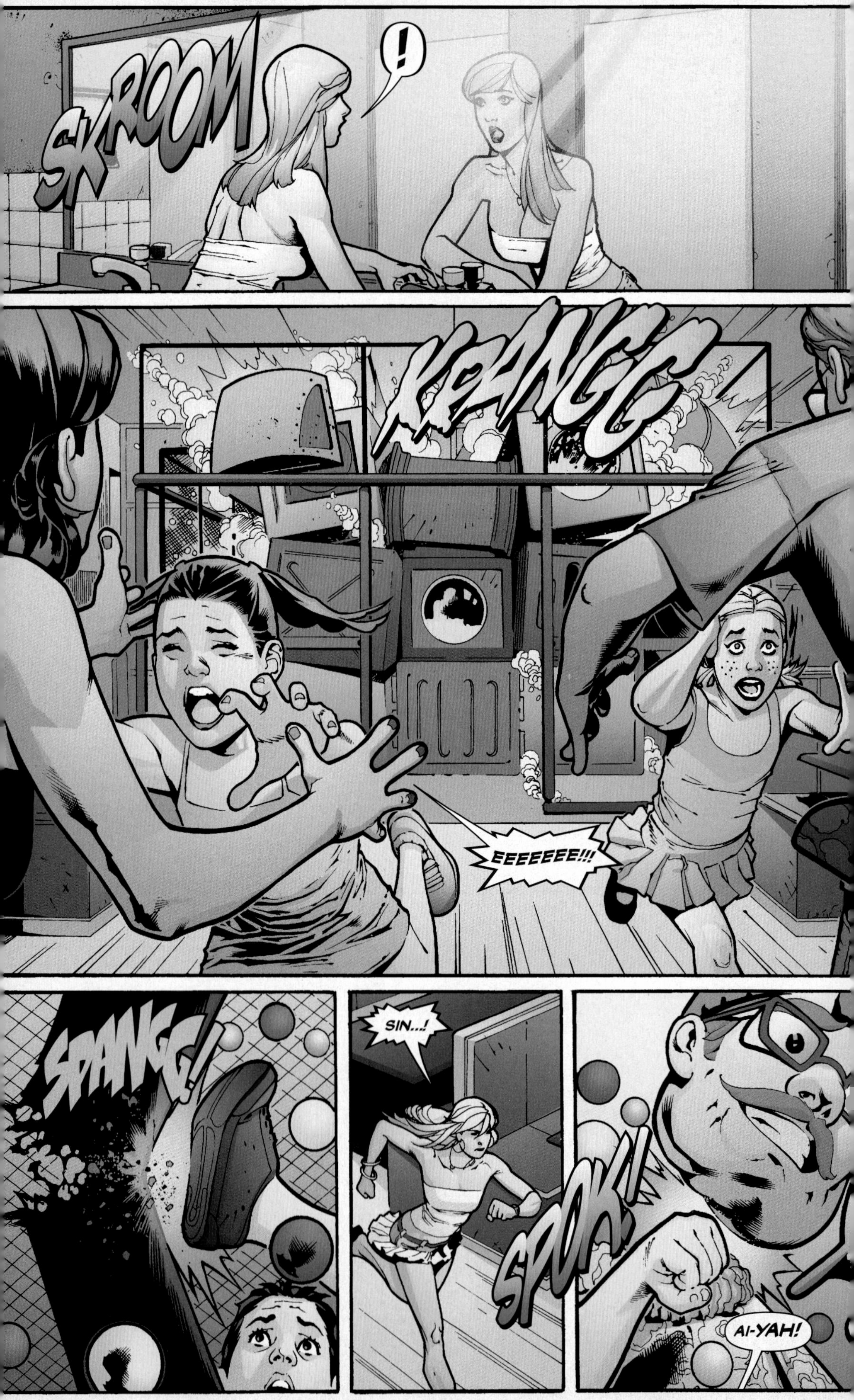
SKROOM
!
KRANGG
EEEEEEE!!!
SPANGG!
SIN...!
SPOK!
AI-YAH!

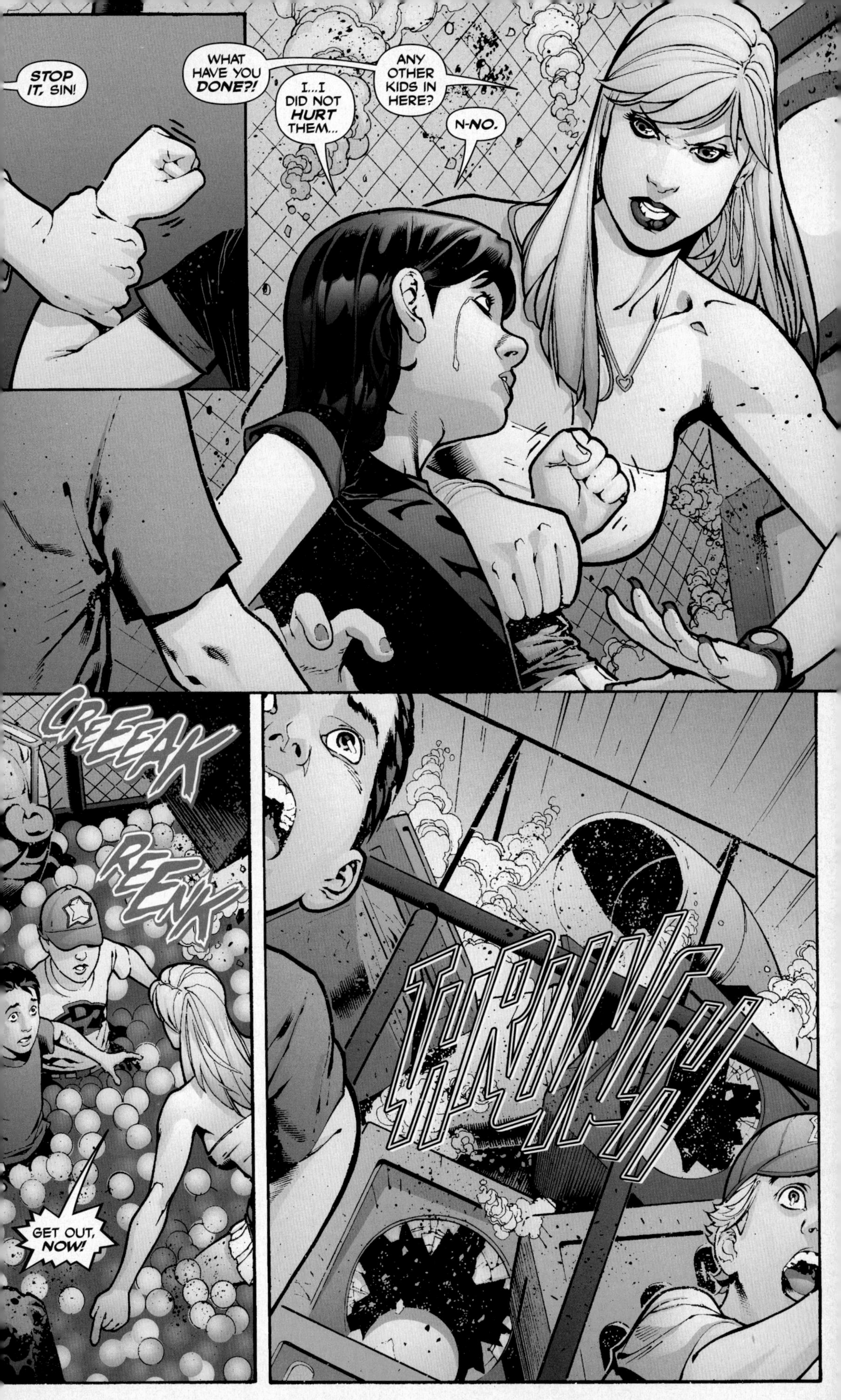
STOP IT, SIN!
WHAT HAVE YOU DONE?!
I...I DID NOT HURT THEM...
ANY OTHER KIDS IN HERE?
N-NO.
CREEEAK
REEENK
GET OUT, NOW!

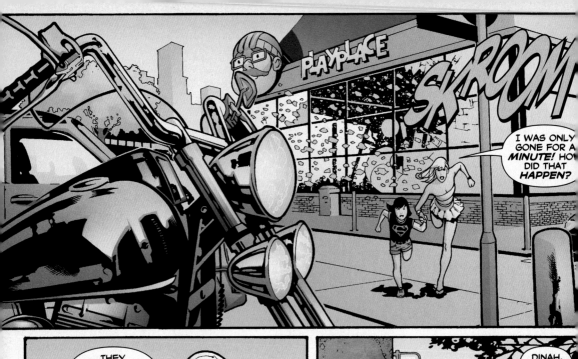

PLAYPLACE

SKROOM

I WAS ONLY GONE FOR A *MINUTE!* HOW DID THAT *HAPPEN?*

THEY *WANTED* TO FIGHT! THEY TRY TO *HIT* ME! I...I HAD TO *SHOW* THEM...

DINAH, DINAH, DINAH...

...YOU ALWAYS WERE A *TROUBLE-MAGNET*...

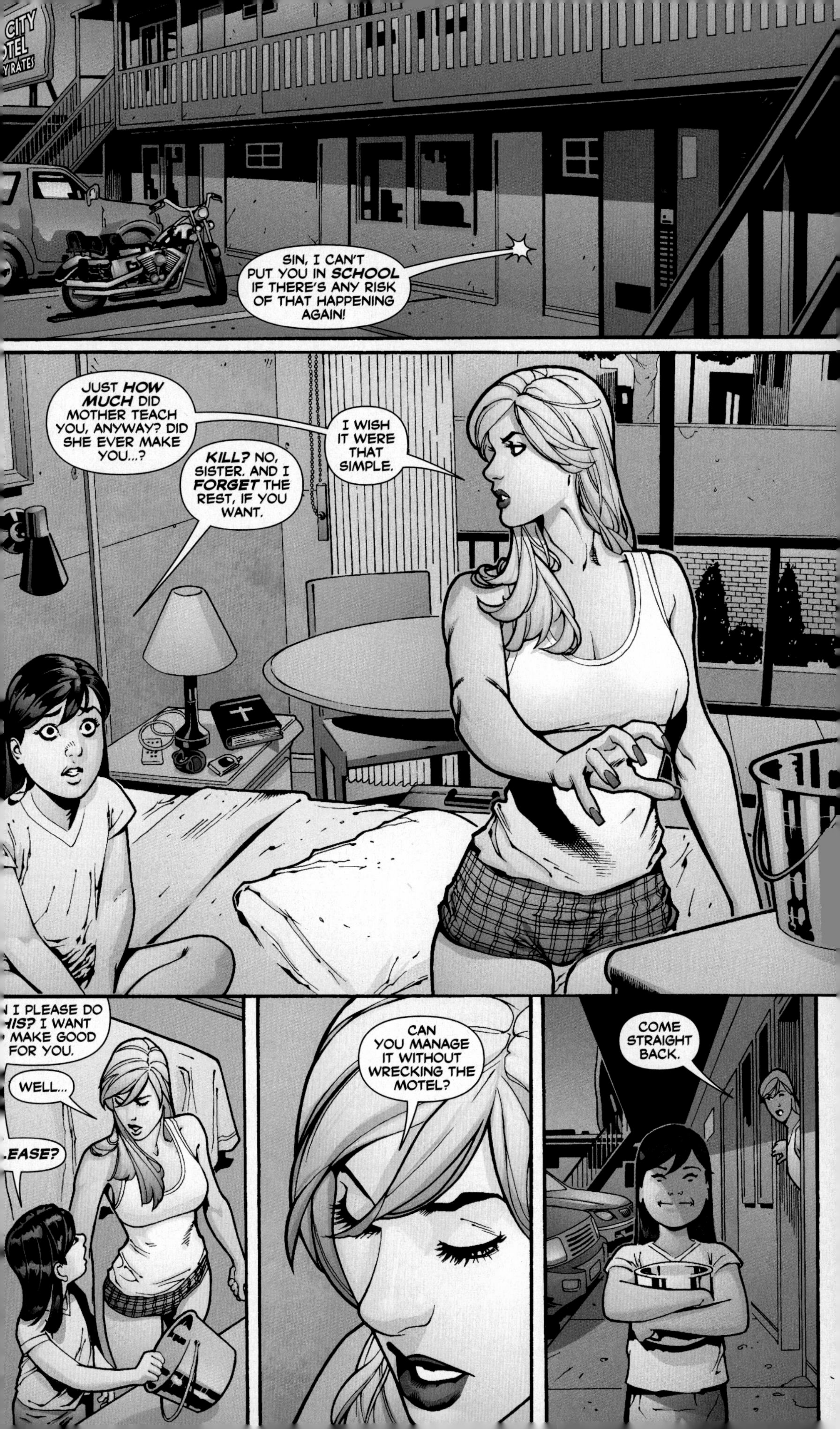

CITY
OTEL
Y RATES
SIN, I CAN'T PUT YOU IN SCHOOL IF THERE'S ANY RISK OF THAT HAPPENING AGAIN!
JUST HOW MUCH DID MOTHER TEACH YOU, ANYWAY? DID SHE EVER MAKE YOU...?
I WISH IT WERE THAT SIMPLE.
KILL? NO, SISTER. AND I FORGET THE REST, IF YOU WANT.
I PLEASE DO HIS? I WANT MAKE GOOD FOR YOU.
WELL...
EASE?
CAN YOU MANAGE IT WITHOUT WRECKING THE MOTEL?
COME STRAIGHT BACK.

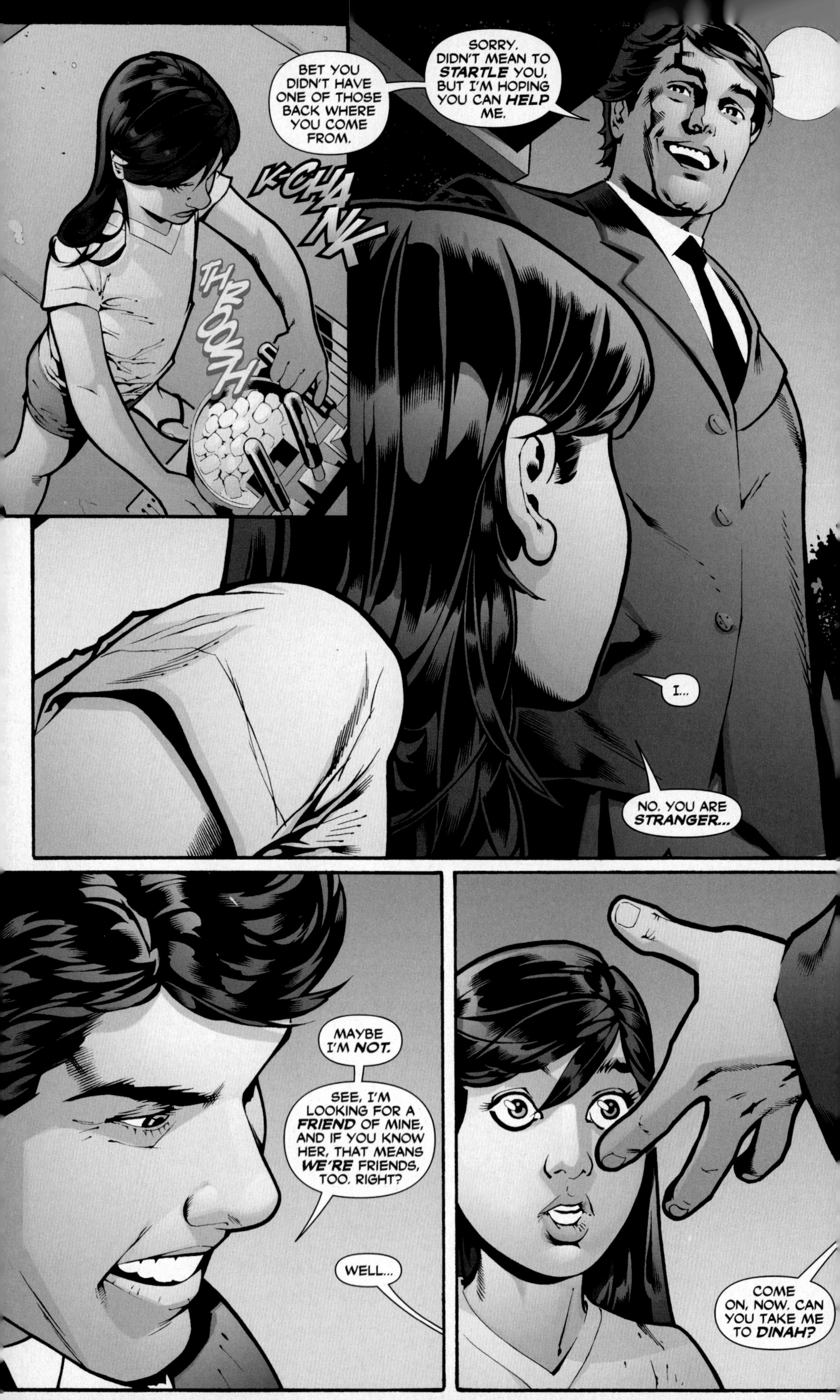
BET YOU DIDN'T HAVE ONE OF THOSE BACK WHERE YOU COME FROM.
K-CHANK
THROOOH
SORRY. DIDN'T MEAN TO STARTLE YOU, BUT I'M HOPING YOU CAN HELP ME.
I...
NO. YOU ARE STRANGER...
MAYBE I'M NOT.
SEE, I'M LOOKING FOR A FRIEND OF MINE, AND IF YOU KNOW HER, THAT MEANS WE'RE FRIENDS, TOO. RIGHT?
WELL...
COME ON, NOW. CAN YOU TAKE ME TO DINAH?

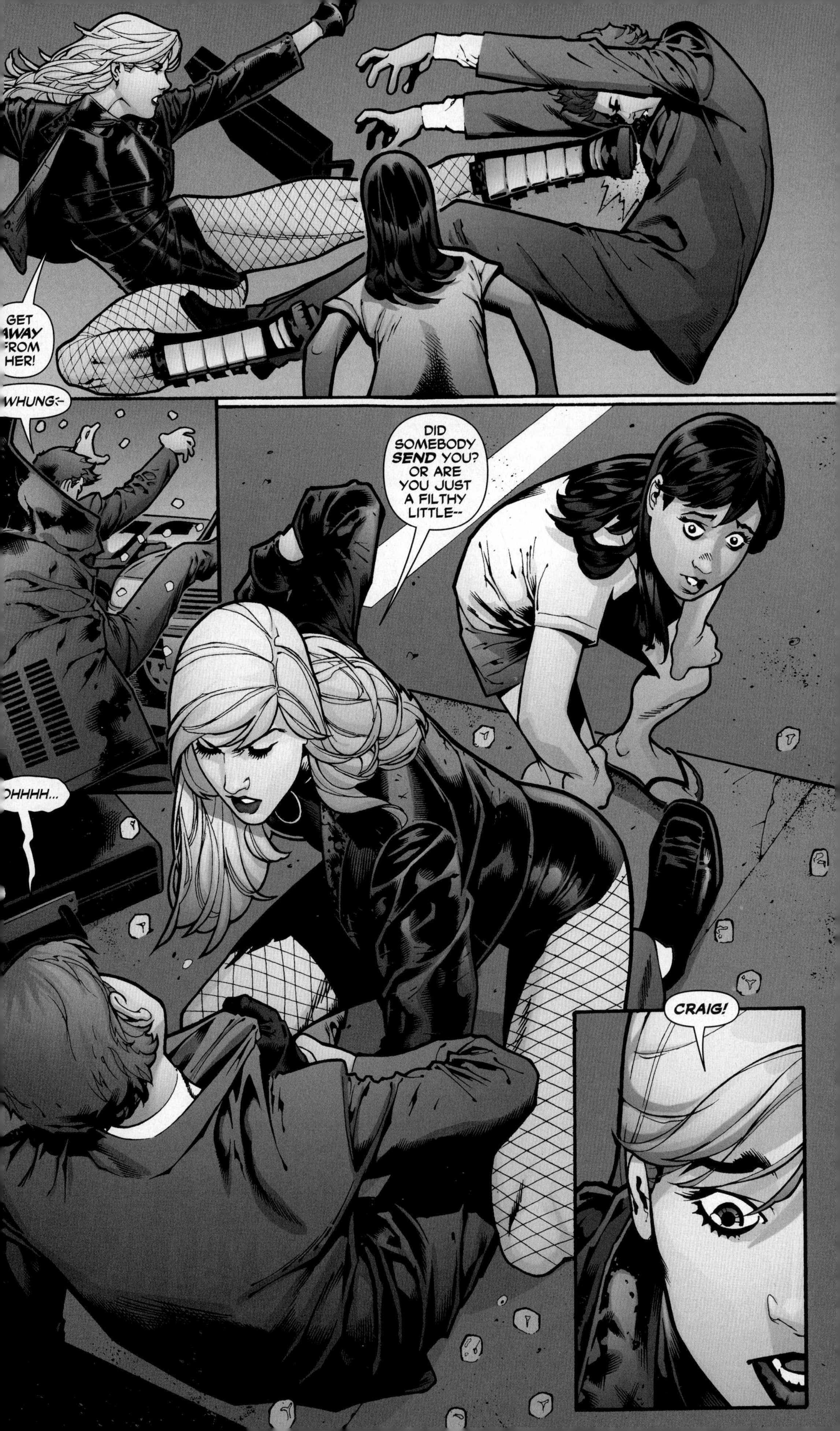

GET AWAY FROM HER!
WHUNG--
DID SOMEBODY SEND YOU? OR ARE YOU JUST A FILTHY LITTLE--
OHHHH...
CRAIG!

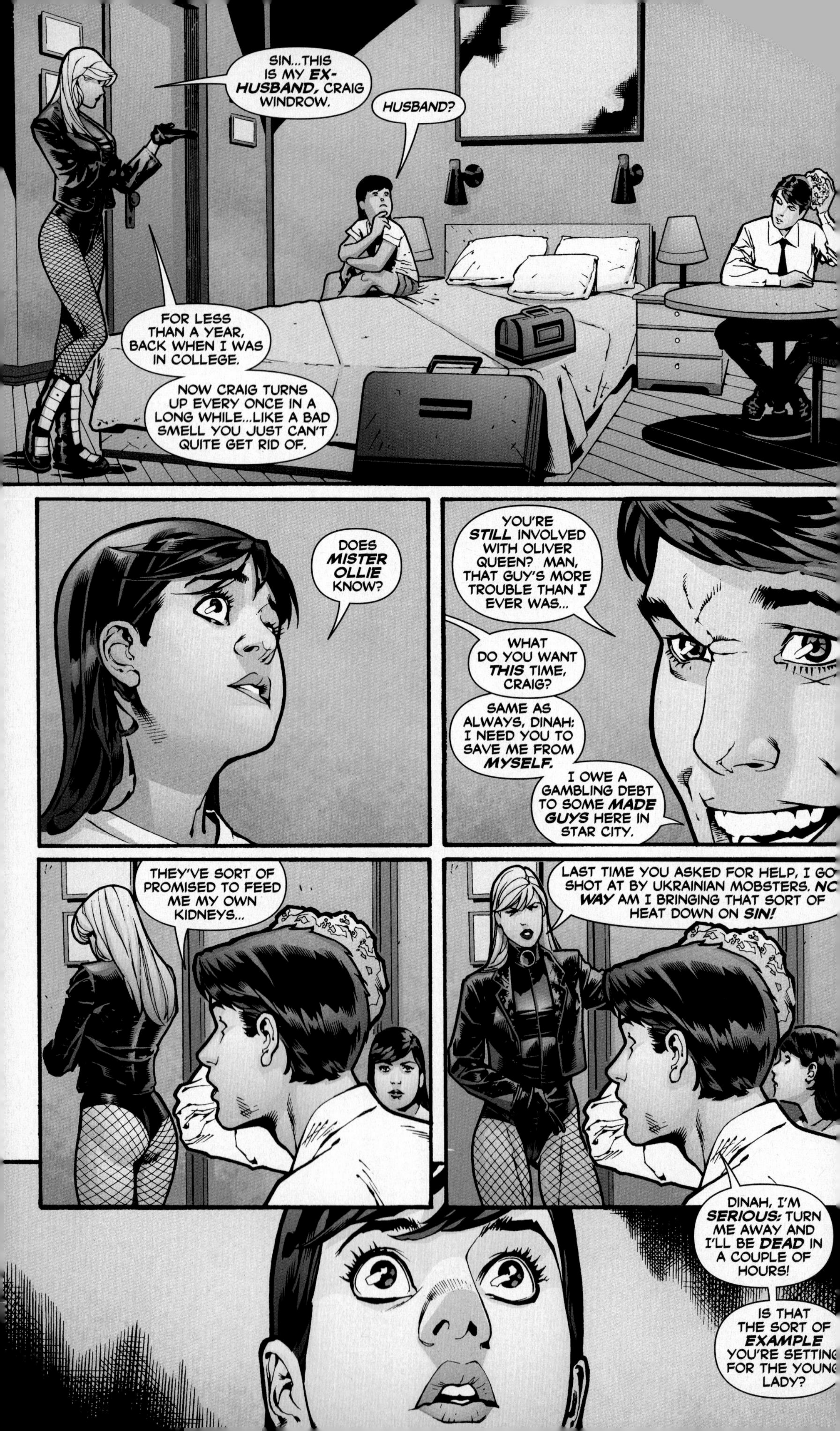

SIN...THIS IS MY EX-HUSBAND, CRAIG WINDROW.
HUSBAND?
FOR LESS THAN A YEAR, BACK WHEN I WAS IN COLLEGE.
NOW CRAIG TURNS UP EVERY ONCE IN A LONG WHILE...LIKE A BAD SMELL YOU JUST CAN'T QUITE GET RID OF.
DOES MISTER OLLIE KNOW?
YOU'RE STILL INVOLVED WITH OLIVER QUEEN? MAN, THAT GUY'S MORE TROUBLE THAN I EVER WAS...
WHAT DO YOU WANT THIS TIME, CRAIG?
SAME AS ALWAYS, DINAH: I NEED YOU TO SAVE ME FROM MYSELF.
I OWE A GAMBLING DEBT TO SOME MADE GUYS HERE IN STAR CITY.
THEY'VE SORT OF PROMISED TO FEED ME MY OWN KIDNEYS...
LAST TIME YOU ASKED FOR HELP, I GO SHOT AT BY UKRAINIAN MOBSTERS. NO WAY AM I BRINGING THAT SORT OF HEAT DOWN ON SIN!
DINAH, I'M SERIOUS: TURN ME AWAY AND I'LL BE DEAD IN A COUPLE OF HOURS!
IS THAT THE SORT OF EXAMPLE YOU'RE SETTING FOR THE YOUNG LADY?

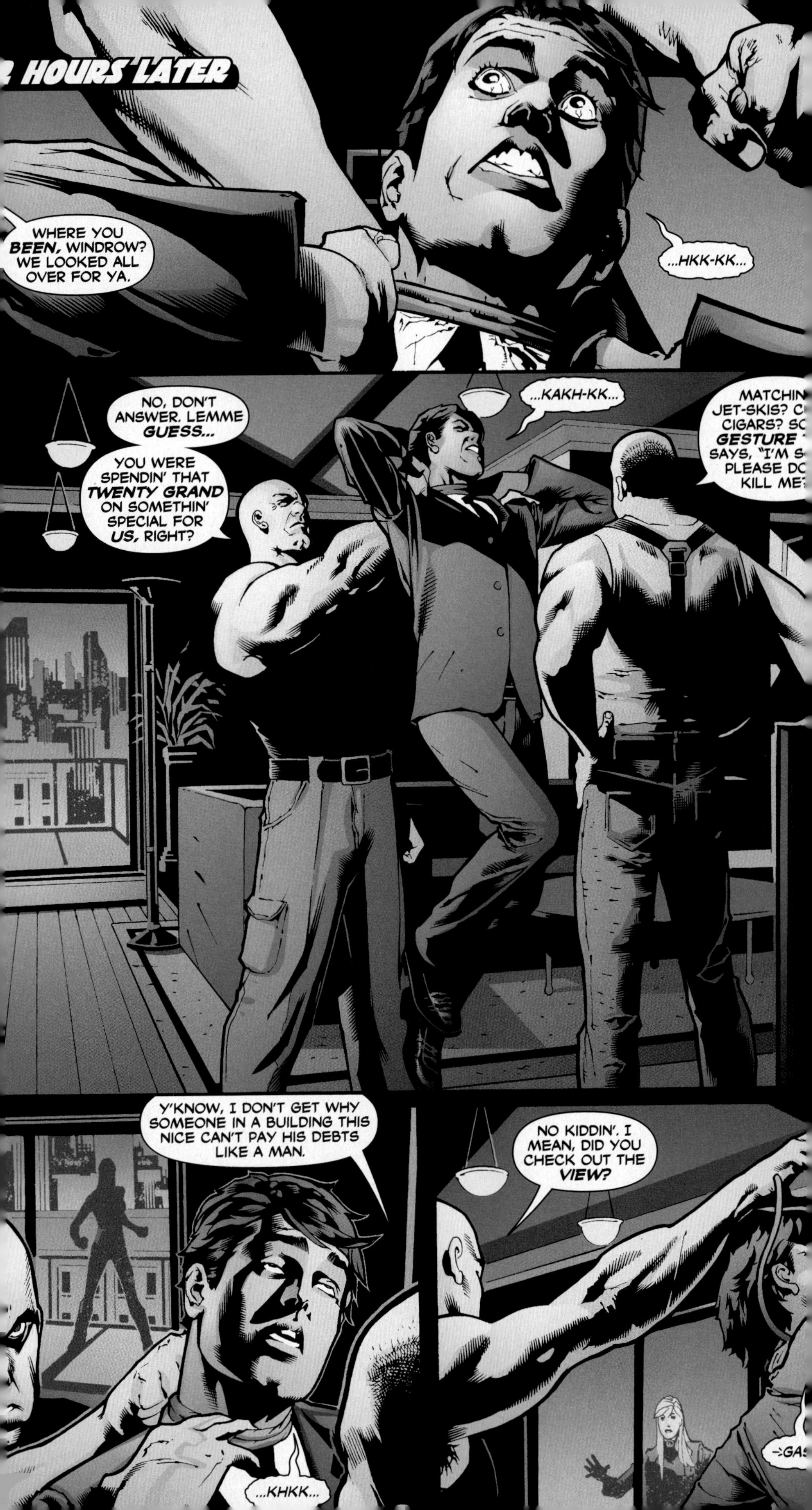

HOURS LATER
WHERE YOU BEEN, WINDROW? WE LOOKED ALL OVER FOR YA.
...HKK-KK...
NO, DON'T ANSWER. LEMME GUESS...
YOU WERE SPENDIN' THAT TWENTY GRAND ON SOMETHIN' SPECIAL FOR US, RIGHT?
...KAKH-KK...
MATCHIN
JET-SKIS?
CIGARS?
GESTURE
SAYS, "I'M
PLEASE DO
KILL ME
Y'KNOW, I DON'T GET WHY SOMEONE IN A BUILDING THIS NICE CAN'T PAY HIS DEBTS LIKE A MAN.
NO KIDDIN'. I MEAN, DID YOU CHECK OUT THE VIEW?
...KHKK...

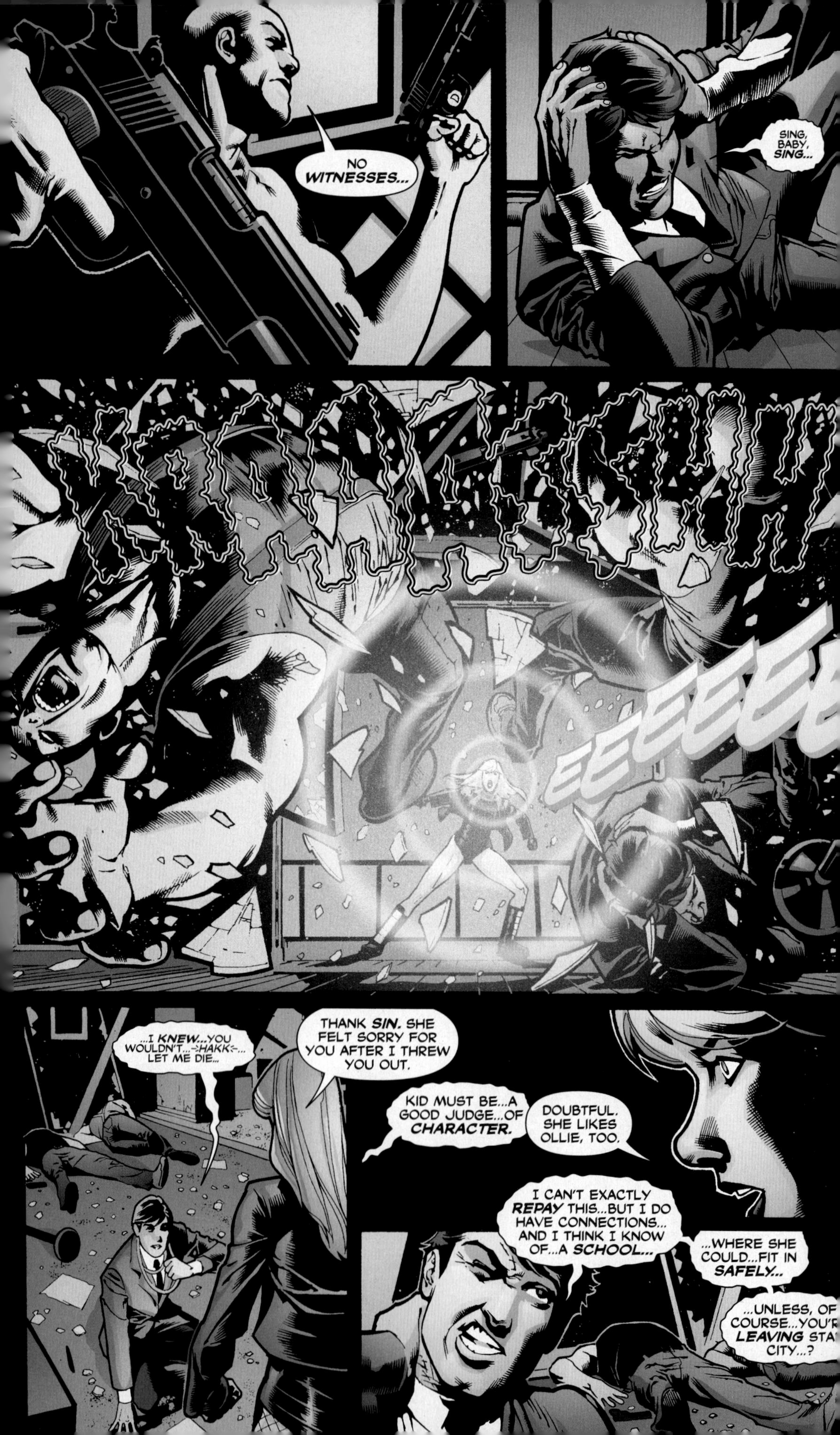
NO WITNESSES...
SING, BABY, SING...
...I KNEW...YOU WOULDN'T...<HAKK<...LET ME DIE...
THANK SIN. SHE FELT SORRY FOR YOU AFTER I THREW YOU OUT.
KID MUST BE...A GOOD JUDGE...OF CHARACTER.
DOUBTFUL. SHE LIKES OLLIE, TOO.
I CAN'T EXACTLY REPAY THIS...BUT I DO HAVE CONNECTIONS... AND I THINK I KNOW OF...A SCHOOL...
...WHERE SHE COULD...FIT IN SAFELY...
...UNLESS, OF COURSE...YOU'R LEAVING STA CITY...?

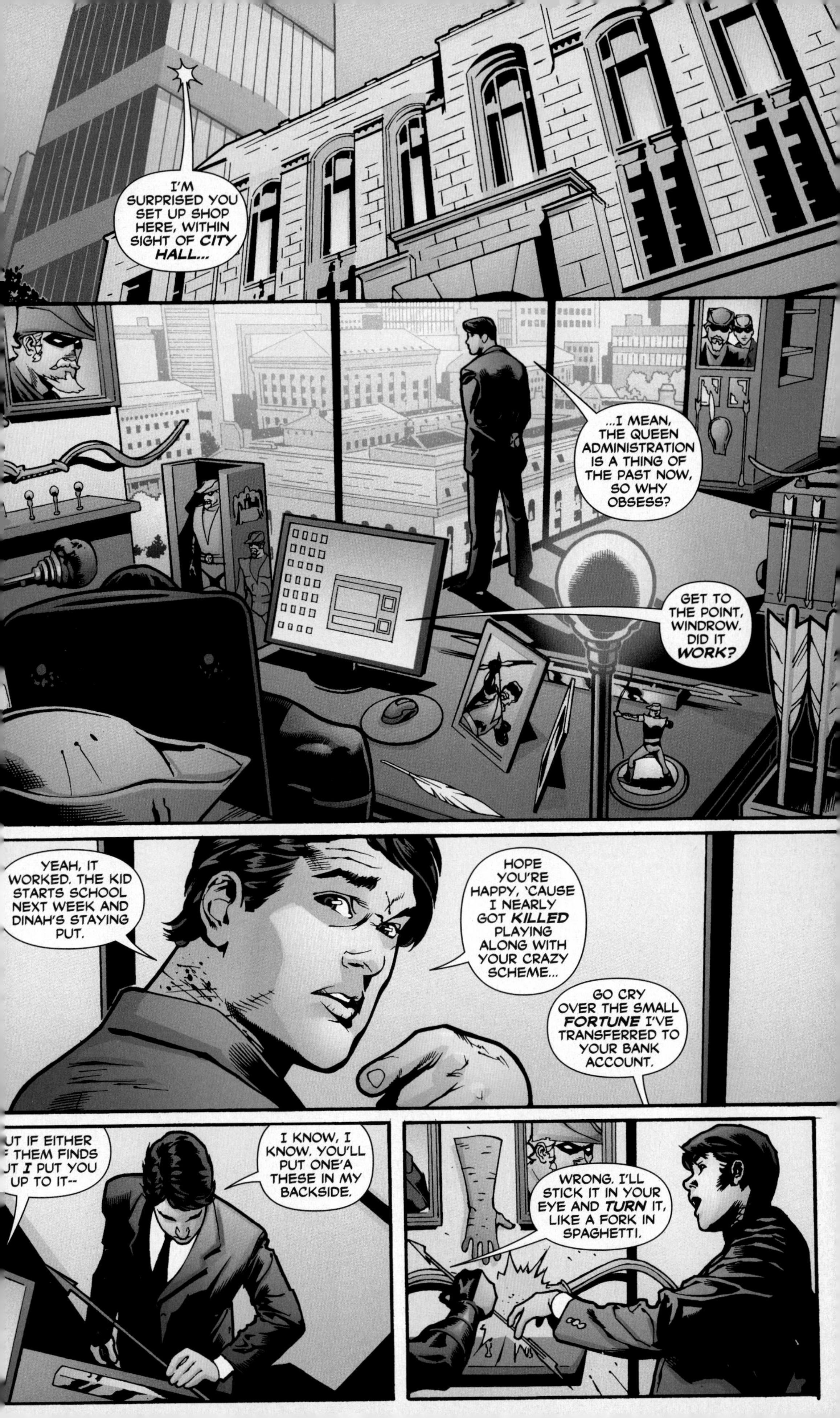
I'M SURPRISED YOU SET UP SHOP HERE, WITHIN SIGHT OF *CITY HALL...*
...I MEAN, THE QUEEN ADMINISTRATION IS A THING OF THE PAST NOW, SO WHY OBSESS?
GET TO THE POINT, WINDROW. DID IT *WORK?*
YEAH, IT WORKED. THE KID STARTS SCHOOL NEXT WEEK AND DINAH'S STAYING PUT.
HOPE YOU'RE HAPPY, 'CAUSE I NEARLY GOT *KILLED* PLAYING ALONG WITH YOUR CRAZY SCHEME...
GO CRY OVER THE SMALL *FORTUNE* I'VE TRANSFERRED TO YOUR BANK ACCOUNT.
UT IF EITHER F THEM FINDS UT *I* PUT YOU UP TO IT--
I KNOW, I KNOW. YOU'LL PUT ONE'A THESE IN MY BACKSIDE.
WRONG. I'LL STICK IT IN YOUR EYE AND *TURN* IT, LIKE A FORK IN SPAGHETTI.

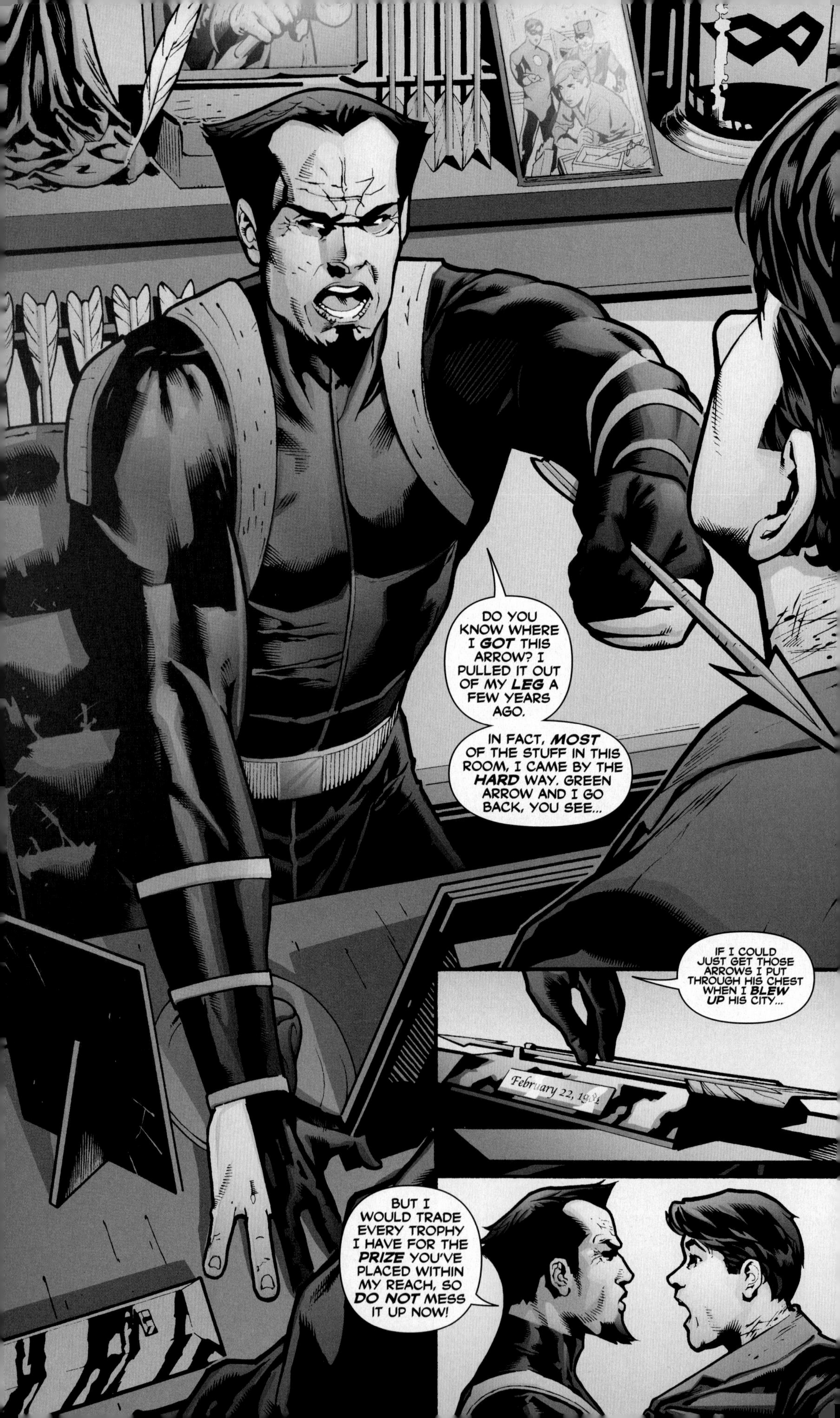
DO YOU KNOW WHERE I GOT THIS ARROW? I PULLED IT OUT OF MY LEG A FEW YEARS AGO.
IN FACT, MOST OF THE STUFF IN THIS ROOM, I CAME BY THE HARD WAY. GREEN ARROW AND I GO BACK, YOU SEE...
IF I COULD JUST GET THOSE ARROWS I PUT THROUGH HIS CHEST WHEN I BLEW UP HIS CITY...
February 22, 1984
BUT I WOULD TRADE EVERY TROPHY I HAVE FOR THE PRIZE YOU'VE PLACED WITHIN MY REACH, SO DO NOT MESS IT UP NOW!

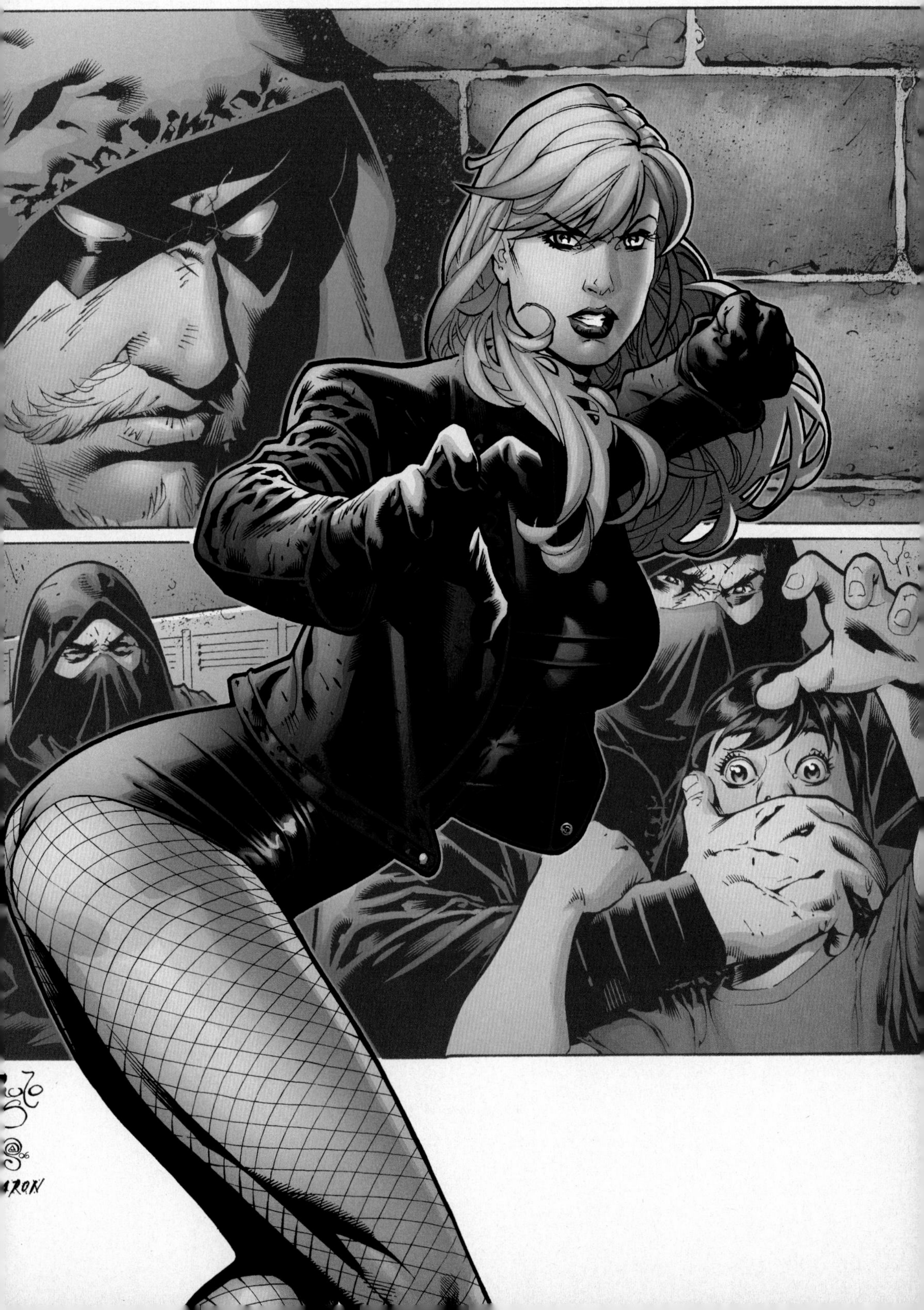

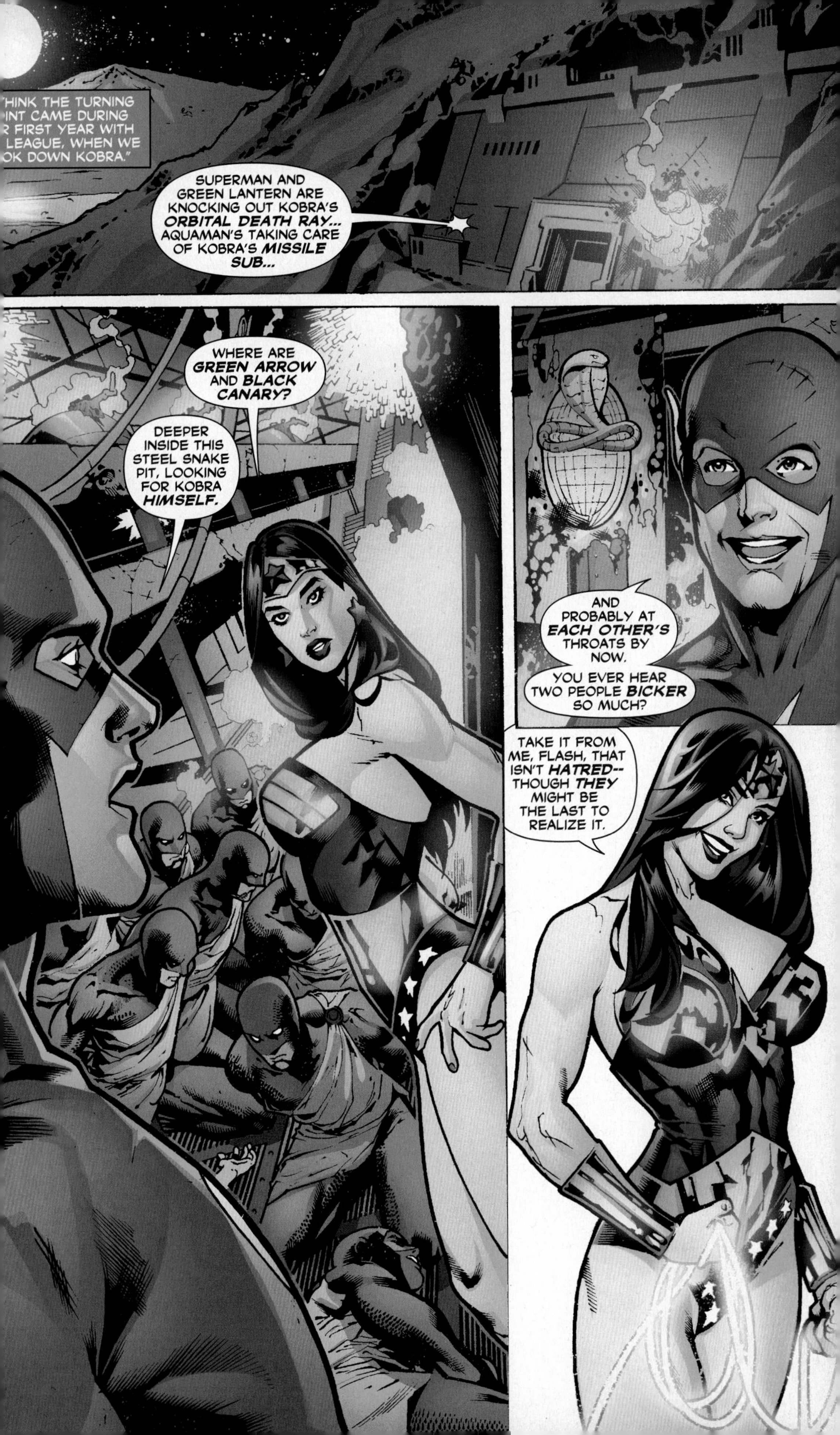
"THINK THE TURNING
POINT CAME DURING
R FIRST YEAR WITH
LEAGUE, WHEN WE
OK DOWN KOBRA."
SUPERMAN AND GREEN LANTERN ARE KNOCKING OUT KOBRA'S ORBITAL DEATH RAY... AQUAMAN'S TAKING CARE OF KOBRA'S MISSILE SUB...
WHERE ARE GREEN ARROW AND BLACK CANARY?
DEEPER INSIDE THIS STEEL SNAKE PIT, LOOKING FOR KOBRA HIMSELF.
AND PROBABLY AT EACH OTHER'S THROATS BY NOW.
YOU EVER HEAR TWO PEOPLE BICKER SO MUCH?
TAKE IT FROM ME, FLASH, THAT ISN'T HATRED-- THOUGH THEY MIGHT BE THE LAST TO REALIZE IT.

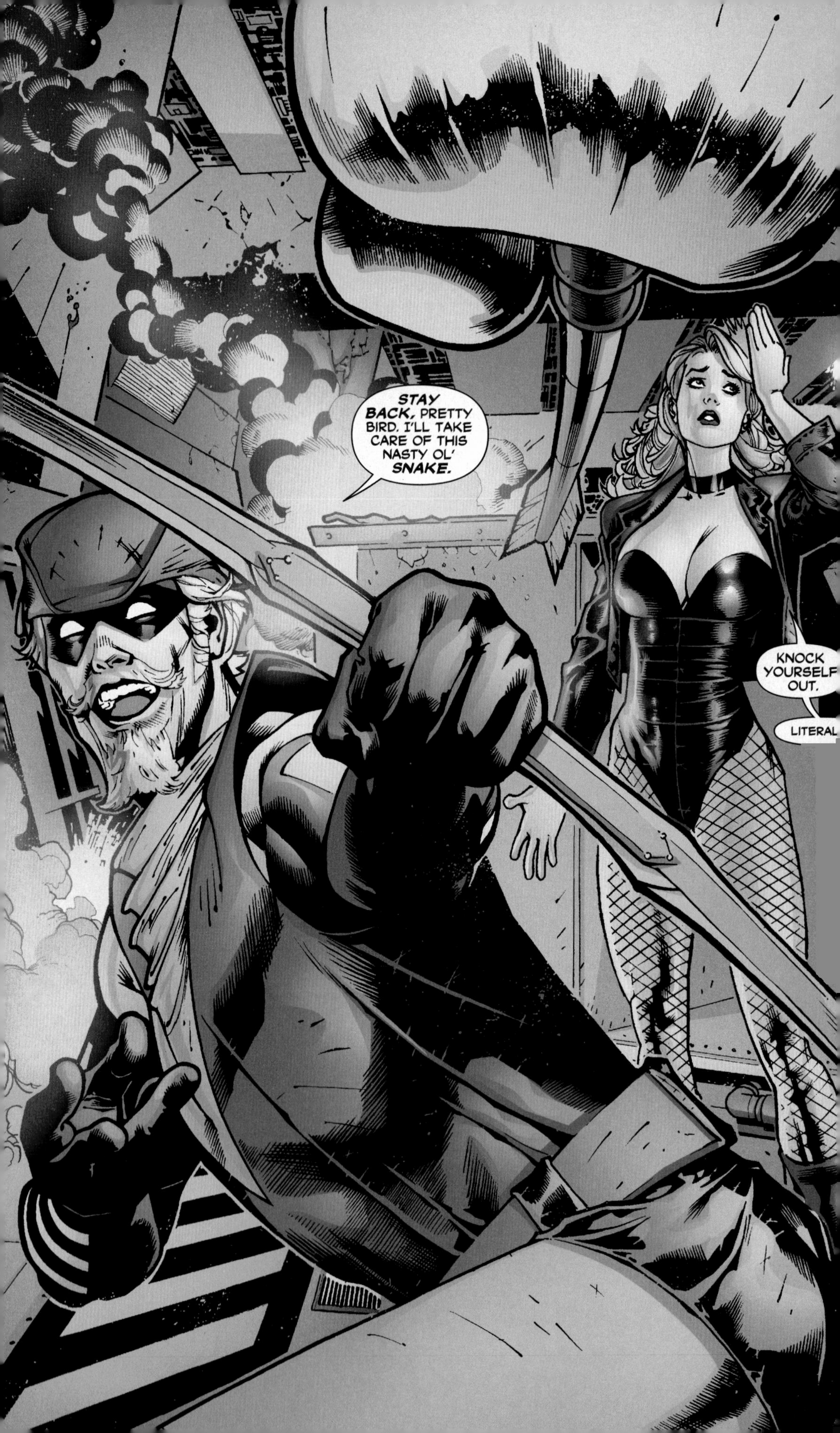
STAY BACK, PRETTY BIRD. I'LL TAKE CARE OF THIS NASTY OL' SNAKE.
KNOCK YOURSELF OUT.
LITERAL

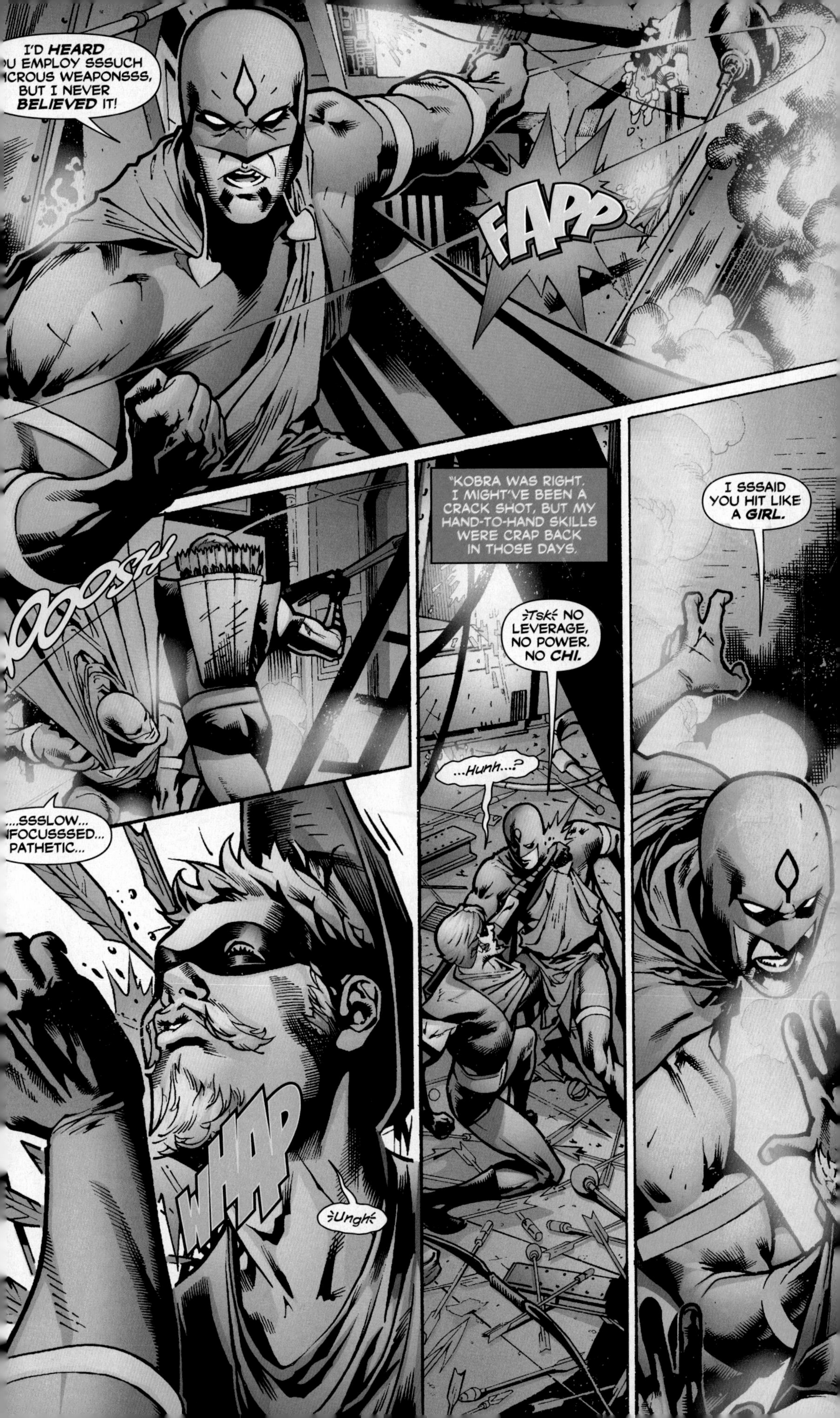
I'D HEARD
OU EMPLOY SSSUCH
ICROUS WEAPONSSS,
BUT I NEVER
BELIEVED IT!
FAPP
OOOSH
...SSSLOW...
IFOCUSSSED...
PATHETIC...
WHAP
Ungh
"KOBRA WAS RIGHT. I MIGHT'VE BEEN A CRACK SHOT, BUT MY HAND-TO-HAND SKILLS WERE CRAP BACK IN THOSE DAYS.
Tsk NO LEVERAGE, NO POWER. NO CHI.
...Hunh...?
I SSSAID YOU HIT LIKE A GIRL.

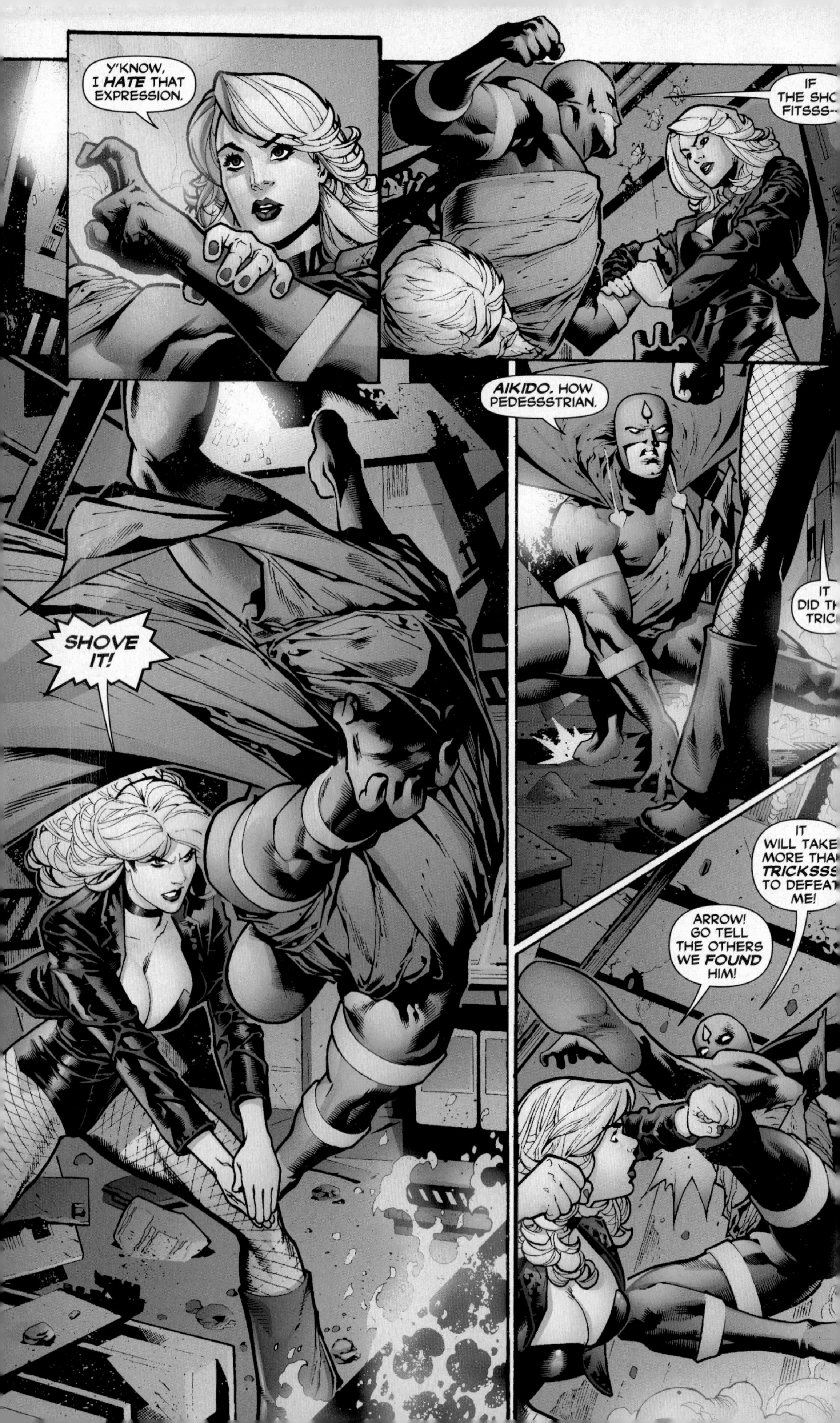
Y'KNOW, I HATE THAT EXPRESSION.
IF THE SHO FITSSS--
AIKIDO. HOW PEDESSSTRIAN.
IT DID TH TRIC
SHOVE IT!
IT WILL TAKE MORE THA TRICKSSS TO DEFEAT ME!
ARROW! GO TELL THE OTHERS WE FOUND HIM!

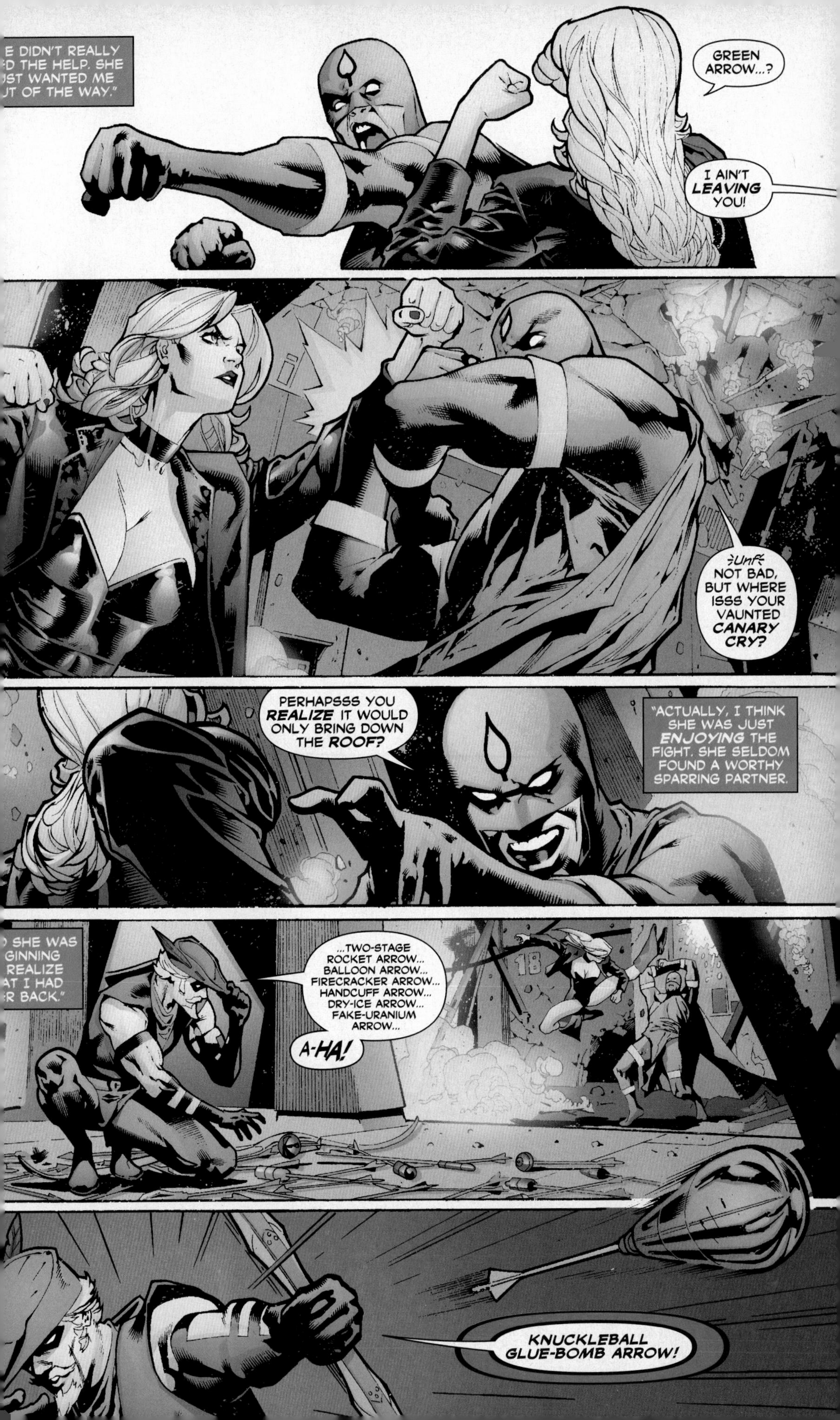
E DIDN'T REALLY
ED THE HELP. SHE
JST WANTED ME
UT OF THE WAY."
GREEN ARROW...?
I AIN'T LEAVING YOU!
Unf NOT BAD, BUT WHERE ISSS YOUR VAUNTED CANARY CRY?
PERHAPSSS YOU REALIZE IT WOULD ONLY BRING DOWN THE ROOF?
"ACTUALLY, I THINK SHE WAS JUST ENJOYING THE FIGHT. SHE SELDOM FOUND A WORTHY SPARRING PARTNER.
SHE WAS
GINNING
REALIZE
AT I HAD
R BACK."
...TWO-STAGE ROCKET ARROW... BALLOON ARROW... FIRECRACKER ARROW... HANDCUFF ARROW... DRY-ICE ARROW... FAKE-URANIUM ARROW...
A-HA!
KNUCKLEBALL GLUE-BOMB ARROW!

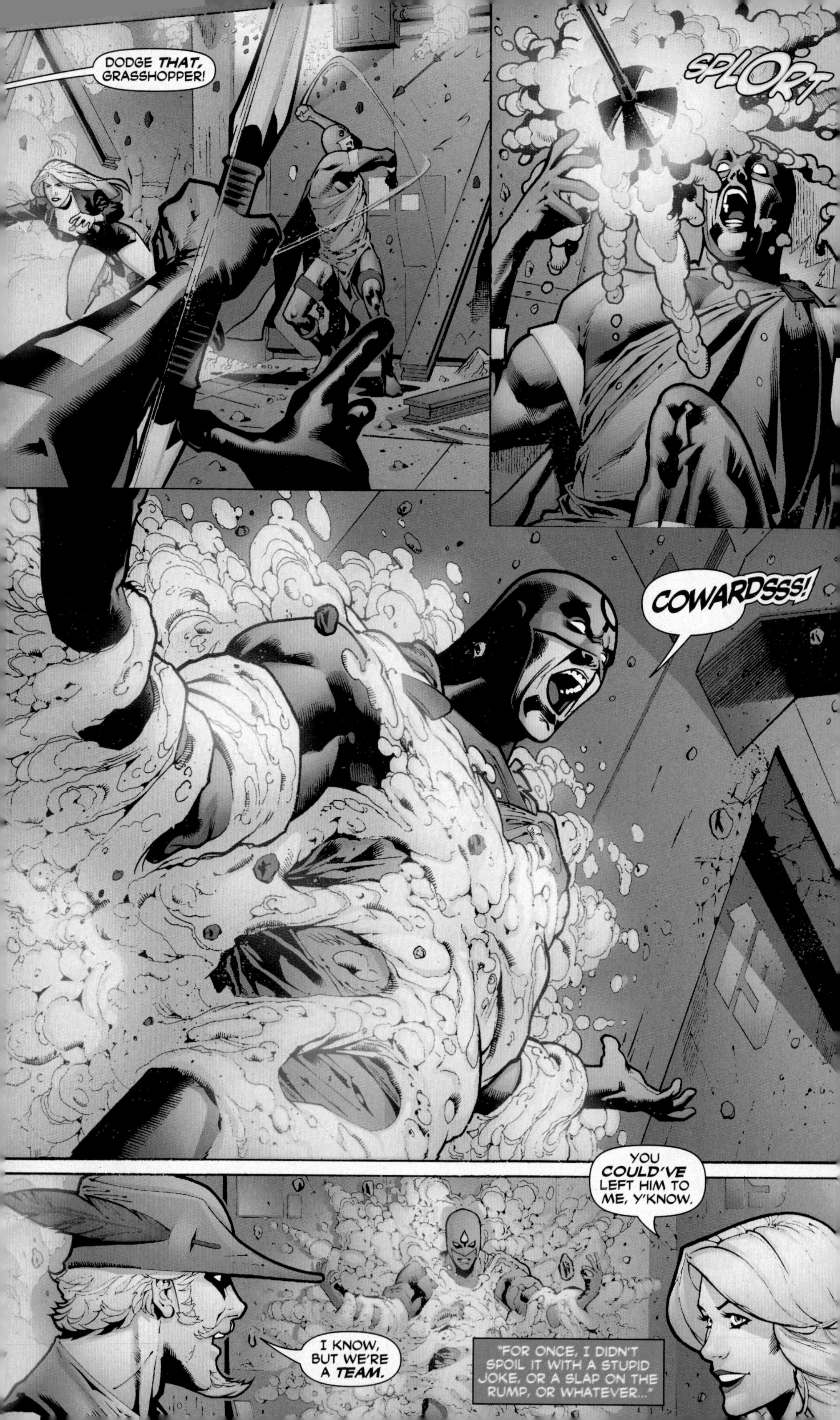
DODGE THAT, GRASSHOPPER!
SPLORT
COWARDSSS!
YOU COULD'VE LEFT HIM TO ME, Y'KNOW.
I KNOW, BUT WE'RE A TEAM.
"FOR ONCE, I DIDN'T SPOIL IT WITH A STUPID JOKE, OR A SLAP ON THE RUMP, OR WHATEVER..."

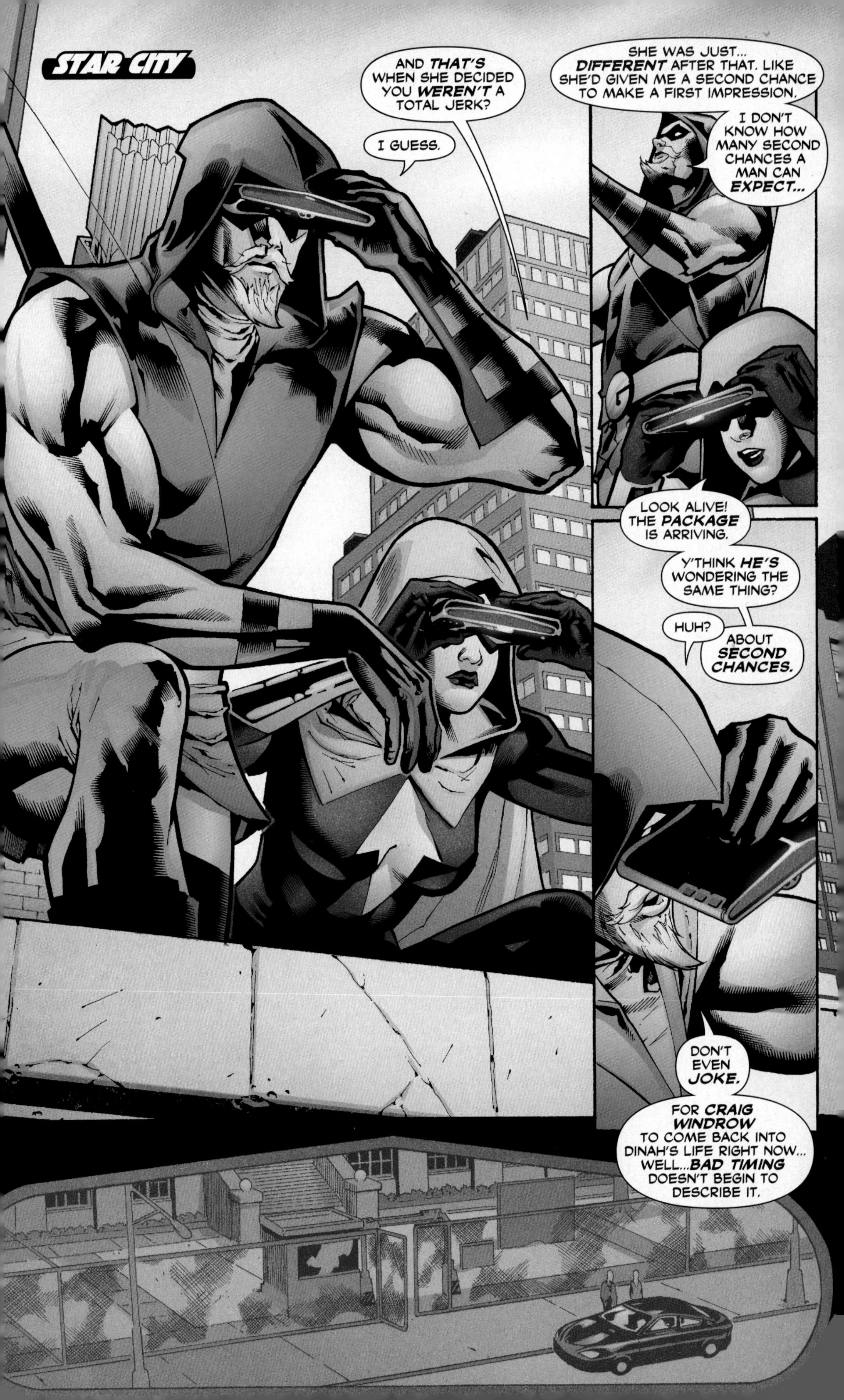
STAR CITY
AND THAT'S WHEN SHE DECIDED YOU WEREN'T A TOTAL JERK?
I GUESS.
SHE WAS JUST... DIFFERENT AFTER THAT. LIKE SHE'D GIVEN ME A SECOND CHANCE TO MAKE A FIRST IMPRESSION.
I DON'T KNOW HOW MANY SECOND CHANCES A MAN CAN EXPECT...
LOOK ALIVE! THE PACKAGE IS ARRIVING.
Y'THINK HE'S WONDERING THE SAME THING?
HUH?
ABOUT SECOND CHANCES.
DON'T EVEN JOKE.
FOR CRAIG WINDROW TO COME BACK INTO DINAH'S LIFE RIGHT NOW... WELL...BAD TIMING DOESN'T BEGIN TO DESCRIBE IT.

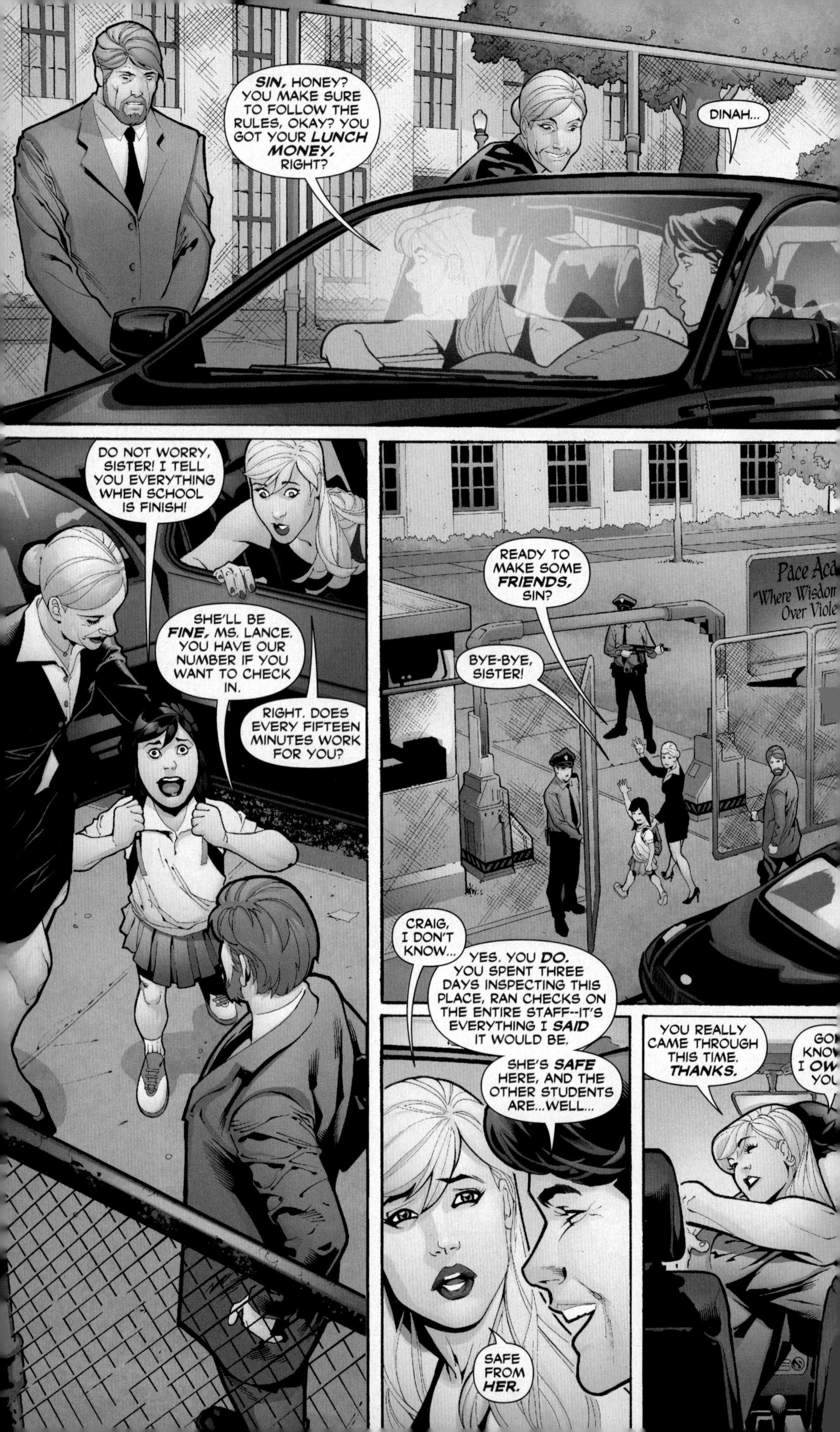
SIN, HONEY? YOU MAKE SURE TO FOLLOW THE RULES, OKAY? YOU GOT YOUR LUNCH MONEY, RIGHT?
DINAH...
DO NOT WORRY, SISTER! I TELL YOU EVERYTHING WHEN SCHOOL IS FINISH!
SHE'LL BE FINE, MS. LANCE. YOU HAVE OUR NUMBER IF YOU WANT TO CHECK IN.
RIGHT. DOES EVERY FIFTEEN MINUTES WORK FOR YOU?
READY TO MAKE SOME FRIENDS, SIN?
BYE-BYE, SISTER!
CRAIG, I DON'T KNOW...
YES. YOU DO. YOU SPENT THREE DAYS INSPECTING THIS PLACE, RAN CHECKS ON THE ENTIRE STAFF--IT'S EVERYTHING I SAID IT WOULD BE.
SHE'S SAFE HERE, AND THE OTHER STUDENTS ARE...WELL...
SAFE FROM HER.
YOU REALLY CAME THROUGH THIS TIME. THANKS.

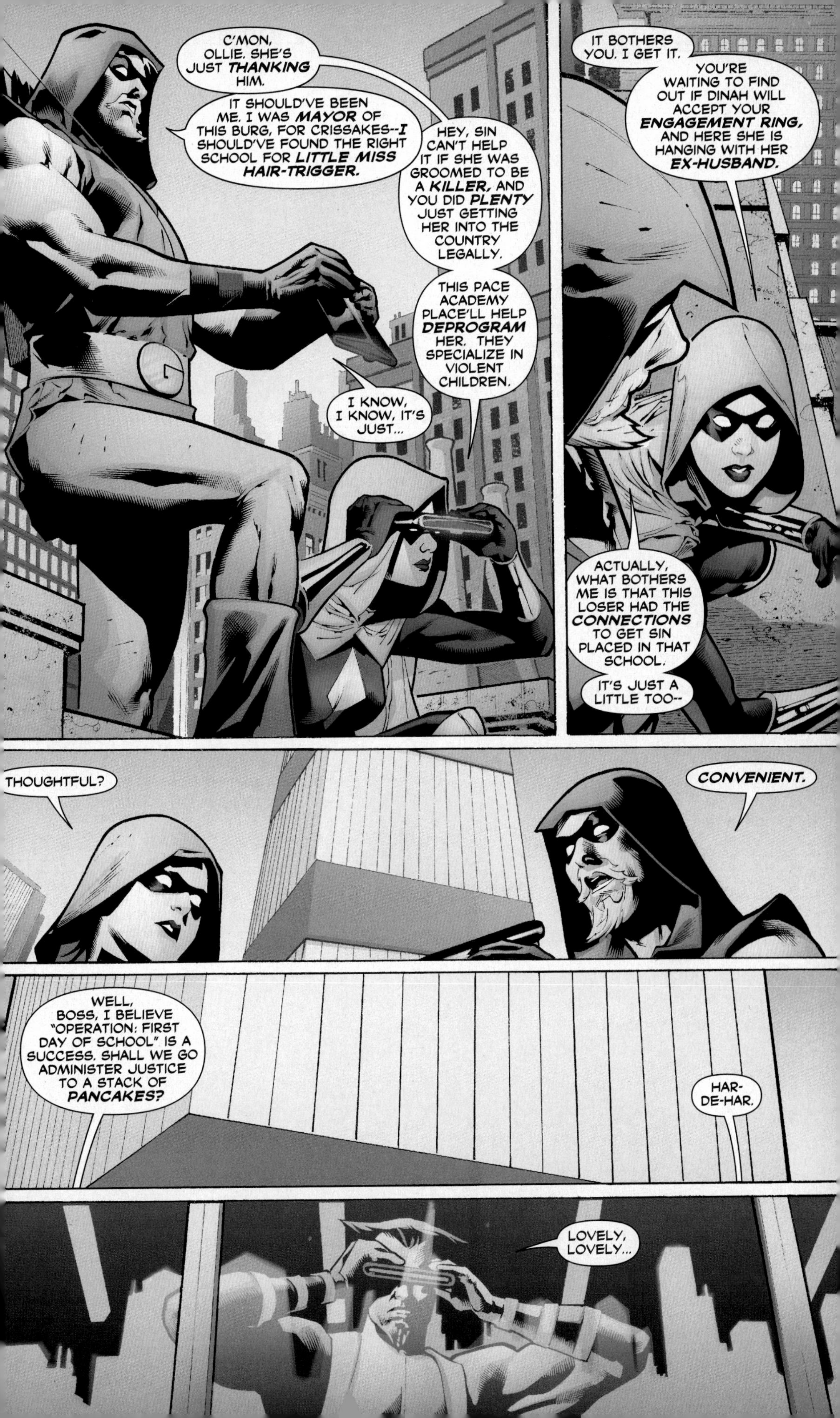
C'MON, OLLIE. SHE'S JUST THANKING HIM.
IT SHOULD'VE BEEN ME. I WAS MAYOR OF THIS BURG, FOR CRISSAKES--I SHOULD'VE FOUND THE RIGHT SCHOOL FOR LITTLE MISS HAIR-TRIGGER.
HEY, SIN CAN'T HELP IT IF SHE WAS GROOMED TO BE A KILLER, AND YOU DID PLENTY JUST GETTING HER INTO THE COUNTRY LEGALLY.
THIS PACE ACADEMY PLACE'LL HELP DEPROGRAM HER. THEY SPECIALIZE IN VIOLENT CHILDREN.
I KNOW, I KNOW, IT'S JUST...
IT BOTHERS YOU. I GET IT.
YOU'RE WAITING TO FIND OUT IF DINAH WILL ACCEPT YOUR ENGAGEMENT RING, AND HERE SHE IS HANGING WITH HER EX-HUSBAND.
ACTUALLY, WHAT BOTHERS ME IS THAT THIS LOSER HAD THE CONNECTIONS TO GET SIN PLACED IN THAT SCHOOL.
IT'S JUST A LITTLE TOO--
THOUGHTFUL?
CONVENIENT.
WELL, BOSS, I BELIEVE "OPERATION: FIRST DAY OF SCHOOL" IS A SUCCESS. SHALL WE GO ADMINISTER JUSTICE TO A STACK OF PANCAKES?
HAR-DE-HAR.
LOVELY, LOVELY...

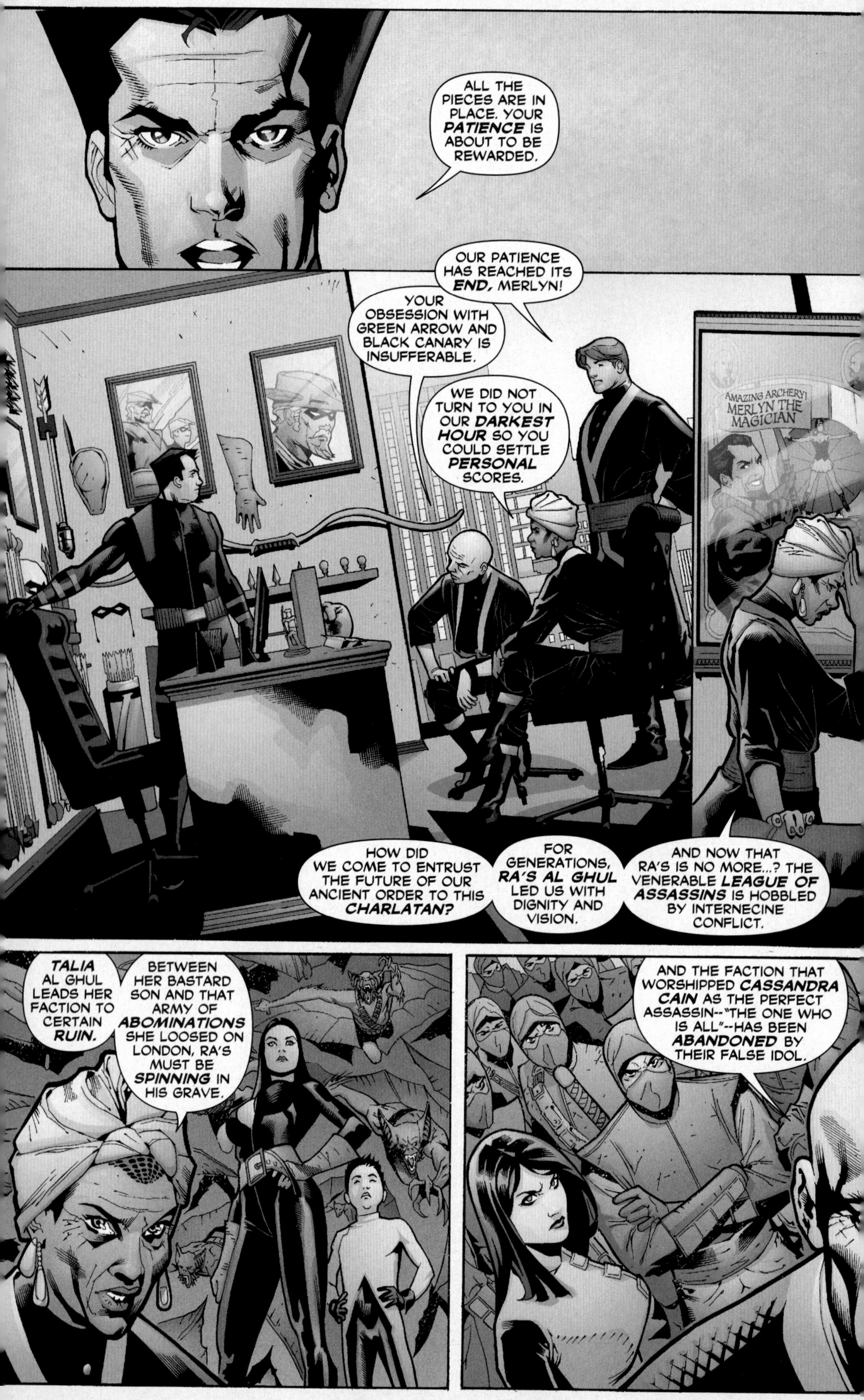
ALL THE PIECES ARE IN PLACE. YOUR PATIENCE IS ABOUT TO BE REWARDED.
OUR PATIENCE HAS REACHED ITS END, MERLYN!
YOUR OBSESSION WITH GREEN ARROW AND BLACK CANARY IS INSUFFERABLE.
WE DID NOT TURN TO YOU IN OUR DARKEST HOUR SO YOU COULD SETTLE PERSONAL SCORES.
AMAZING ARCHERY! MERLYN THE MAGICIAN
HOW DID WE COME TO ENTRUST THE FUTURE OF OUR ANCIENT ORDER TO THIS CHARLATAN?
FOR GENERATIONS, RA'S AL GHUL LED US WITH DIGNITY AND VISION.
AND NOW THAT RA'S IS NO MORE...? THE VENERABLE LEAGUE OF ASSASSINS IS HOBBLED BY INTERNECINE CONFLICT.
TALIA AL GHUL LEADS HER FACTION TO CERTAIN RUIN.
BETWEEN HER BASTARD SON AND THAT ARMY OF ABOMINATIONS SHE LOOSED ON LONDON, RA'S MUST BE SPINNING IN HIS GRAVE.
AND THE FACTION THAT WORSHIPPED CASSANDRA CAIN AS THE PERFECT ASSASSIN--"THE ONE WHO IS ALL"--HAS BEEN ABANDONED BY THEIR FALSE IDOL.

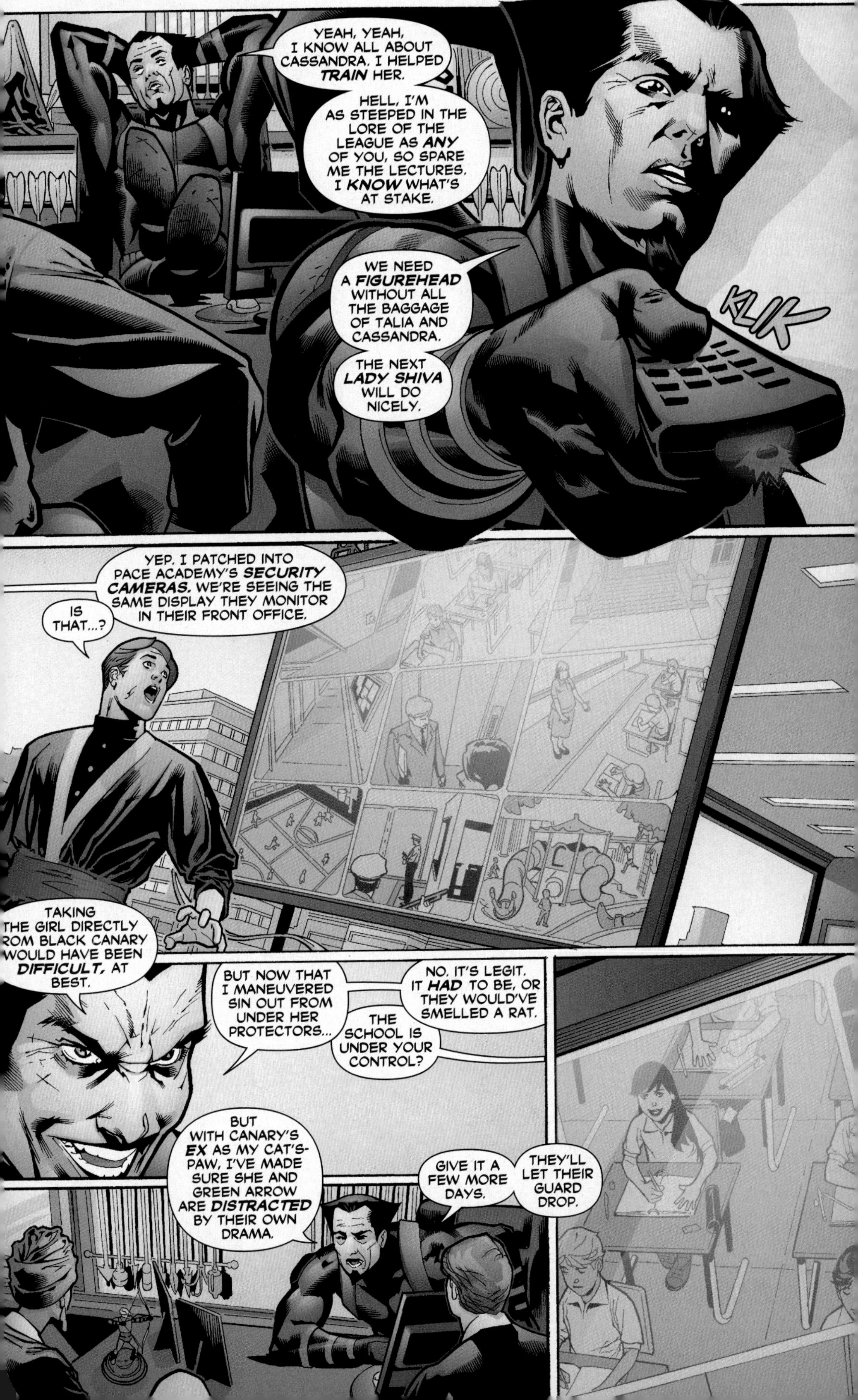

YEAH, YEAH, I KNOW ALL ABOUT CASSANDRA. I HELPED TRAIN HER.
HELL, I'M AS STEEPED IN THE LORE OF THE LEAGUE AS ANY OF YOU, SO SPARE ME THE LECTURES. I KNOW WHAT'S AT STAKE.
WE NEED A FIGUREHEAD WITHOUT ALL THE BAGGAGE OF TALIA AND CASSANDRA.
THE NEXT LADY SHIVA WILL DO NICELY.
KLIK
YEP. I PATCHED INTO PACE ACADEMY'S SECURITY CAMERAS. WE'RE SEEING THE SAME DISPLAY THEY MONITOR IN THEIR FRONT OFFICE.
IS THAT...?
TAKING THE GIRL DIRECTLY ROM BLACK CANARY WOULD HAVE BEEN DIFFICULT, AT BEST.
BUT NOW THAT I MANEUVERED SIN OUT FROM UNDER HER PROTECTORS...
THE SCHOOL IS UNDER YOUR CONTROL?
NO, IT'S LEGIT. IT HAD TO BE, OR THEY WOULD'VE SMELLED A RAT.
BUT WITH CANARY'S EX AS MY CAT'S-PAW, I'VE MADE SURE SHE AND GREEN ARROW ARE DISTRACTED BY THEIR OWN DRAMA.
GIVE IT A FEW MORE DAYS.
THEY'LL LET THEIR GUARD DROP.

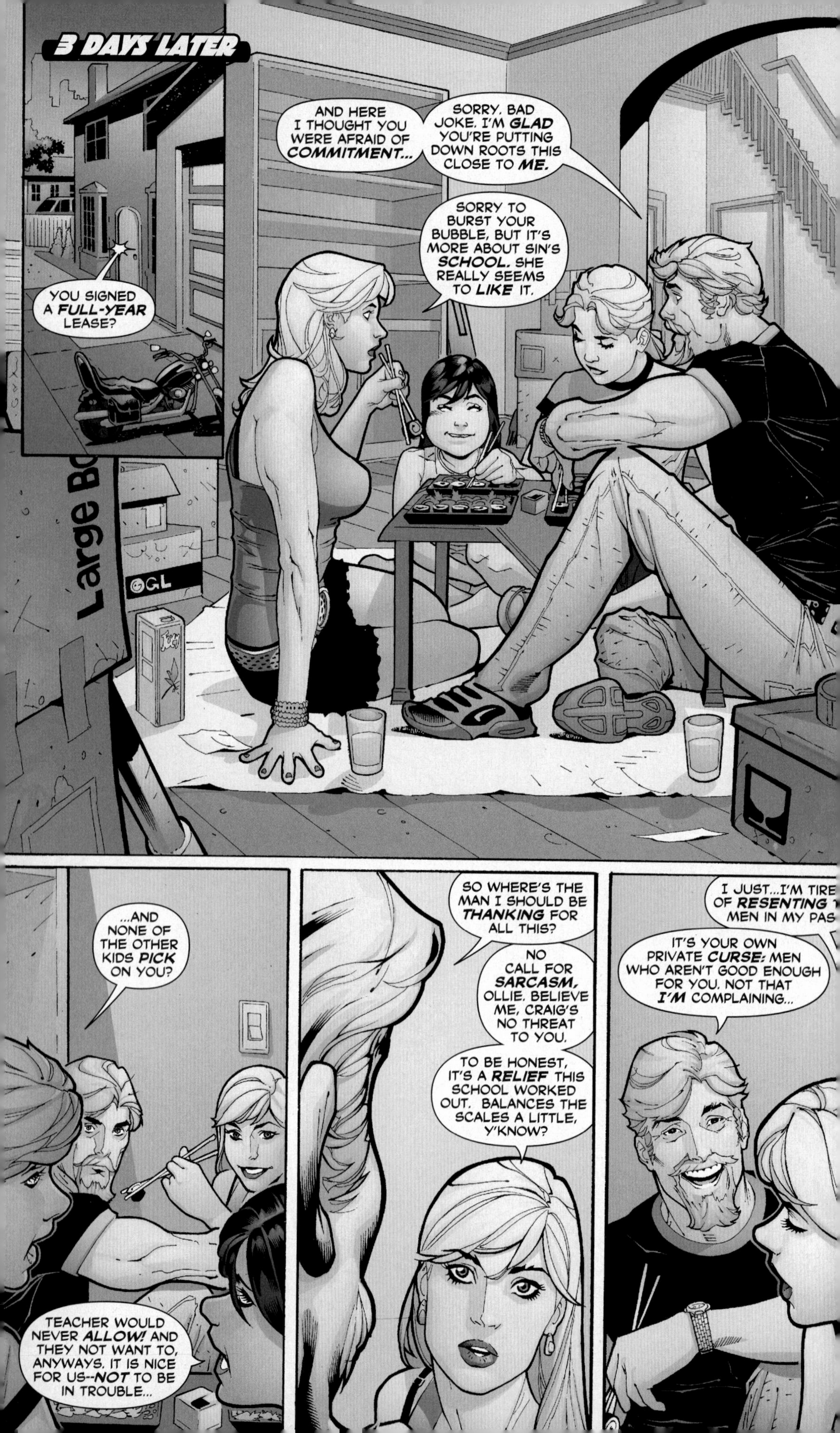
3 DAYS LATER
YOU SIGNED A FULL-YEAR LEASE?
AND HERE I THOUGHT YOU WERE AFRAID OF COMMITMENT...
SORRY. BAD JOKE. I'M GLAD YOU'RE PUTTING DOWN ROOTS THIS CLOSE TO ME.
SORRY TO BURST YOUR BUBBLE, BUT IT'S MORE ABOUT SIN'S SCHOOL. SHE REALLY SEEMS TO LIKE IT.
Large Bo
GL
...AND NONE OF THE OTHER KIDS PICK ON YOU?
TEACHER WOULD NEVER ALLOW! AND THEY NOT WANT TO, ANYWAYS. IT IS NICE FOR US--NOT TO BE IN TROUBLE...
SO WHERE'S THE MAN I SHOULD BE THANKING FOR ALL THIS?
NO CALL FOR SARCASM, OLLIE. BELIEVE ME, CRAIG'S NO THREAT TO YOU.
TO BE HONEST, IT'S A RELIEF THIS SCHOOL WORKED OUT. BALANCES THE SCALES A LITTLE, Y'KNOW?
I JUST...I'M TIRE OF RESENTING MEN IN MY PAS
IT'S YOUR OWN PRIVATE CURSE: MEN WHO AREN'T GOOD ENOUGH FOR YOU. NOT THAT I'M COMPLAINING...

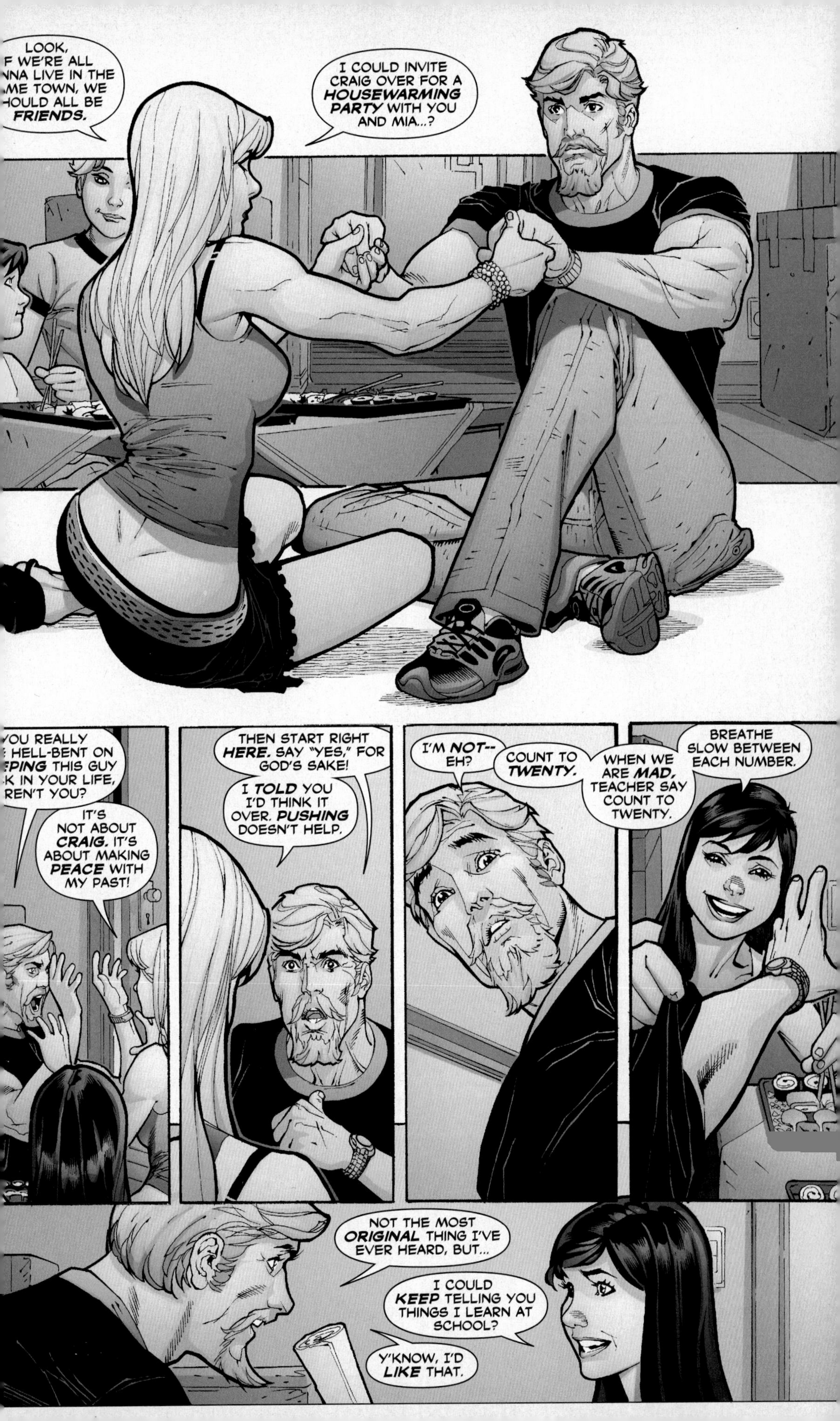

LOOK, F WE'RE ALL NNA LIVE IN THE ME TOWN, WE HOULD ALL BE FRIENDS.
I COULD INVITE CRAIG OVER FOR A HOUSEWARMING PARTY WITH YOU AND MIA...?
OU REALLY HELL-BENT ON PING THIS GUY K IN YOUR LIFE, REN'T YOU?
IT'S NOT ABOUT CRAIG. IT'S ABOUT MAKING PEACE WITH MY PAST!
THEN START RIGHT HERE. SAY "YES," FOR GOD'S SAKE!
I TOLD YOU I'D THINK IT OVER. PUSHING DOESN'T HELP.
I'M NOT-- EH?
COUNT TO TWENTY.
WHEN WE ARE MAD, TEACHER SAY COUNT TO TWENTY.
BREATHE SLOW BETWEEN EACH NUMBER.
NOT THE MOST ORIGINAL THING I'VE EVER HEARD, BUT...
I COULD KEEP TELLING YOU THINGS I LEARN AT SCHOOL?
Y'KNOW, I'D LIKE THAT.

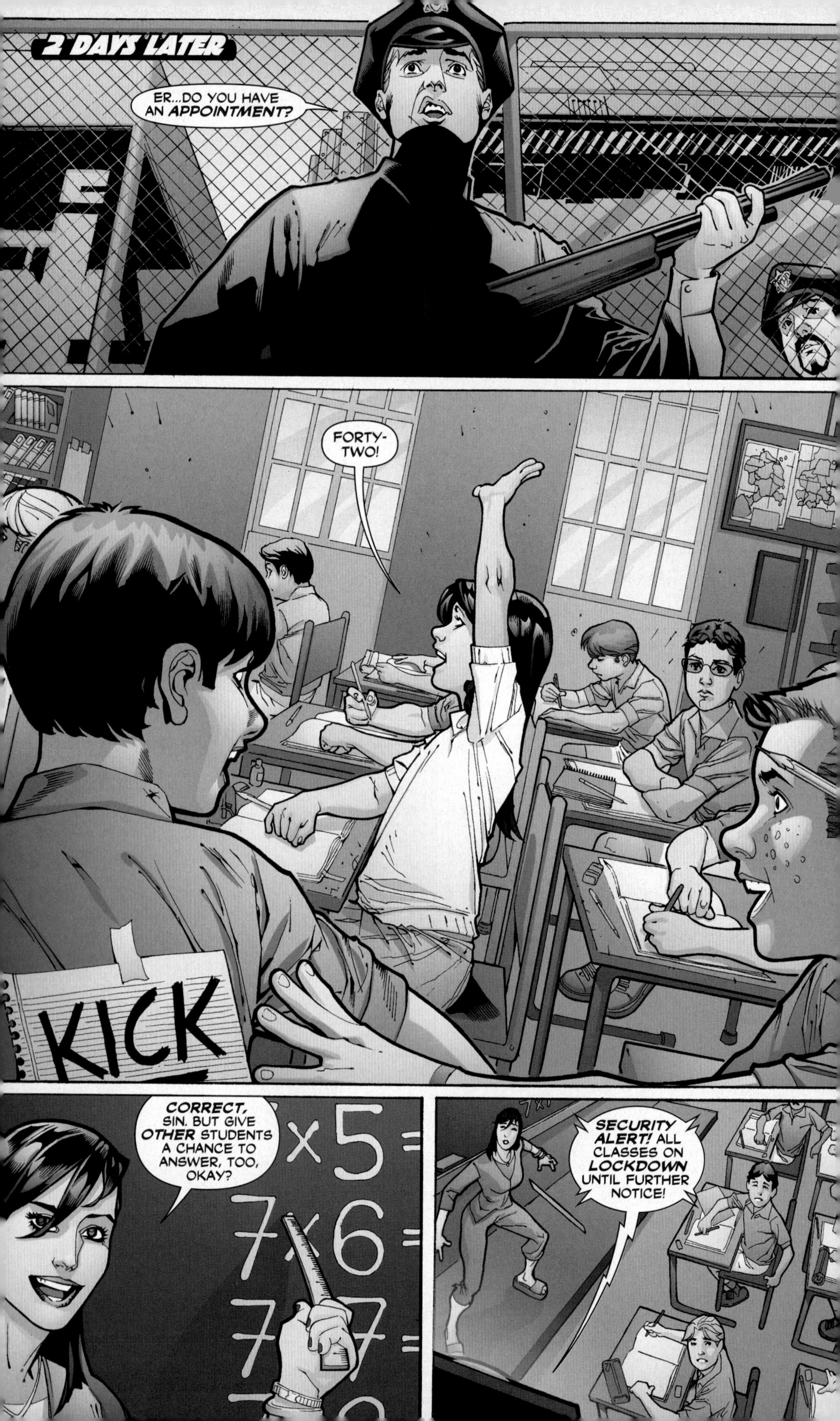
2 DAYS LATER
ER...DO YOU HAVE AN APPOINTMENT?
FORTY-TWO!
KICK
CORRECT, SIN. BUT GIVE OTHER STUDENTS A CHANCE TO ANSWER, TOO, OKAY?
SECURITY ALERT! ALL CLASSES ON LOCKDOWN UNTIL FURTHER NOTICE!

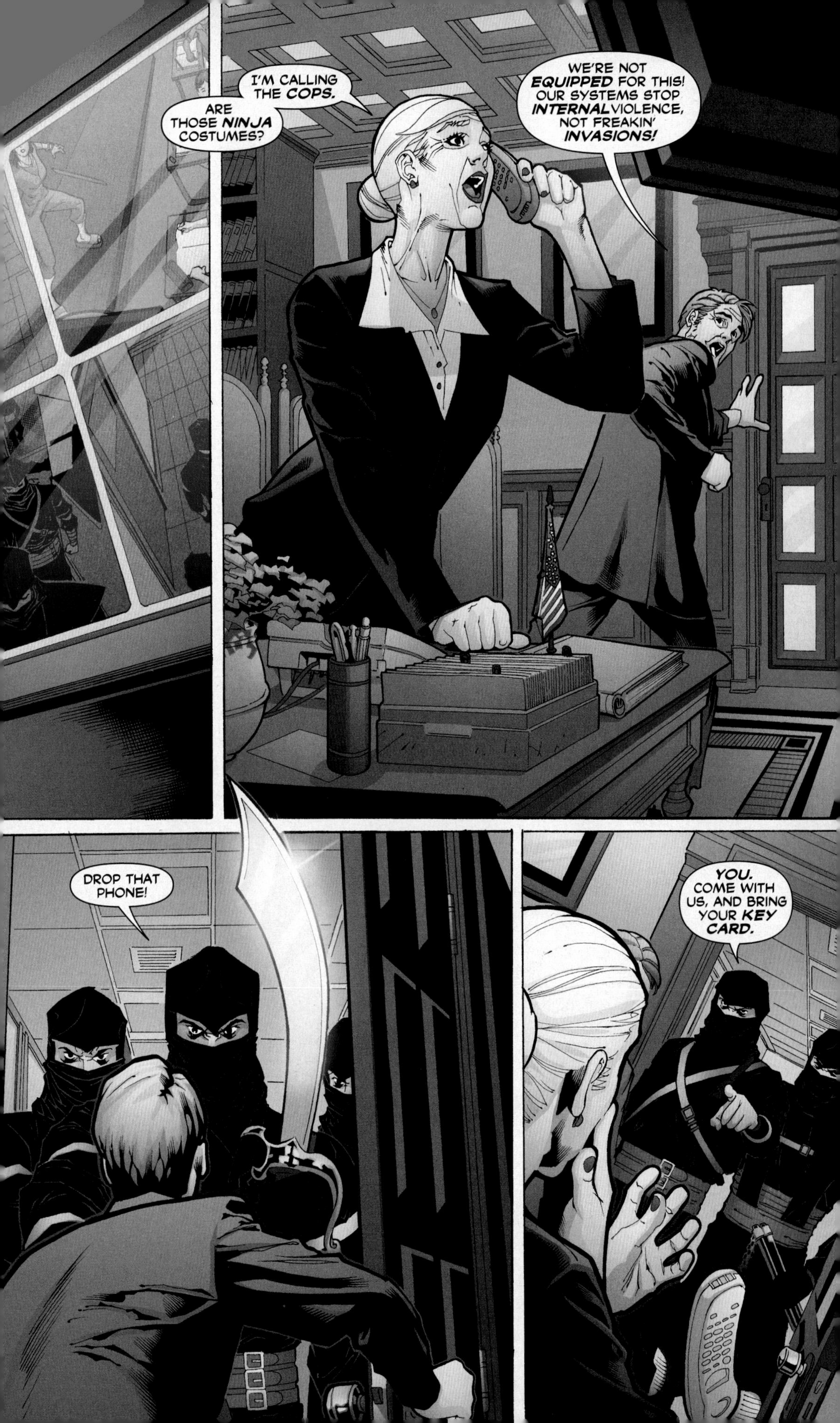
ARE THOSE NINJA COSTUMES?
I'M CALLING THE COPS.
WE'RE NOT EQUIPPED FOR THIS! OUR SYSTEMS STOP INTERNAL VIOLENCE, NOT FREAKIN' INVASIONS!
DROP THAT PHONE!
YOU. COME WITH US, AND BRING YOUR KEY CARD.

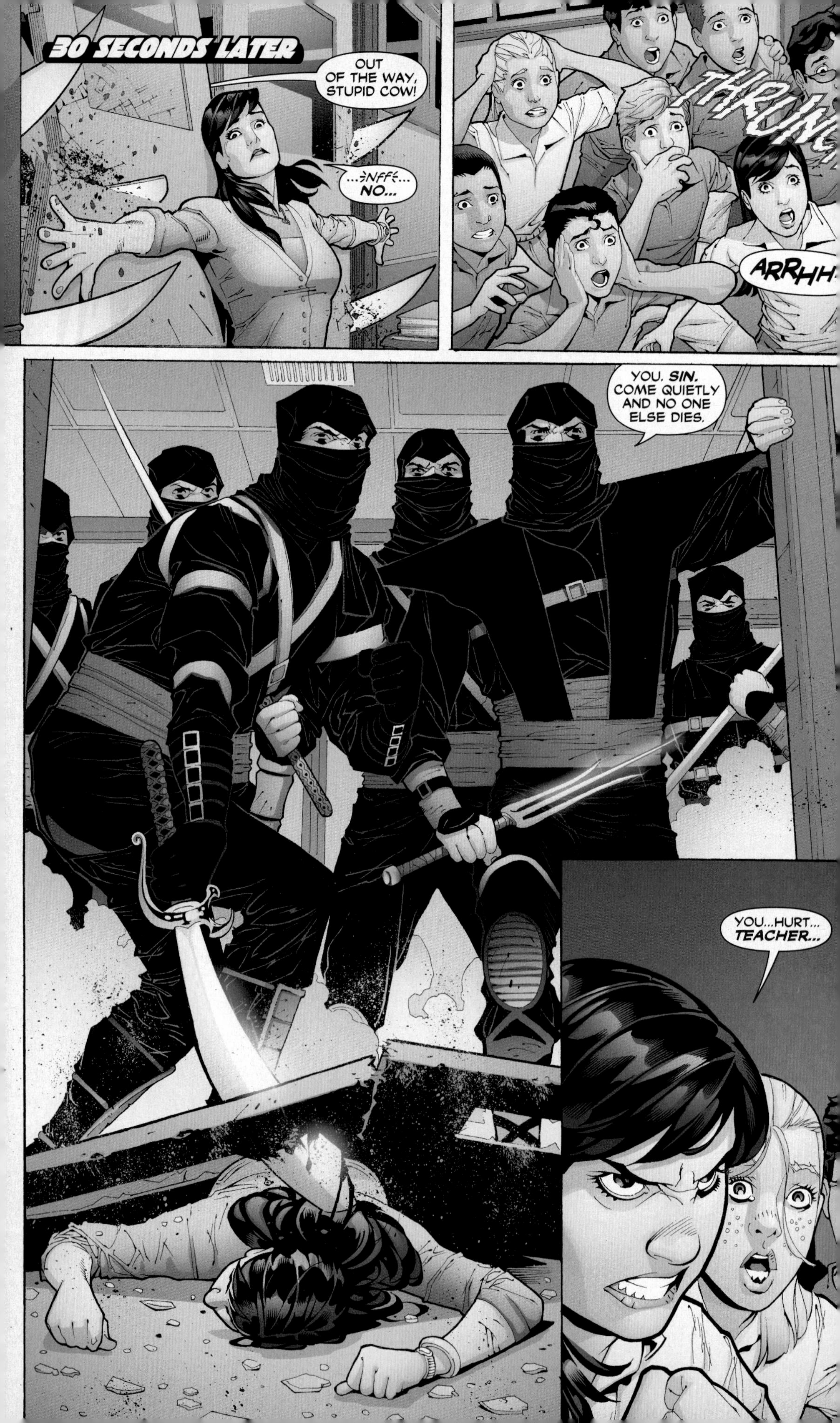

30 SECONDS LATER
OUT OF THE WAY, STUPID COW!
...NFF... NO...
THRUNG
ARRHH
YOU. SIN. COME QUIETLY AND NO ONE ELSE DIES.
YOU...HURT... TEACHER...

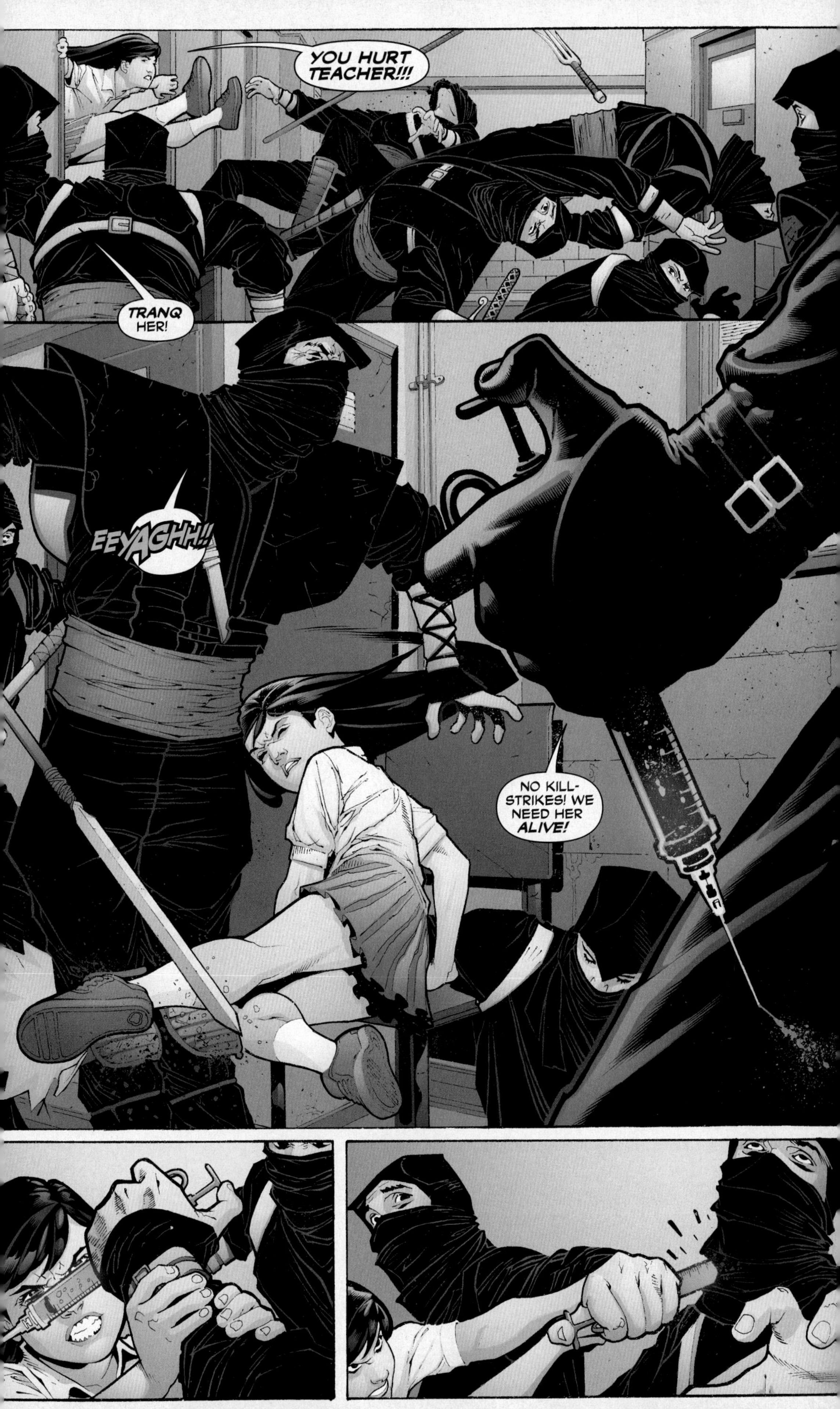
YOU HURT TEACHER!!!
TRANQ HER!
EEYAGHH!!
NO KILL-STRIKES! WE NEED HER ALIVE!

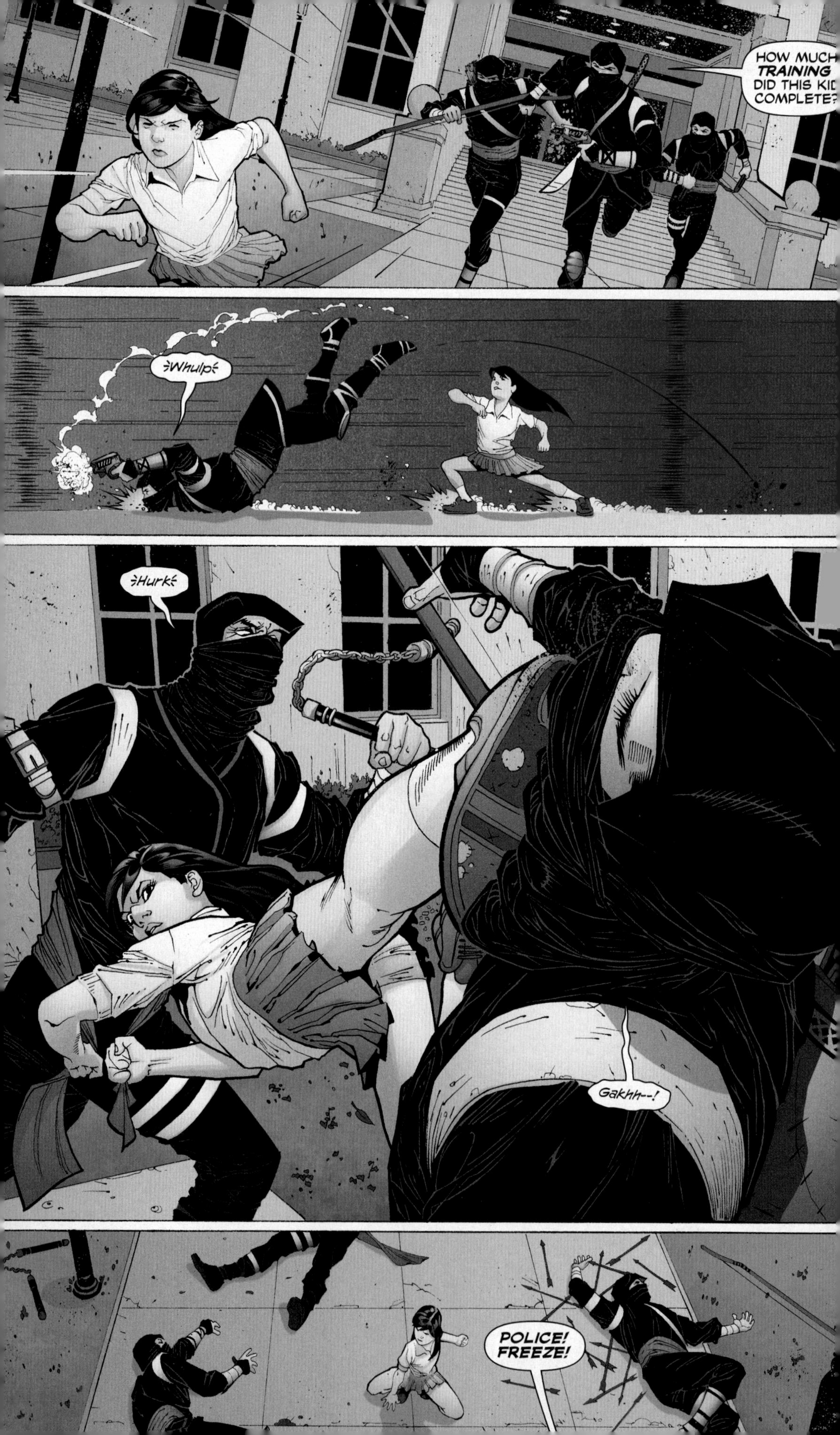
HOW MUCH TRAINING DID THIS KID COMPLETE?
Whulp
Hurk
Gakhh--!
POLICE! FREEZE!

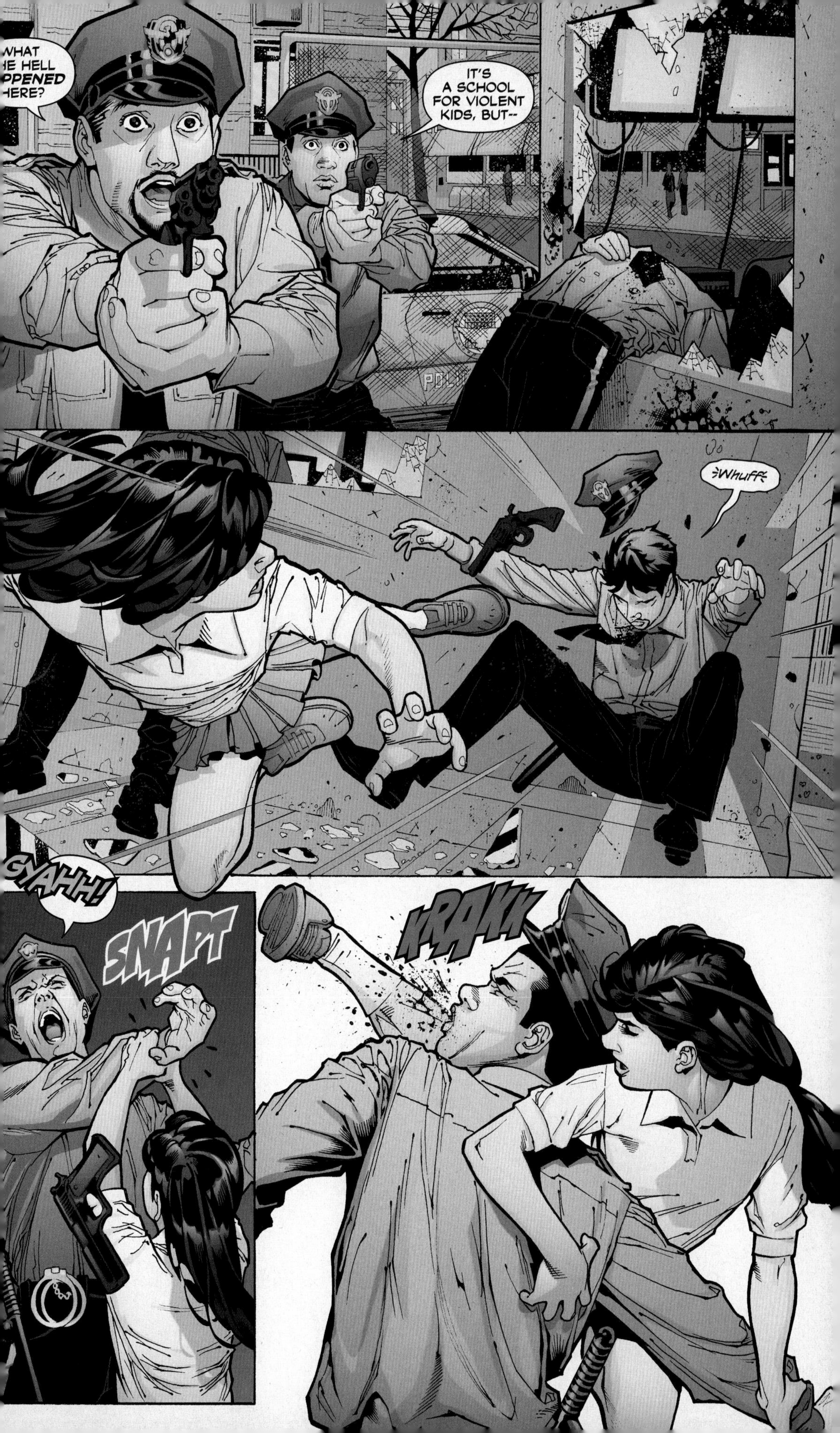
WHAT
HE HELL
PPENED
HERE?
IT'S A SCHOOL FOR VIOLENT KIDS, BUT--
Whuff
GYAHH!
SNAPT
KRAKK

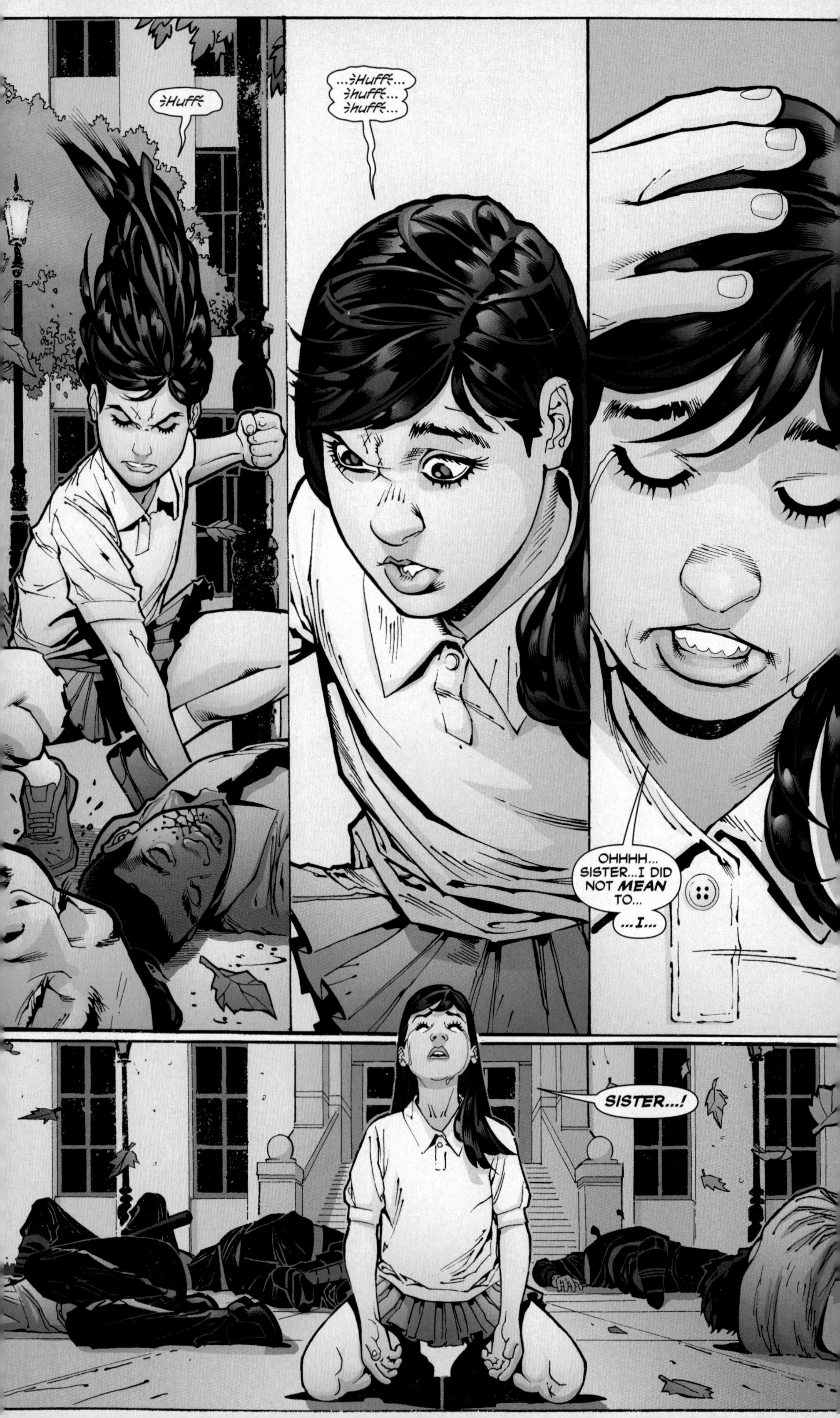

≷Huff≶
...≷Huff≶...
≷huff≶...
≷huff≶...
OHHHH... SISTER...I DID NOT **MEAN** TO...
...I...
SISTER...!

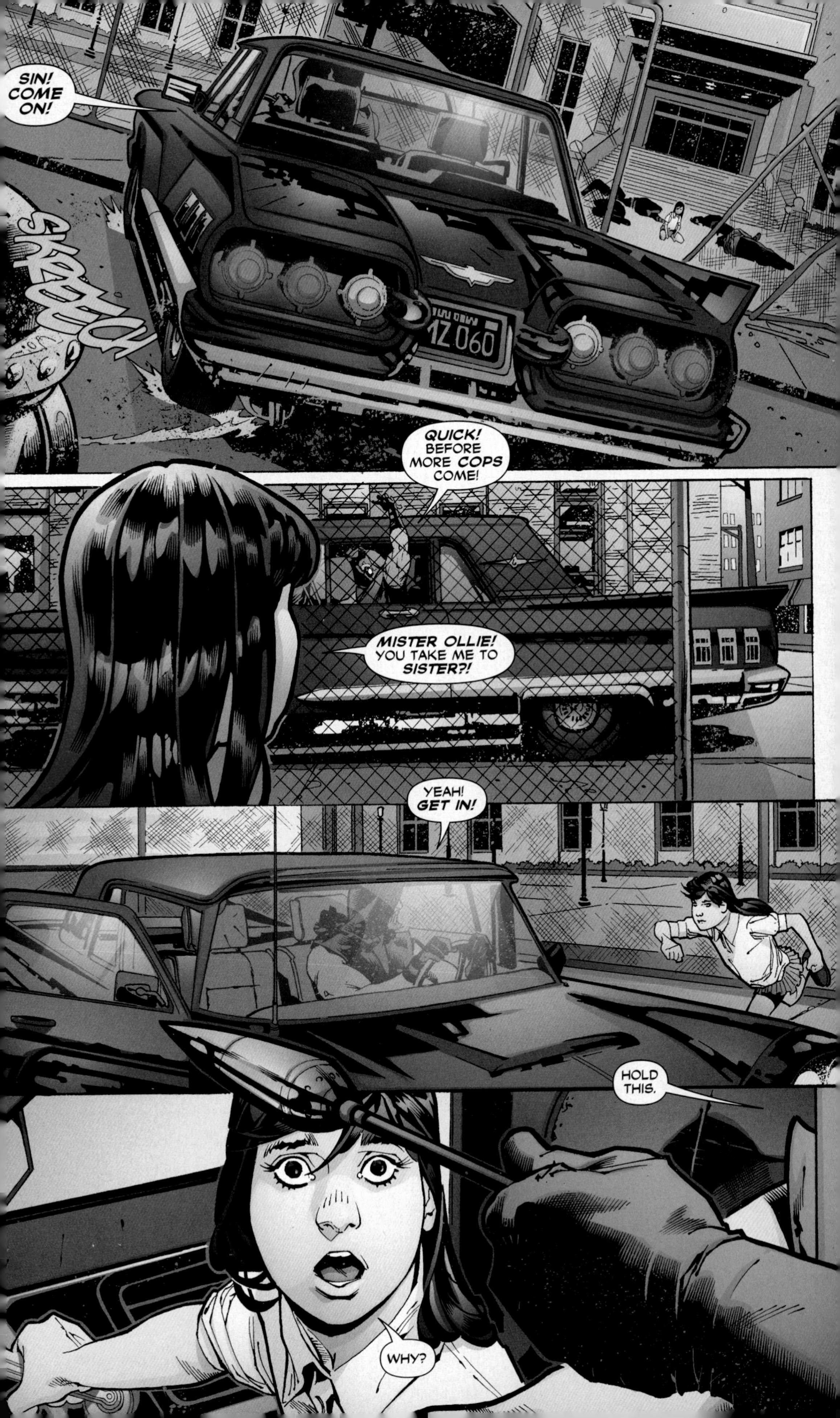
SIN! COME ON!
SKREECH
QUICK! BEFORE MORE COPS COME!
MISTER OLLIE! YOU TAKE ME TO SISTER?!
YEAH! GET IN!
HOLD THIS.
WHY?

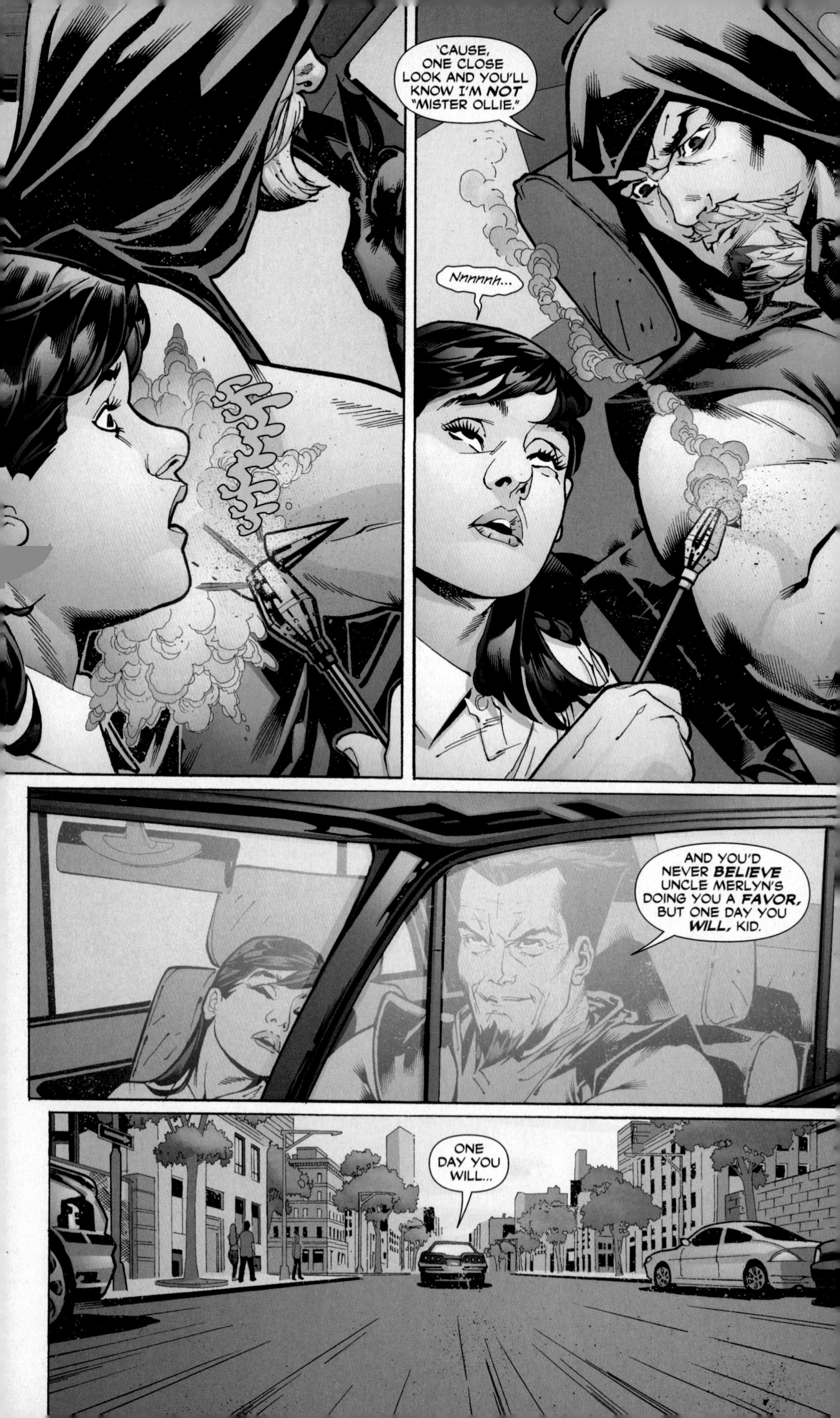
'CAUSE, ONE CLOSE LOOK AND YOU'LL KNOW I'M **NOT** "MISTER OLLIE."
SSSSSS
Nnnnnh...
AND YOU'D NEVER **BELIEVE** UNCLE MERLYN'S DOING YOU A **FAVOR,** BUT ONE DAY YOU **WILL,** KID.
ONE DAY YOU WILL...

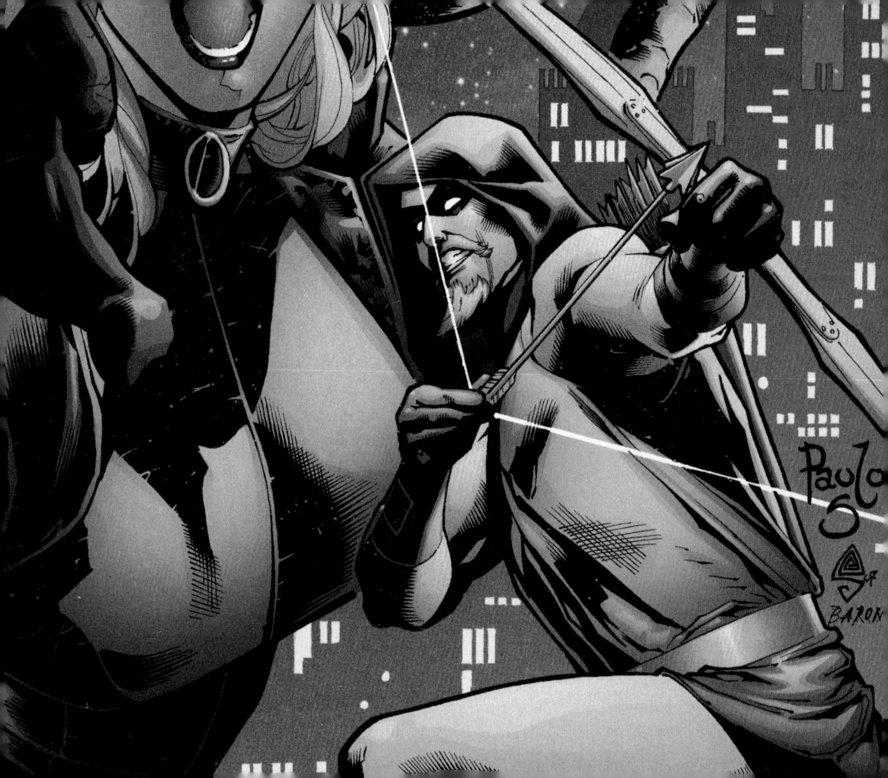
Paulo S
BARON

BLACK CANARY #3

TONY BEDARD
WRITER

MIKE NORTON
THUMBNAILS

PAULO SIQUEIRA
TOM DERENICK
PENCILLERS

AMILTON SANTOS
RODNEY RAMOS
INKERS

I.L.L.
COLORIST

PAT BROSSEAU
LETTERER

PAULO SIQUEIRA & AMILTON SANTOS
WITH DAVID BARON
COVER

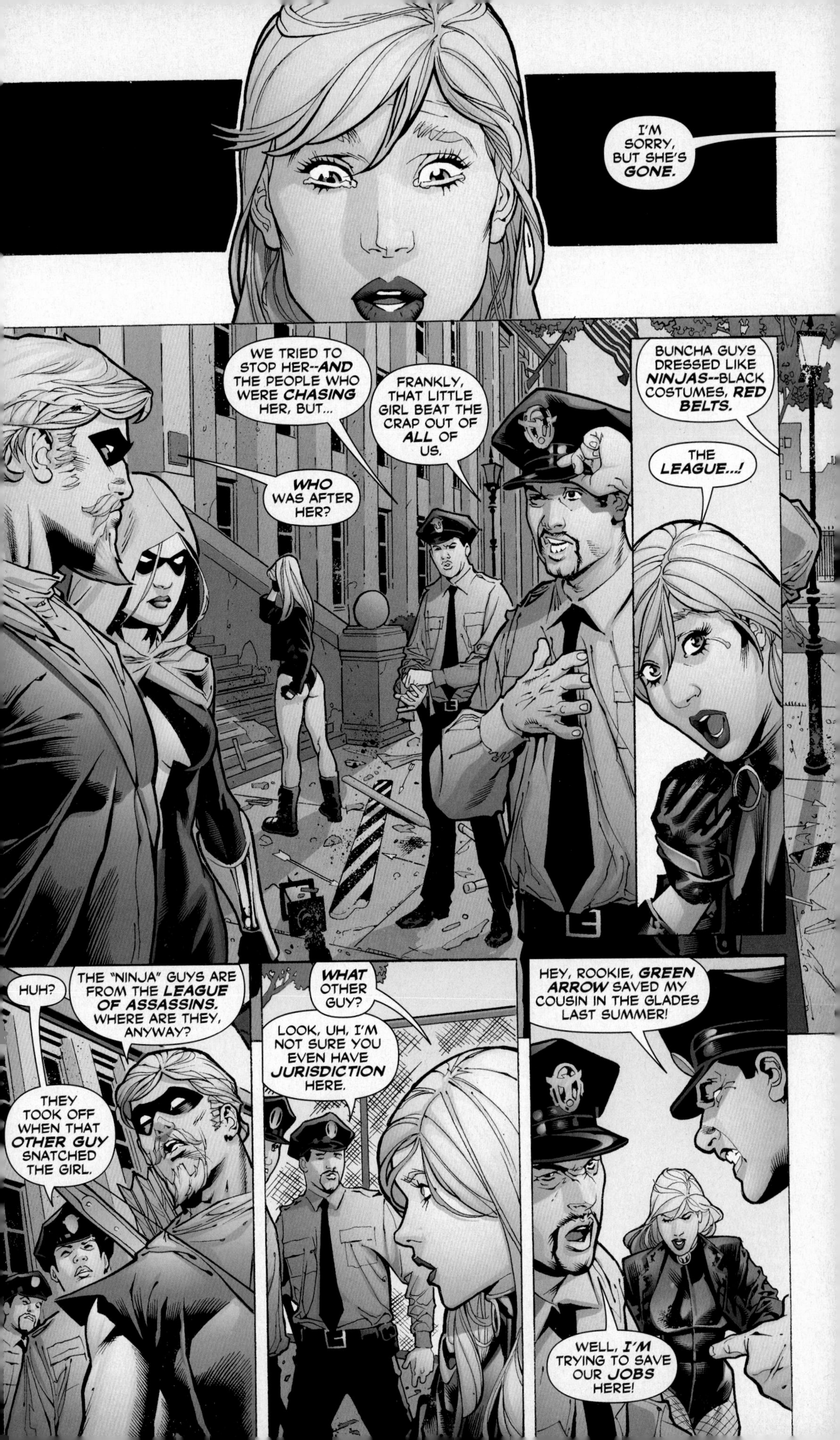
I'M SORRY, BUT SHE'S GONE.
WE TRIED TO STOP HER--AND THE PEOPLE WHO WERE CHASING HER, BUT...
FRANKLY, THAT LITTLE GIRL BEAT THE CRAP OUT OF ALL OF US.
WHO WAS AFTER HER?
BUNCHA GUYS DRESSED LIKE NINJAS--BLACK COSTUMES, RED BELTS.
THE LEAGUE...!
HUH?
THE "NINJA" GUYS ARE FROM THE LEAGUE OF ASSASSINS. WHERE ARE THEY, ANYWAY?
THEY TOOK OFF WHEN THAT OTHER GUY SNATCHED THE GIRL.
WHAT OTHER GUY?
LOOK, UH, I'M NOT SURE YOU EVEN HAVE JURISDICTION HERE.
HEY, ROOKIE, GREEN ARROW SAVED MY COUSIN IN THE GLADES LAST SUMMER!
WELL, I'M TRYING TO SAVE OUR JOBS HERE!

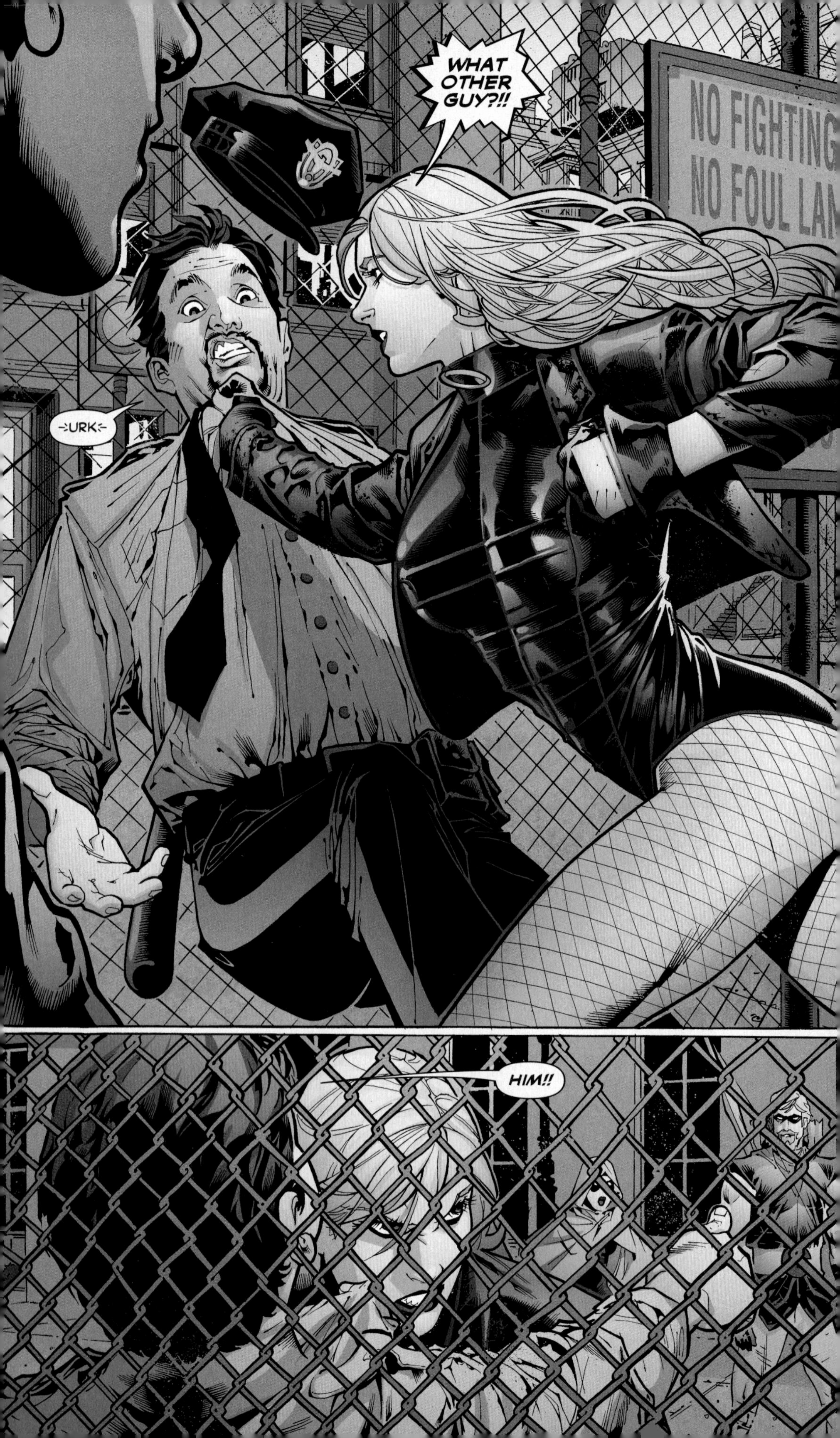
WHAT OTHER GUY?!!
NO FIGHTING
NO FOUL LAN
-URK-
HIM!!

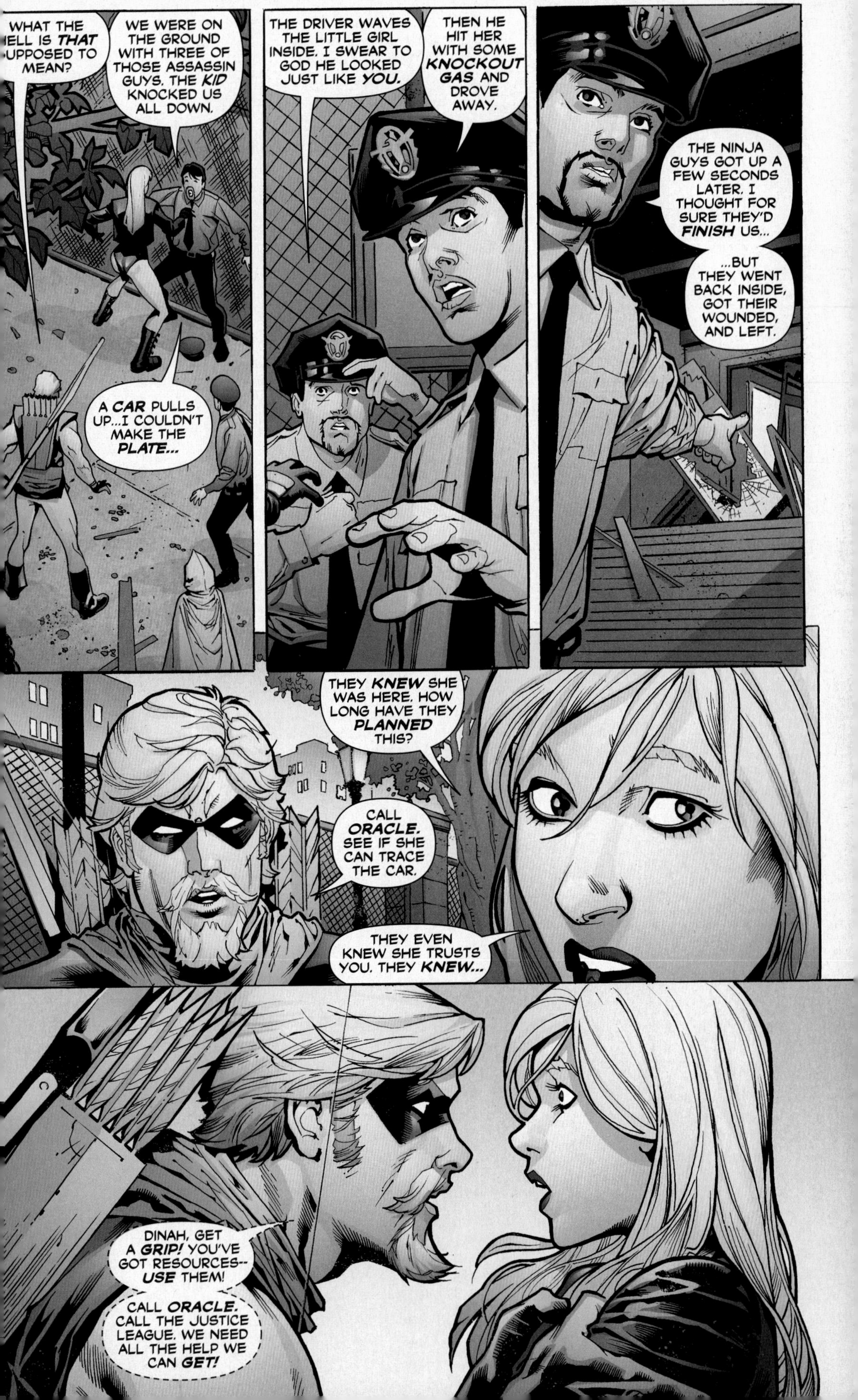
WHAT THE HELL IS THAT SUPPOSED TO MEAN?
WE WERE ON THE GROUND WITH THREE OF THOSE ASSASSIN GUYS. THE KID KNOCKED US ALL DOWN.
A CAR PULLS UP...I COULDN'T MAKE THE PLATE...
THE DRIVER WAVES THE LITTLE GIRL INSIDE. I SWEAR TO GOD HE LOOKED JUST LIKE YOU.
THEN HE HIT HER WITH SOME KNOCKOUT GAS AND DROVE AWAY.
THE NINJA GUYS GOT UP A FEW SECONDS LATER. I THOUGHT FOR SURE THEY'D FINISH US...
...BUT THEY WENT BACK INSIDE, GOT THEIR WOUNDED, AND LEFT.
THEY KNEW SHE WAS HERE. HOW LONG HAVE THEY PLANNED THIS?
CALL ORACLE. SEE IF SHE CAN TRACE THE CAR.
THEY EVEN KNEW SHE TRUSTS YOU. THEY KNEW...
DINAH, GET A GRIP! YOU'VE GOT RESOURCES--USE THEM!
CALL ORACLE. CALL THE JUSTICE LEAGUE. WE NEED ALL THE HELP WE CAN GET!

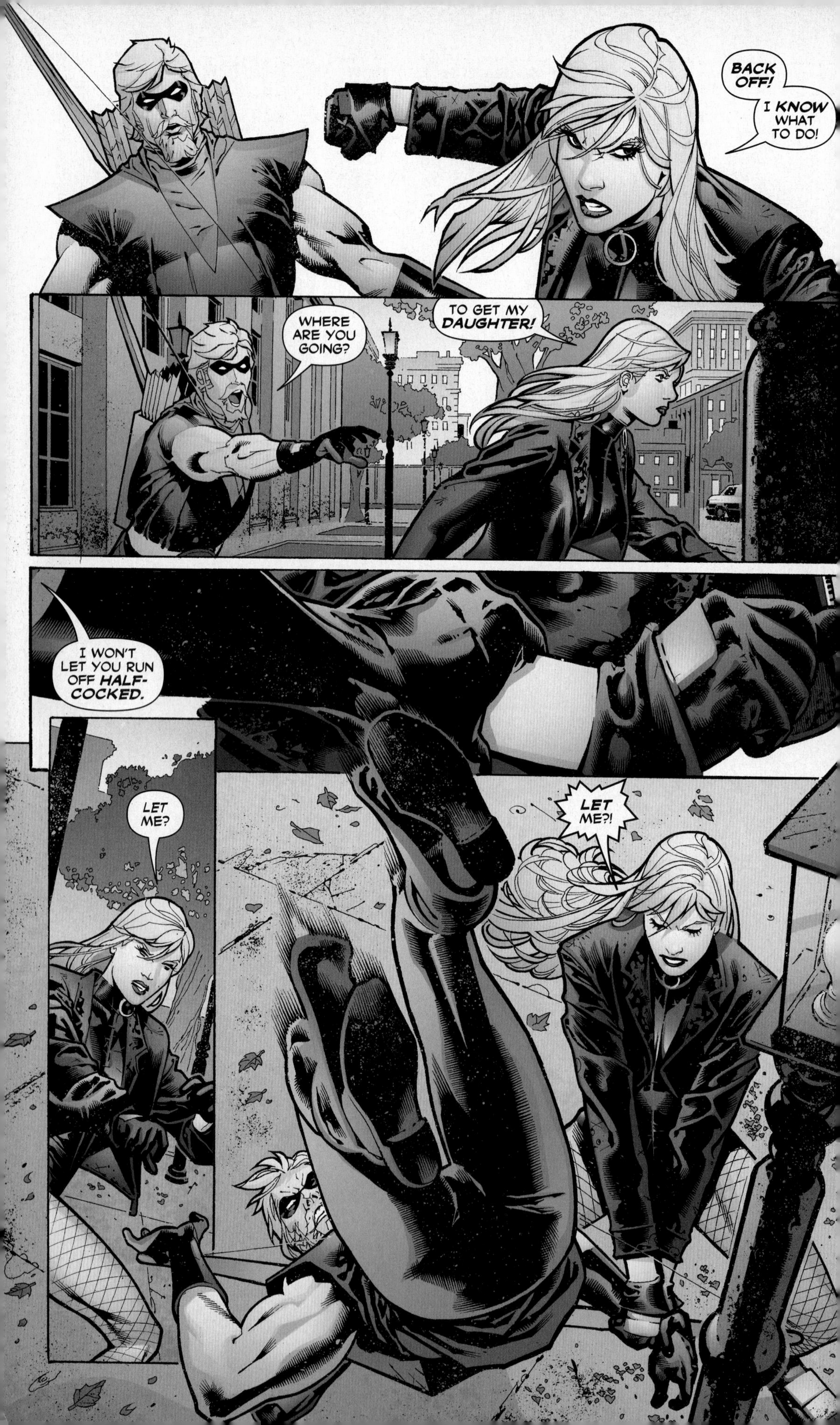
BACK OFF!
I KNOW WHAT TO DO!
WHERE ARE YOU GOING?
TO GET MY DAUGHTER!
I WON'T LET YOU RUN OFF HALF-COCKED.
LET ME?
LET ME?!

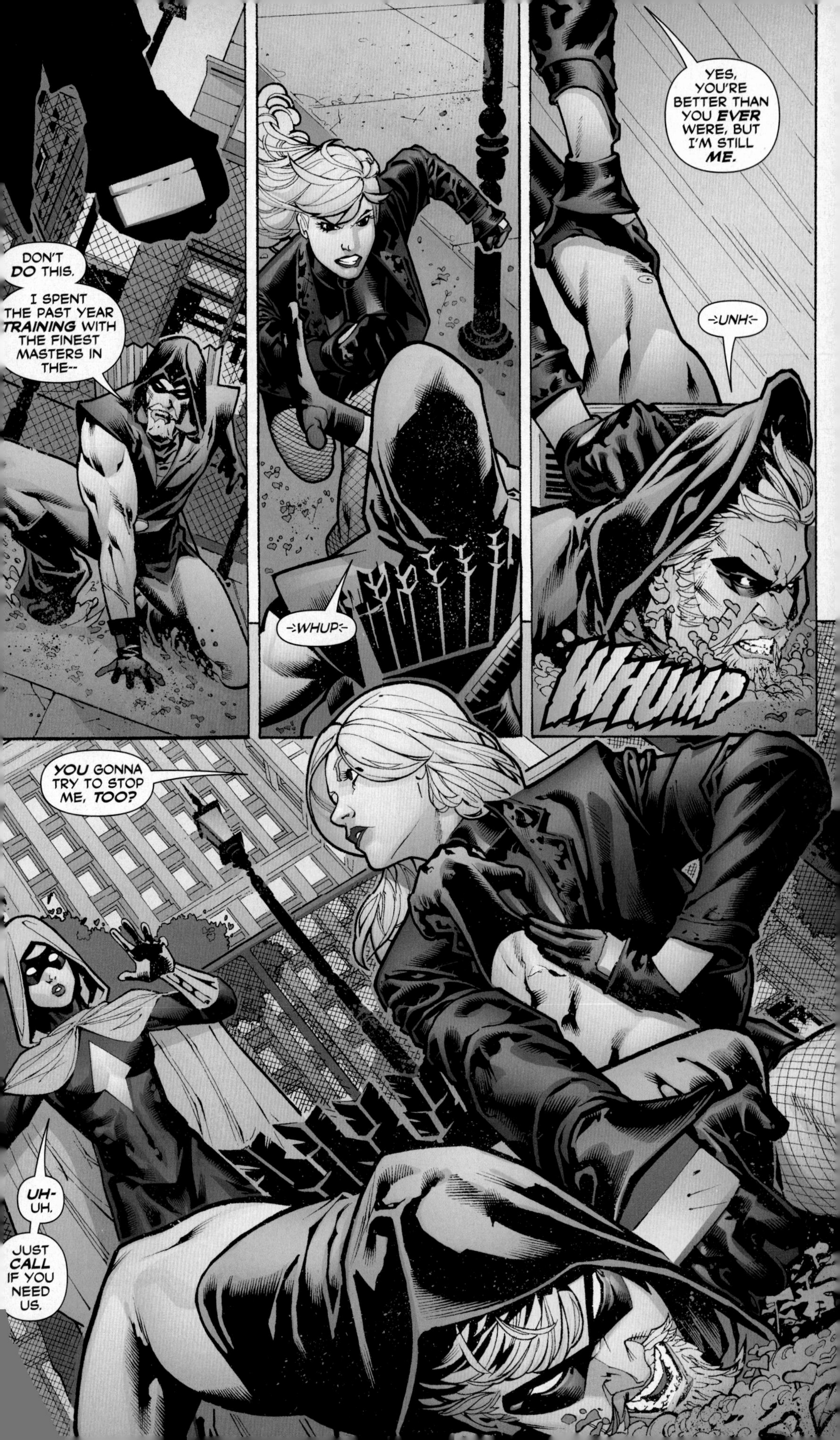
DON'T DO THIS.
I SPENT THE PAST YEAR TRAINING WITH THE FINEST MASTERS IN THE--
-WHUP-
YES, YOU'RE BETTER THAN YOU EVER WERE, BUT I'M STILL ME.
-UNH-
WHUMP
YOU GONNA TRY TO STOP ME, TOO?
UH-UH.
JUST CALL IF YOU NEED US.

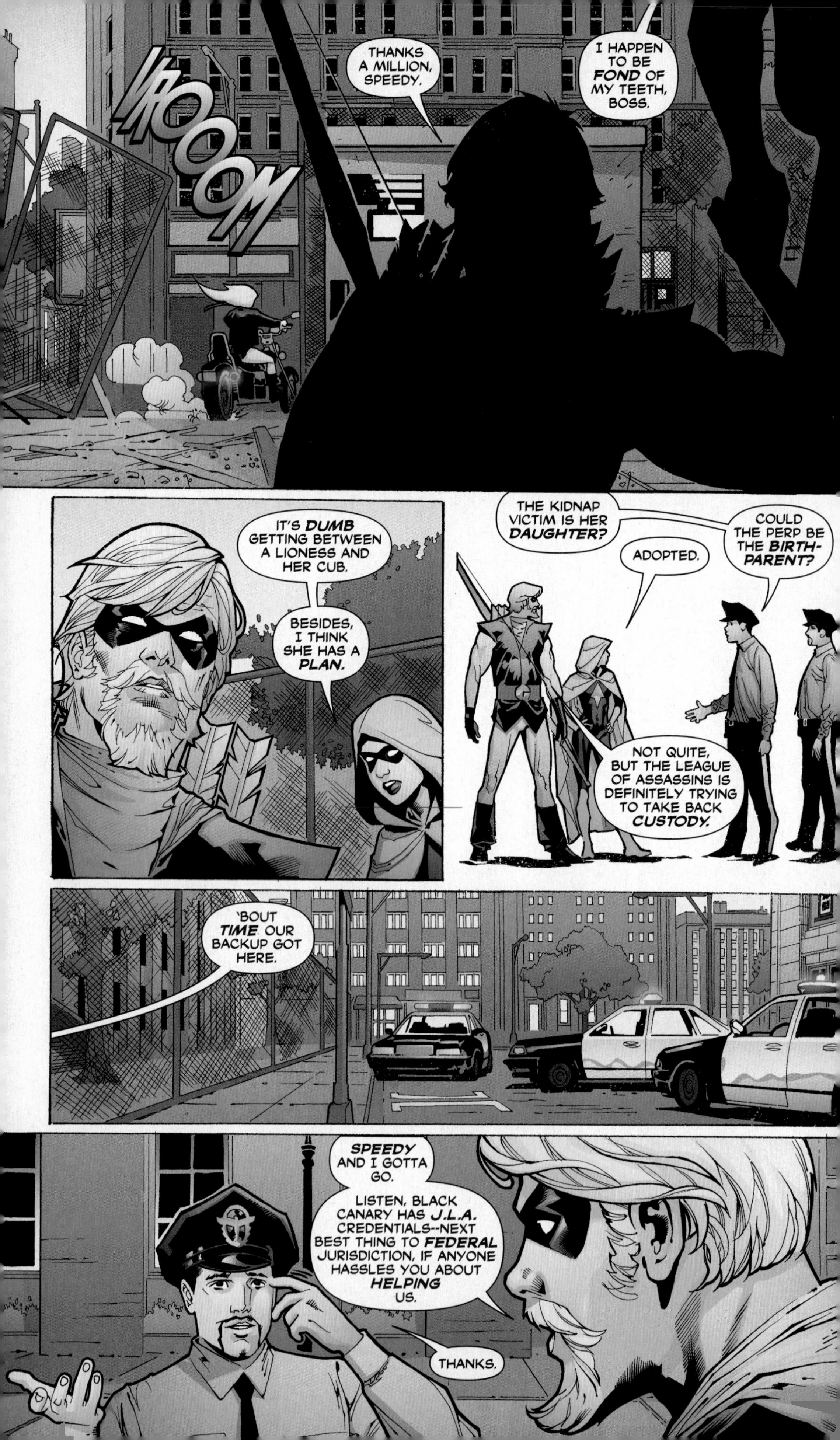
VROOOM
THANKS A MILLION, SPEEDY.
I HAPPEN TO BE FOND OF MY TEETH, BOSS.
IT'S DUMB GETTING BETWEEN A LIONESS AND HER CUB.
BESIDES, I THINK SHE HAS A PLAN.
THE KIDNAP VICTIM IS HER DAUGHTER?
ADOPTED.
COULD THE PERP BE THE BIRTH-PARENT?
NOT QUITE, BUT THE LEAGUE OF ASSASSINS IS DEFINITELY TRYING TO TAKE BACK CUSTODY.
'BOUT TIME OUR BACKUP GOT HERE.
SPEEDY AND I GOTTA GO.
LISTEN, BLACK CANARY HAS J.L.A. CREDENTIALS--NEXT BEST THING TO FEDERAL JURISDICTION, IF ANYONE HASSLES YOU ABOUT HELPING US.
THANKS.

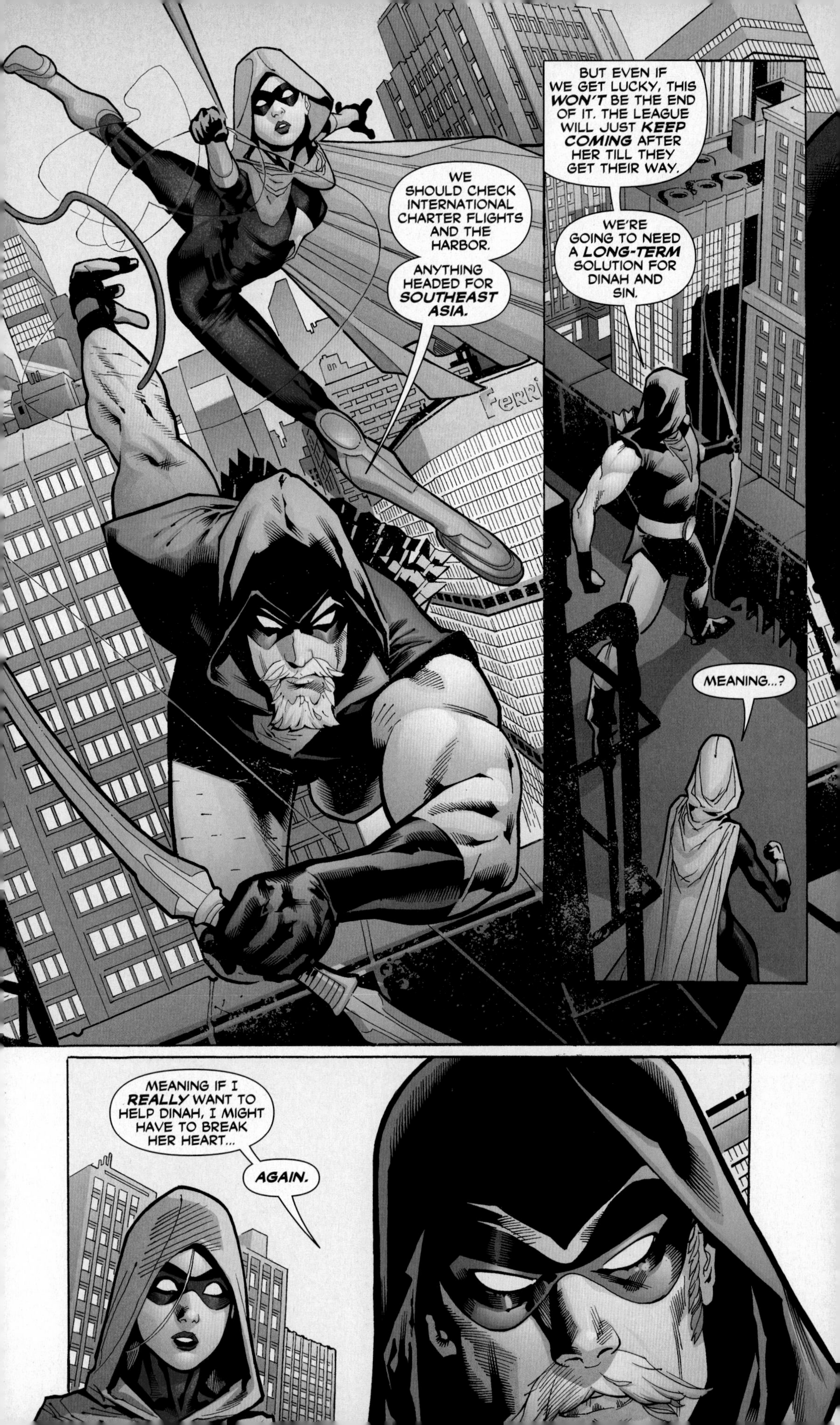
WE SHOULD CHECK INTERNATIONAL CHARTER FLIGHTS AND THE HARBOR.
ANYTHING HEADED FOR SOUTHEAST ASIA.
BUT EVEN IF WE GET LUCKY, THIS WON'T BE THE END OF IT. THE LEAGUE WILL JUST KEEP COMING AFTER HER TILL THEY GET THEIR WAY.
WE'RE GOING TO NEED A LONG-TERM SOLUTION FOR DINAH AND SIN.
MEANING...?
MEANING IF I REALLY WANT TO HELP DINAH, I MIGHT HAVE TO BREAK HER HEART...
AGAIN.

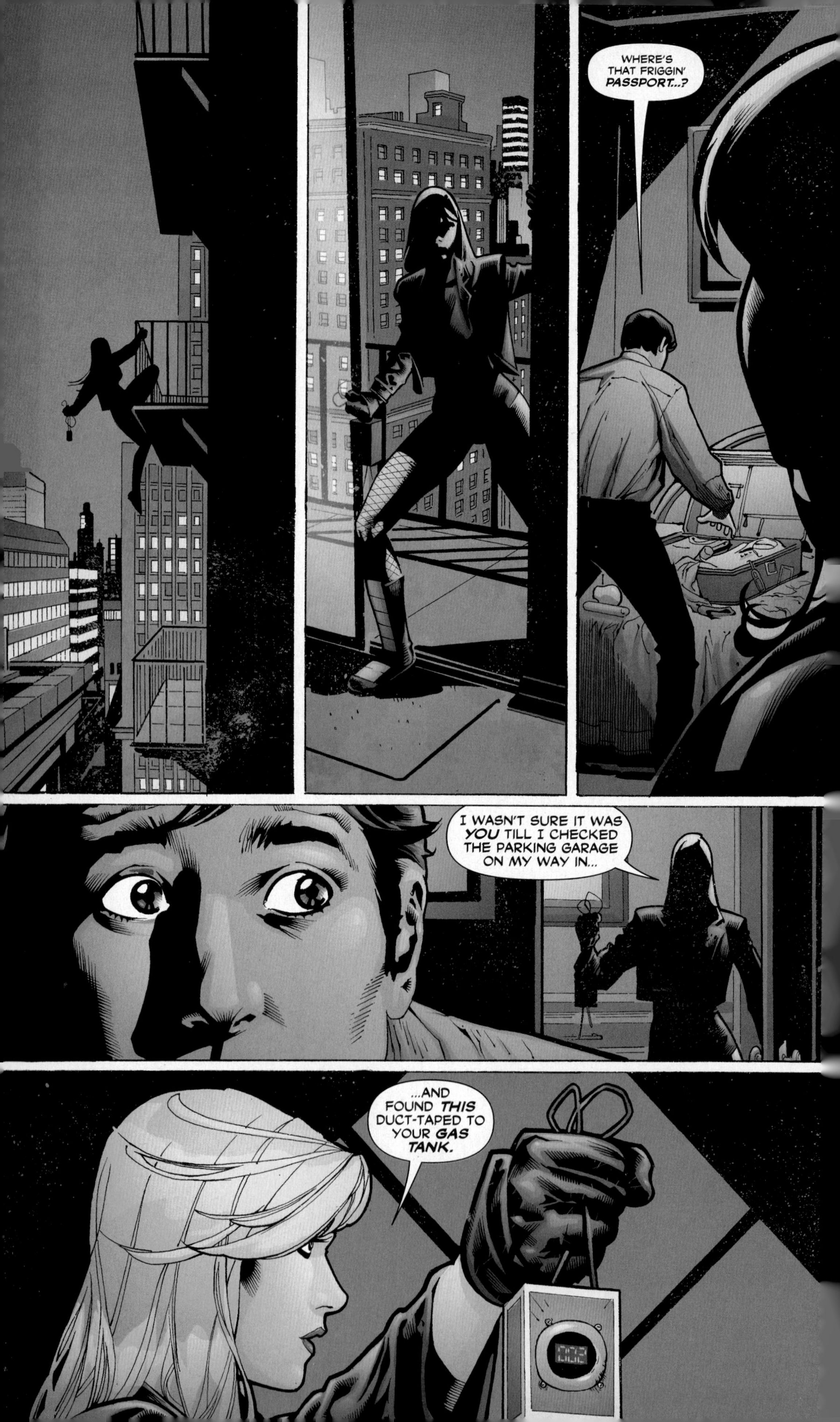
WHERE'S THAT FRIGGIN' PASSPORT...?
I WASN'T SURE IT WAS YOU TILL I CHECKED THE PARKING GARAGE ON MY WAY IN...
...AND FOUND THIS DUCT-TAPED TO YOUR GAS TANK.

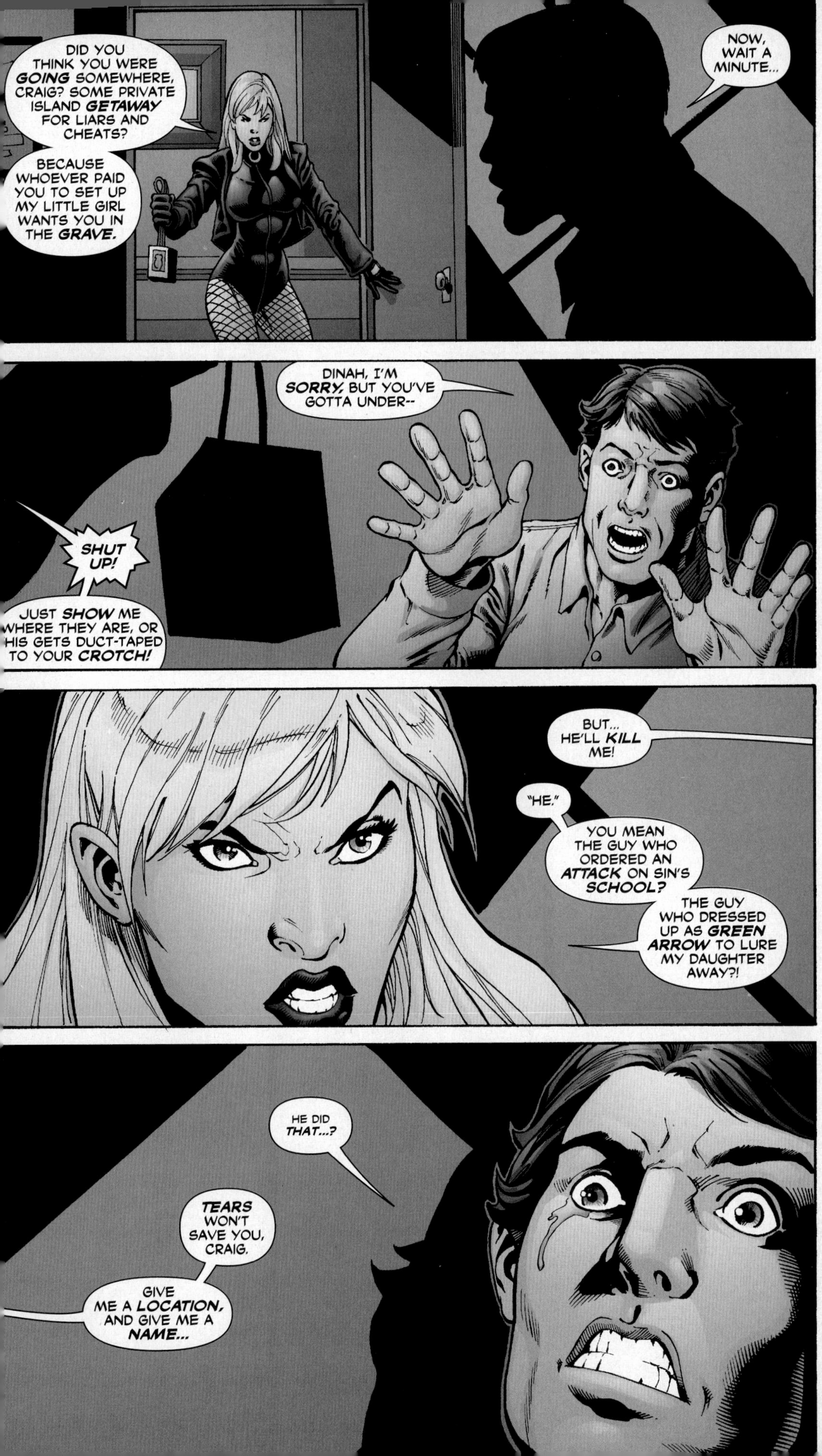
DID YOU THINK YOU WERE GOING SOMEWHERE, CRAIG? SOME PRIVATE ISLAND GETAWAY FOR LIARS AND CHEATS?
BECAUSE WHOEVER PAID YOU TO SET UP MY LITTLE GIRL WANTS YOU IN THE GRAVE.
NOW, WAIT A MINUTE...
DINAH, I'M SORRY, BUT YOU'VE GOTTA UNDER--
SHUT UP!
JUST SHOW ME WHERE THEY ARE, OR HIS GETS DUCT-TAPED TO YOUR CROTCH!
BUT... HE'LL KILL ME!
"HE."
YOU MEAN THE GUY WHO ORDERED AN ATTACK ON SIN'S SCHOOL?
THE GUY WHO DRESSED UP AS GREEN ARROW TO LURE MY DAUGHTER AWAY?!
HE DID THAT...?
TEARS WON'T SAVE YOU, CRAIG.
GIVE ME A LOCATION, AND GIVE ME A NAME...

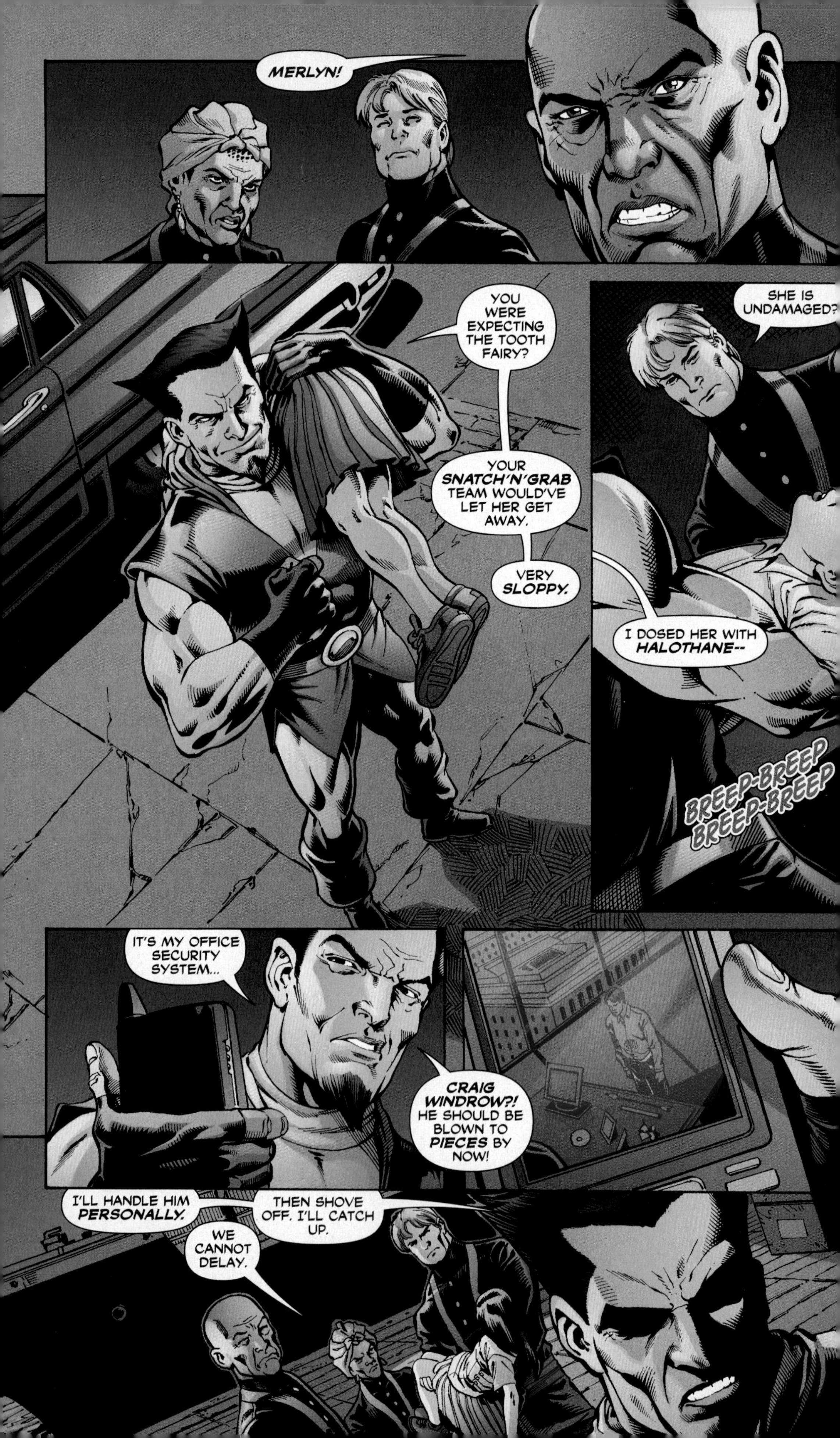
MERLYN!
YOU WERE EXPECTING THE TOOTH FAIRY?
YOUR SNATCH'N'GRAB TEAM WOULD'VE LET HER GET AWAY.
VERY SLOPPY.
SHE IS UNDAMAGED?
I DOSED HER WITH HALOTHANE--
BREEP-BREEP BREEP-BREEP
IT'S MY OFFICE SECURITY SYSTEM...
CRAIG WINDROW?! HE SHOULD BE BLOWN TO PIECES BY NOW!
I'LL HANDLE HIM PERSONALLY.
WE CANNOT DELAY.
THEN SHOVE OFF. I'LL CATCH UP.

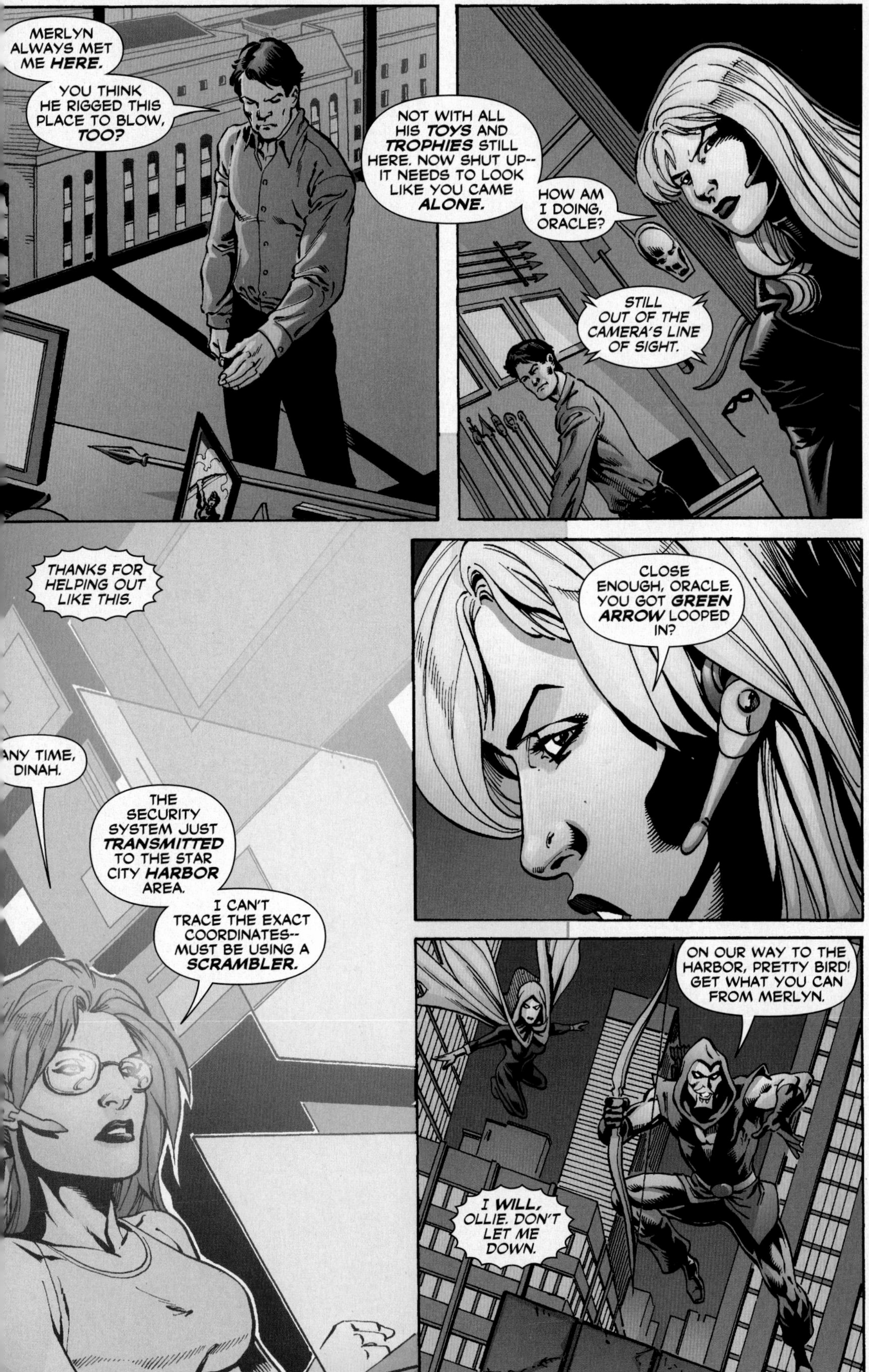

MERLYN ALWAYS MET ME **HERE.**
YOU THINK HE RIGGED THIS PLACE TO BLOW, **TOO?**
NOT WITH ALL HIS **TOYS** AND **TROPHIES** STILL HERE. NOW SHUT UP-- IT NEEDS TO LOOK LIKE YOU CAME **ALONE.**
HOW AM I DOING, ORACLE?
STILL OUT OF THE CAMERA'S LINE OF SIGHT.
THANKS FOR HELPING OUT LIKE THIS.
ANY TIME, DINAH.
THE SECURITY SYSTEM JUST **TRANSMITTED** TO THE STAR CITY **HARBOR** AREA.
I CAN'T TRACE THE EXACT COORDINATES-- MUST BE USING A **SCRAMBLER.**
CLOSE ENOUGH, ORACLE. YOU GOT **GREEN ARROW** LOOPED IN?
ON OUR WAY TO THE HARBOR, PRETTY BIRD! GET WHAT YOU CAN FROM MERLYN.
I **WILL,** OLLIE. DON'T LET ME DOWN.

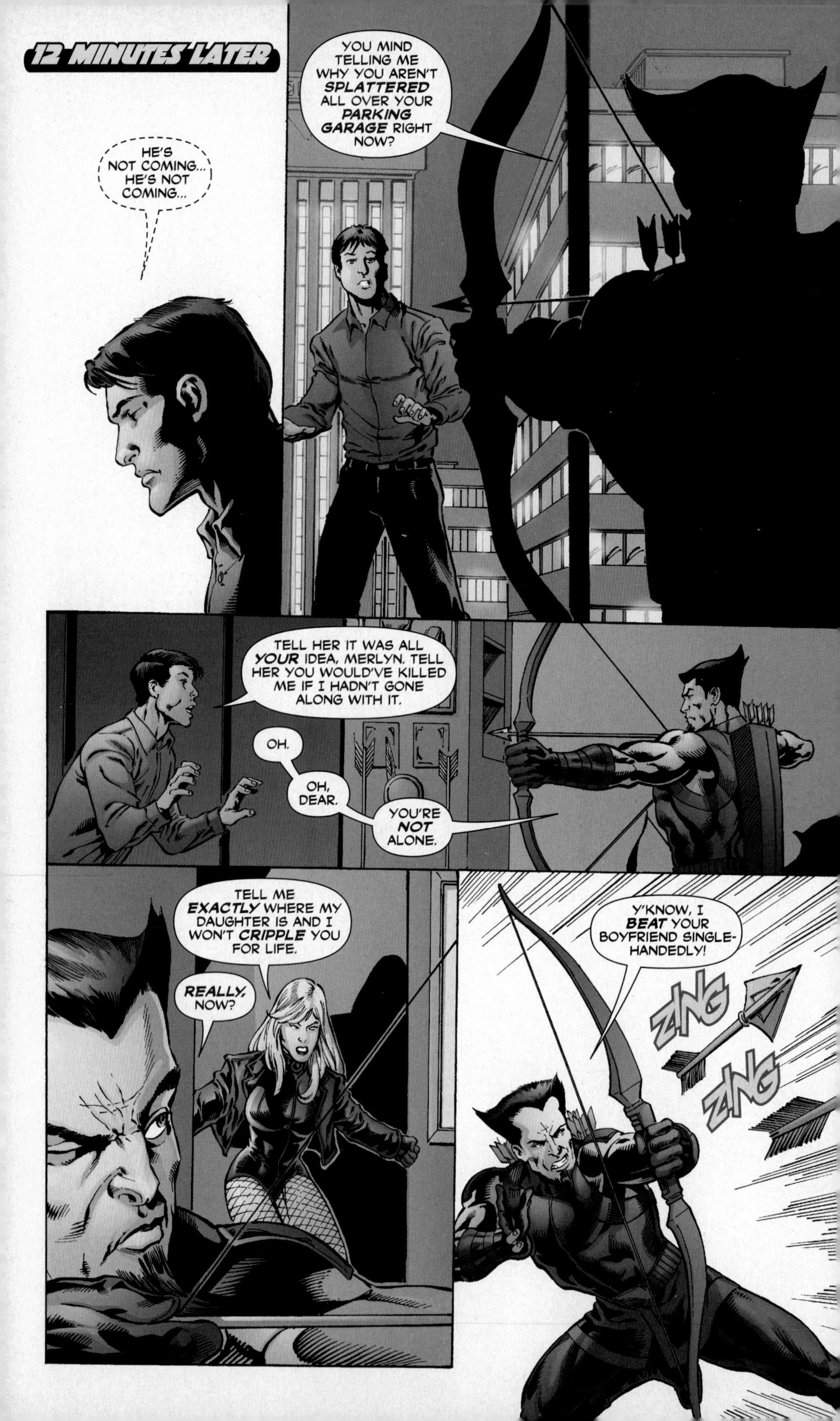
12 MINUTES LATER
HE'S NOT COMING... HE'S NOT COMING...
YOU MIND TELLING ME WHY YOU AREN'T SPLATTERED ALL OVER YOUR PARKING GARAGE RIGHT NOW?
TELL HER IT WAS ALL YOUR IDEA, MERLYN. TELL HER YOU WOULD'VE KILLED ME IF I HADN'T GONE ALONG WITH IT.
OH.
OH, DEAR.
YOU'RE NOT ALONE.
TELL ME EXACTLY WHERE MY DAUGHTER IS AND I WON'T CRIPPLE YOU FOR LIFE.
REALLY, NOW?
Y'KNOW, I BEAT YOUR BOYFRIEND SINGLE-HANDEDLY!
ZING
ZING

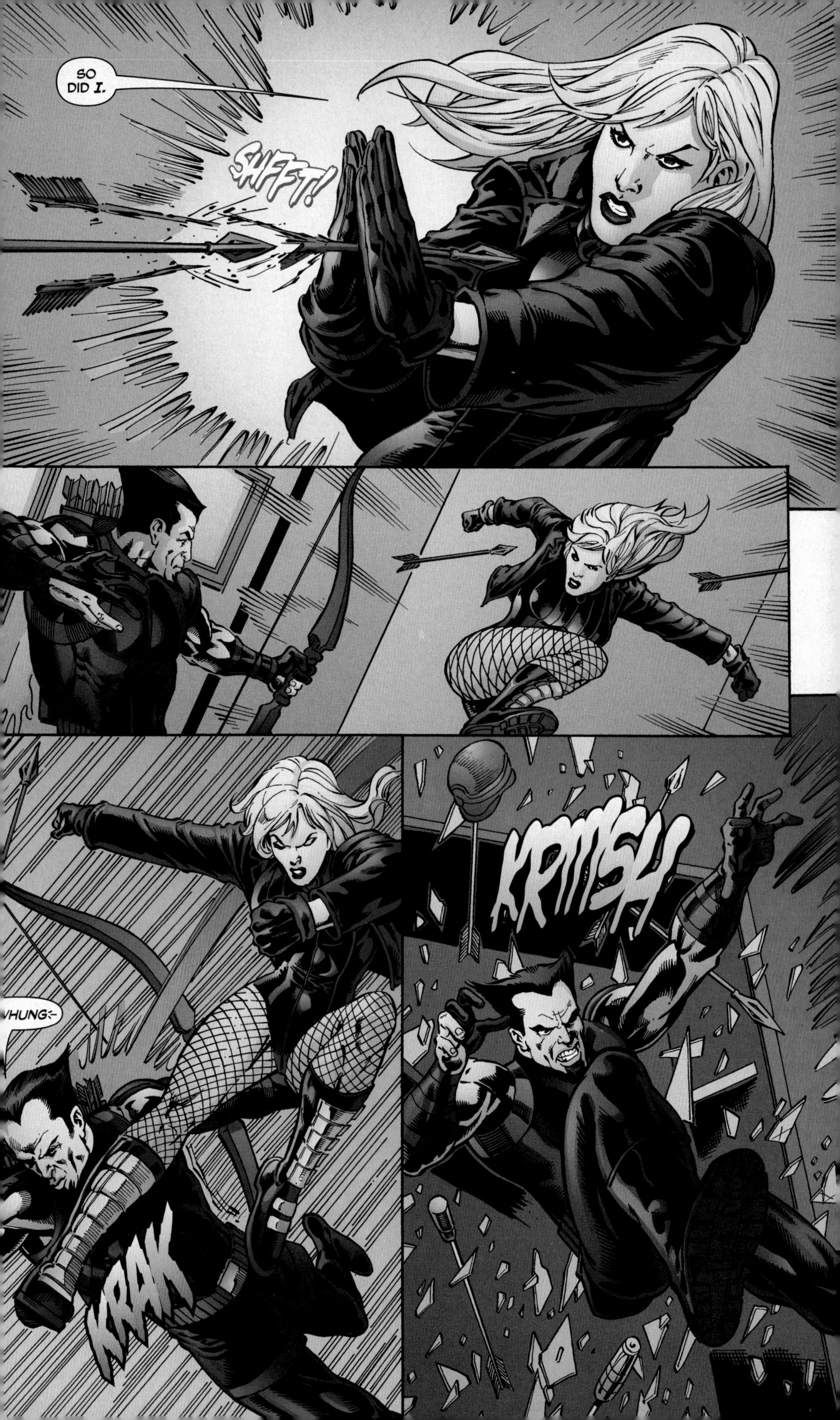

SO DID *I*.
SHFFT!
KRTTSH
WHUNG
KRAK

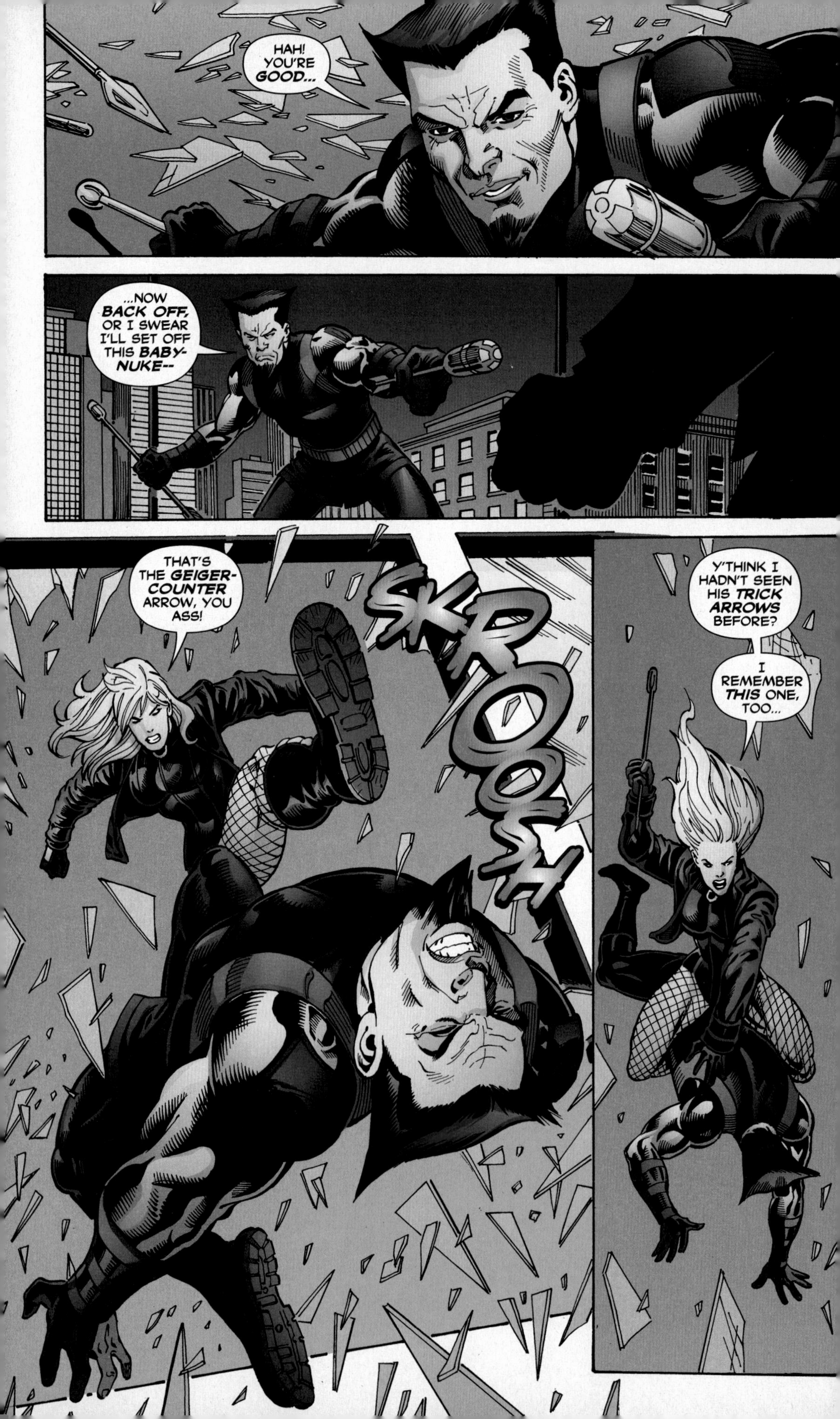

HAH! YOU'RE GOOD...
...NOW BACK OFF, OR I SWEAR I'LL SET OFF THIS BABY-NUKE--
THAT'S THE GEIGER-COUNTER ARROW, YOU ASS!
SKROOOM
Y'THINK I HADN'T SEEN HIS TRICK ARROWS BEFORE?
I REMEMBER THIS ONE, TOO...

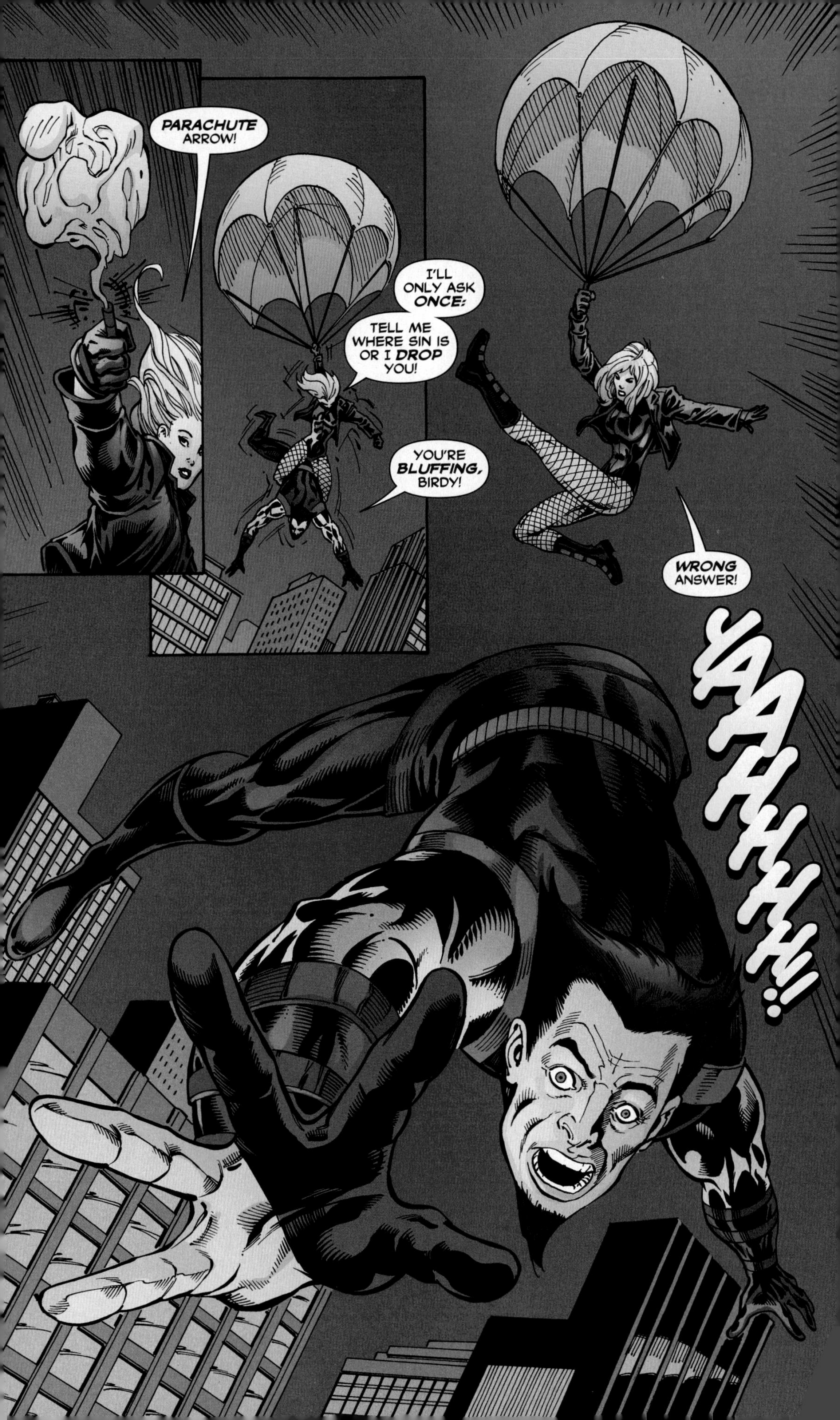
PARACHUTE ARROW!
I'LL ONLY ASK ONCE:
TELL ME WHERE SIN IS OR I DROP YOU!
YOU'RE BLUFFING, BIRDY!
WRONG ANSWER!
YAAHHHH!!

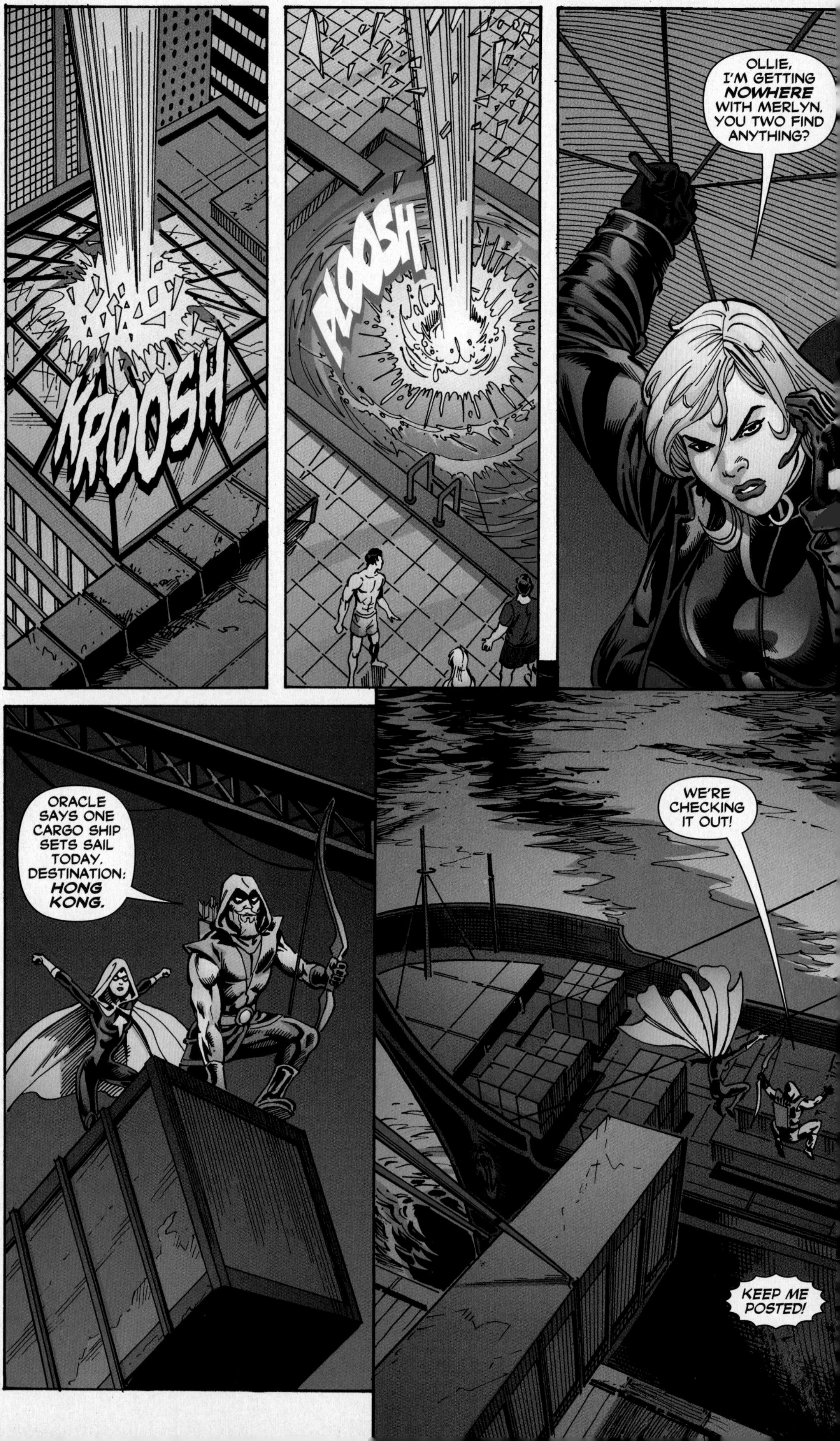
KROOSH
PLOOSH
OLLIE, I'M GETTING NOWHERE WITH MERLYN. YOU TWO FIND ANYTHING?
ORACLE SAYS ONE CARGO SHIP SETS SAIL TODAY. DESTINATION: HONG KONG.
WE'RE CHECKING IT OUT!
KEEP ME POSTED!

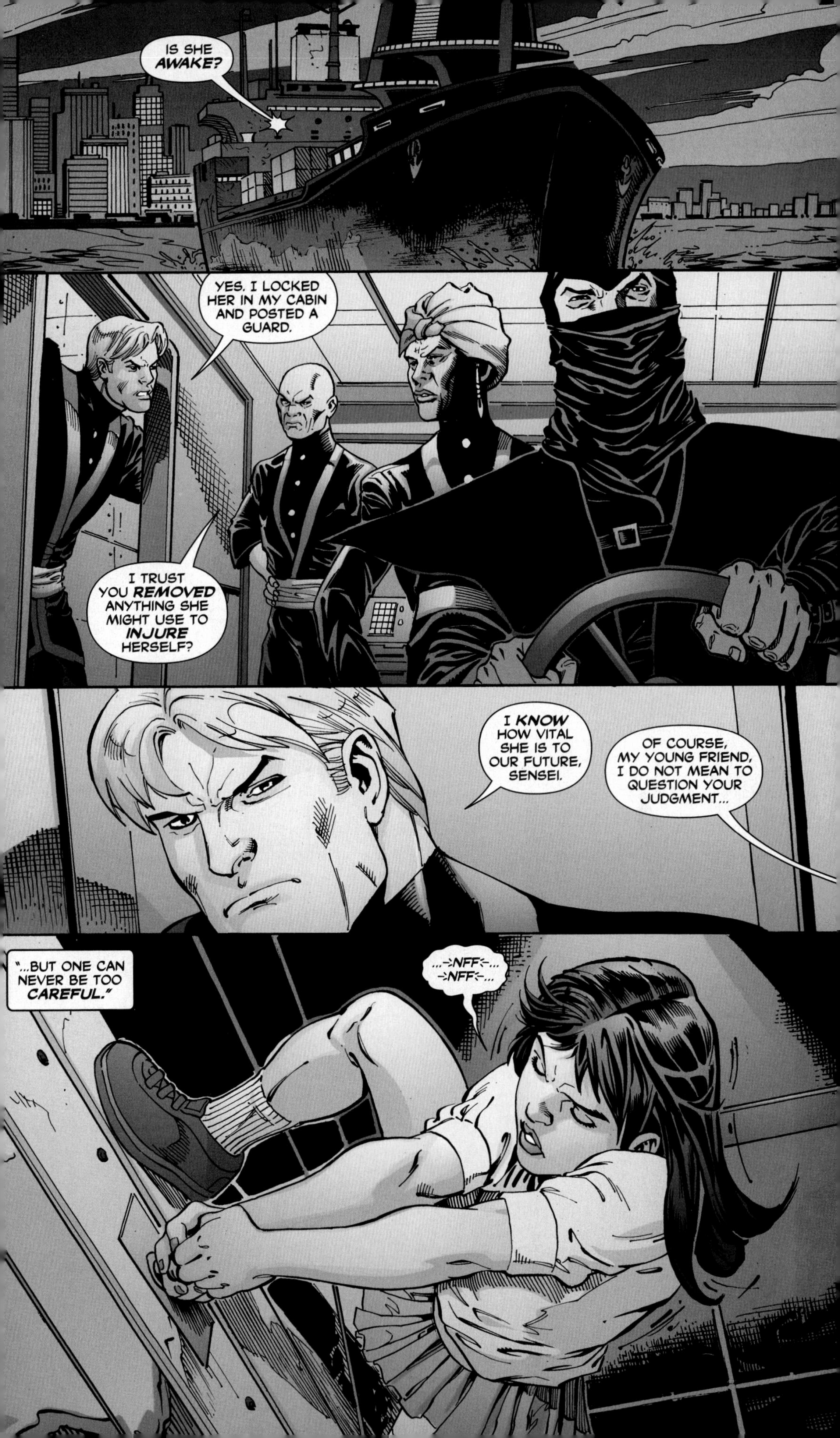
IS SHE *AWAKE?*
YES. I LOCKED HER IN MY CABIN AND POSTED A GUARD.
I TRUST YOU *REMOVED* ANYTHING SHE MIGHT USE TO *INJURE* HERSELF?
I *KNOW* HOW VITAL SHE IS TO OUR FUTURE, SENSEI.
OF COURSE, MY YOUNG FRIEND, I DO NOT MEAN TO QUESTION YOUR JUDGMENT...
"...BUT ONE CAN NEVER BE TOO *CAREFUL.*"
...*NFF*...
NFF...

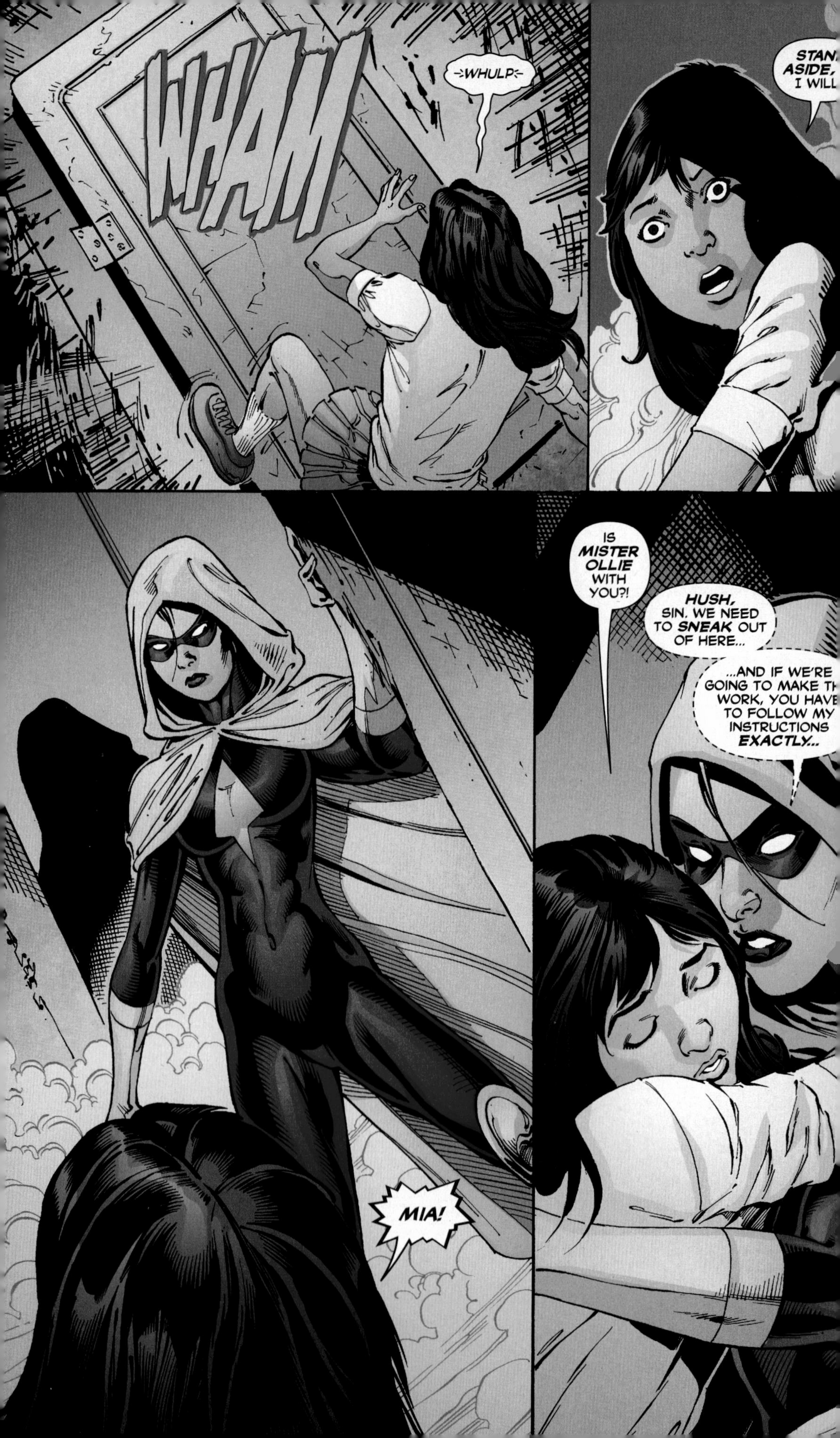
WHAM
-WHULP-
STAN
ASIDE,
I WILL
IS MISTER OLLIE WITH YOU?!
HUSH, SIN. WE NEED TO SNEAK OUT OF HERE...
...AND IF WE'RE GOING TO MAKE TH WORK, YOU HAVE TO FOLLOW MY INSTRUCTIONS EXACTLY...
MIA!

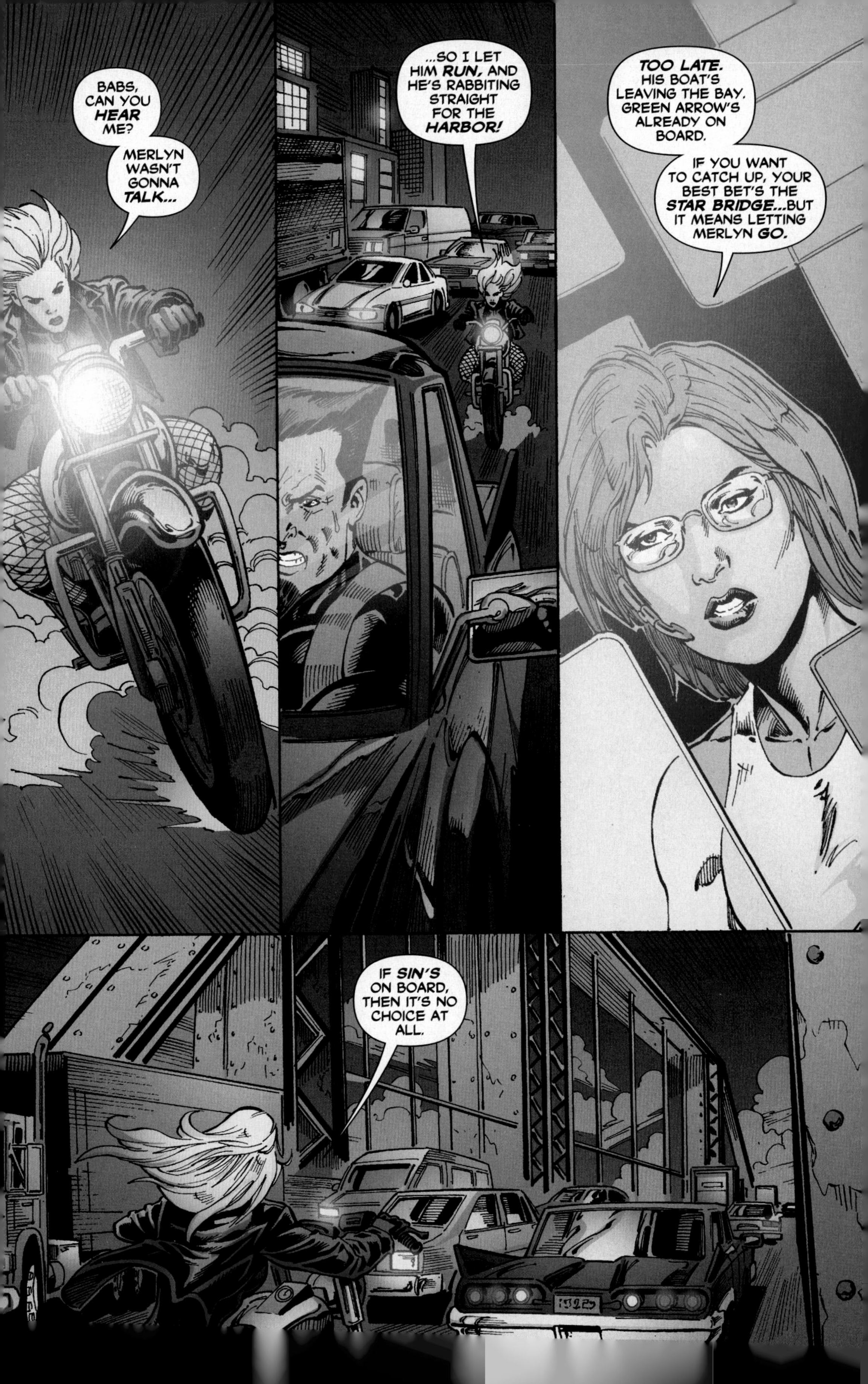
BABS, CAN YOU HEAR ME?
MERLYN WASN'T GONNA TALK...
...SO I LET HIM RUN, AND HE'S RABBITING STRAIGHT FOR THE HARBOR!
TOO LATE. HIS BOAT'S LEAVING THE BAY. GREEN ARROW'S ALREADY ON BOARD.
IF YOU WANT TO CATCH UP, YOUR BEST BET'S THE STAR BRIDGE...BUT IT MEANS LETTING MERLYN GO.
IF SIN'S ON BOARD, THEN IT'S NO CHOICE AT ALL.

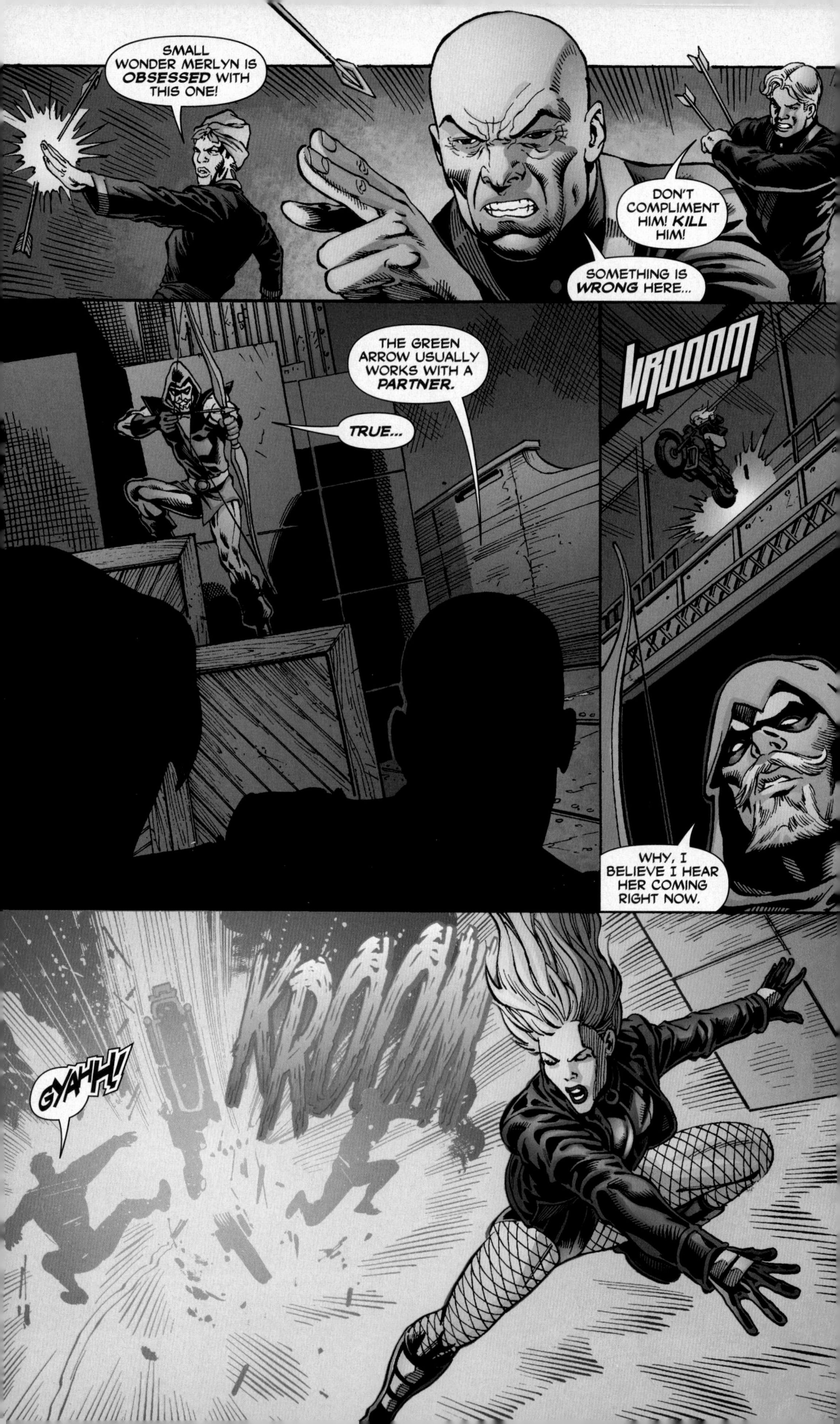
SMALL WONDER MERLYN IS OBSESSED WITH THIS ONE!
DON'T COMPLIMENT HIM! KILL HIM!
SOMETHING IS WRONG HERE...
THE GREEN ARROW USUALLY WORKS WITH A PARTNER.
TRUE...
VROOOM
WHY, I BELIEVE I HEAR HER COMING RIGHT NOW.
KROOM
GYAHH!

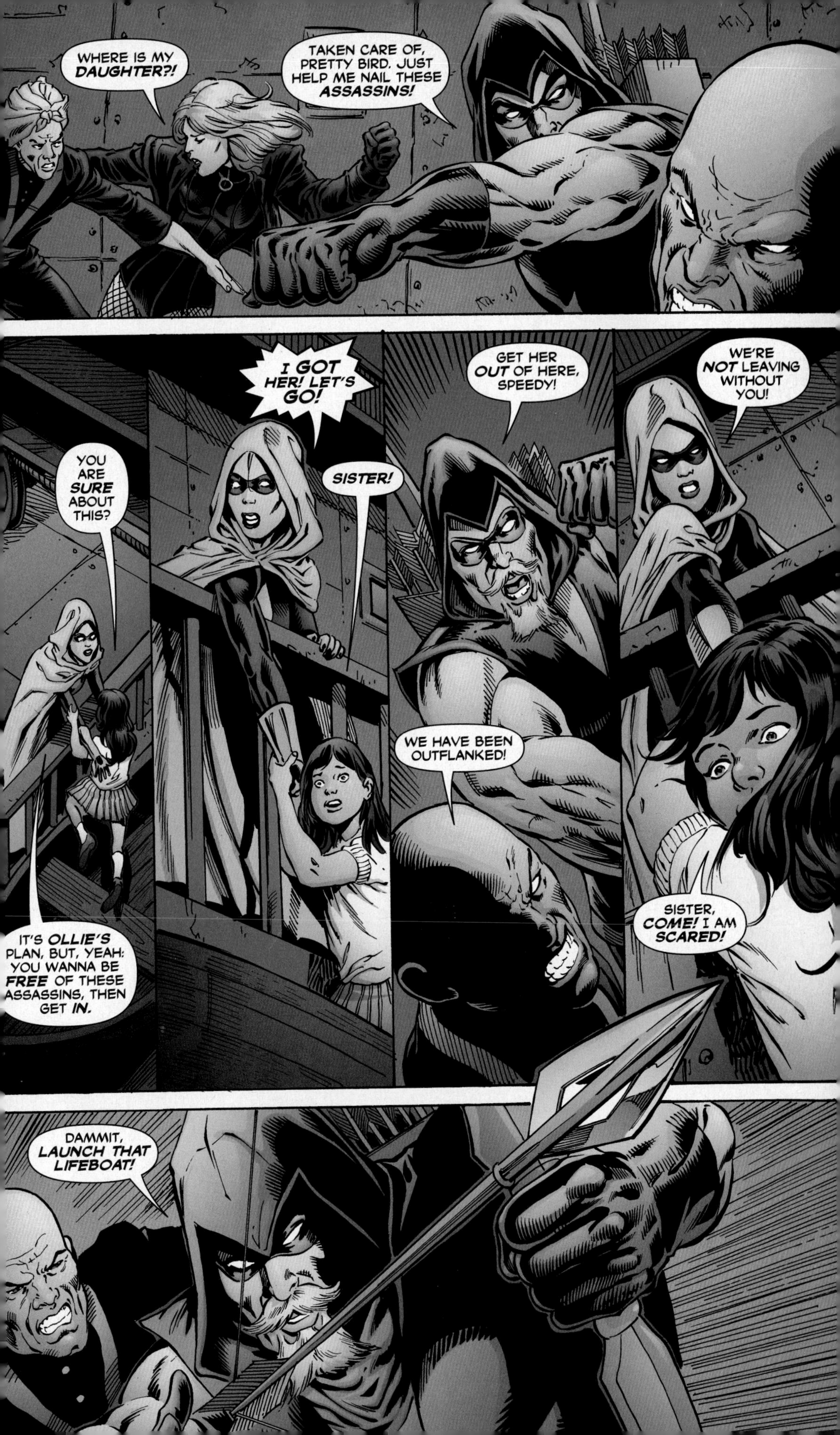
WHERE IS MY DAUGHTER?!
TAKEN CARE OF, PRETTY BIRD. JUST HELP ME NAIL THESE ASSASSINS!
YOU ARE SURE ABOUT THIS?
IT'S OLLIE'S PLAN, BUT, YEAH: YOU WANNA BE FREE OF THESE ASSASSINS, THEN GET IN.
I GOT HER! LET'S GO!
SISTER!
GET HER OUT OF HERE, SPEEDY!
WE HAVE BEEN OUTFLANKED!
WE'RE NOT LEAVING WITHOUT YOU!
SISTER, COME! I AM SCARED!
DAMMIT, LAUNCH THAT LIFEBOAT!

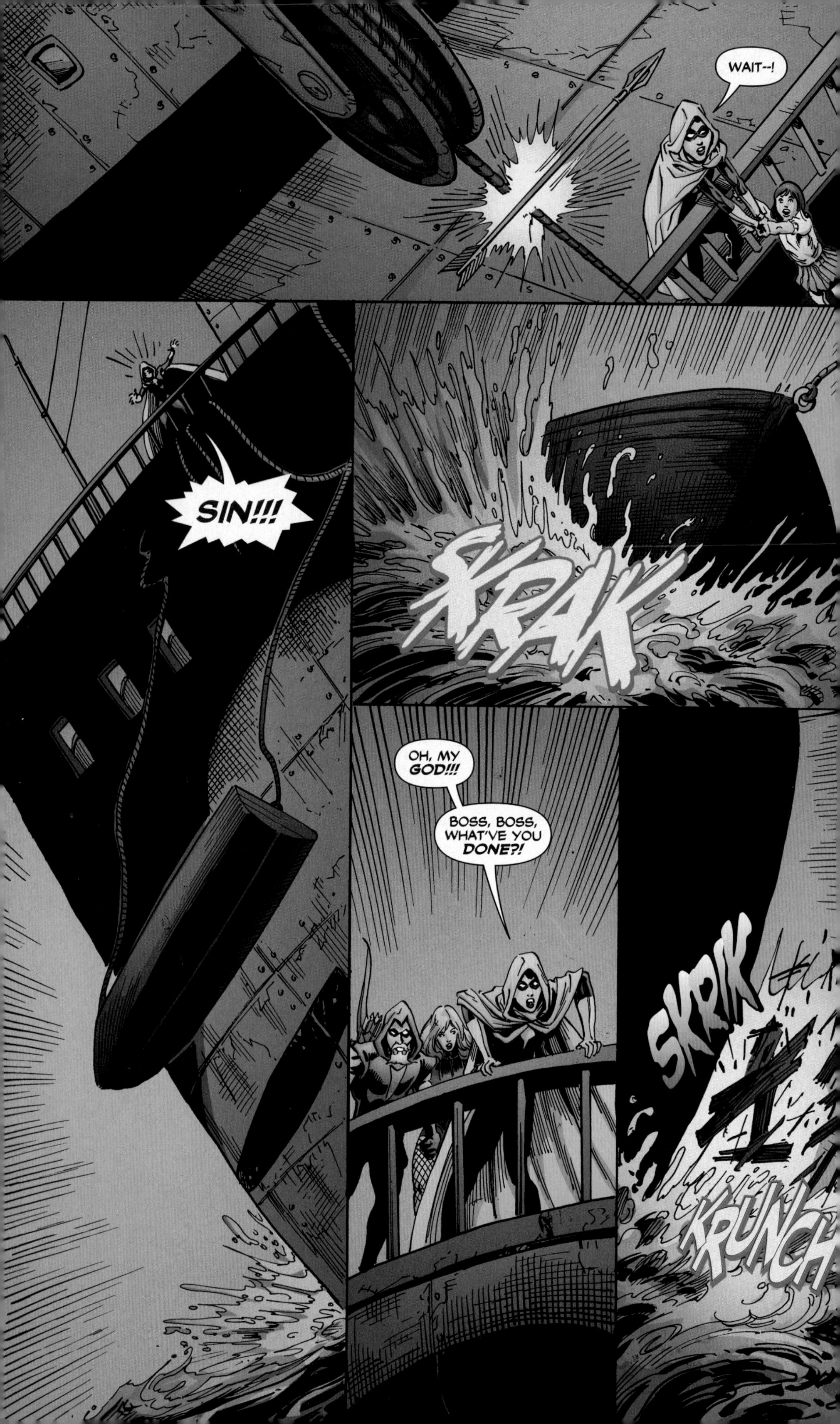
WAIT--!
SIN!!!
SKRAK
OH, MY GOD!!!
BOSS, BOSS, WHAT'VE YOU DONE?!
SKRIK
KRUNCH

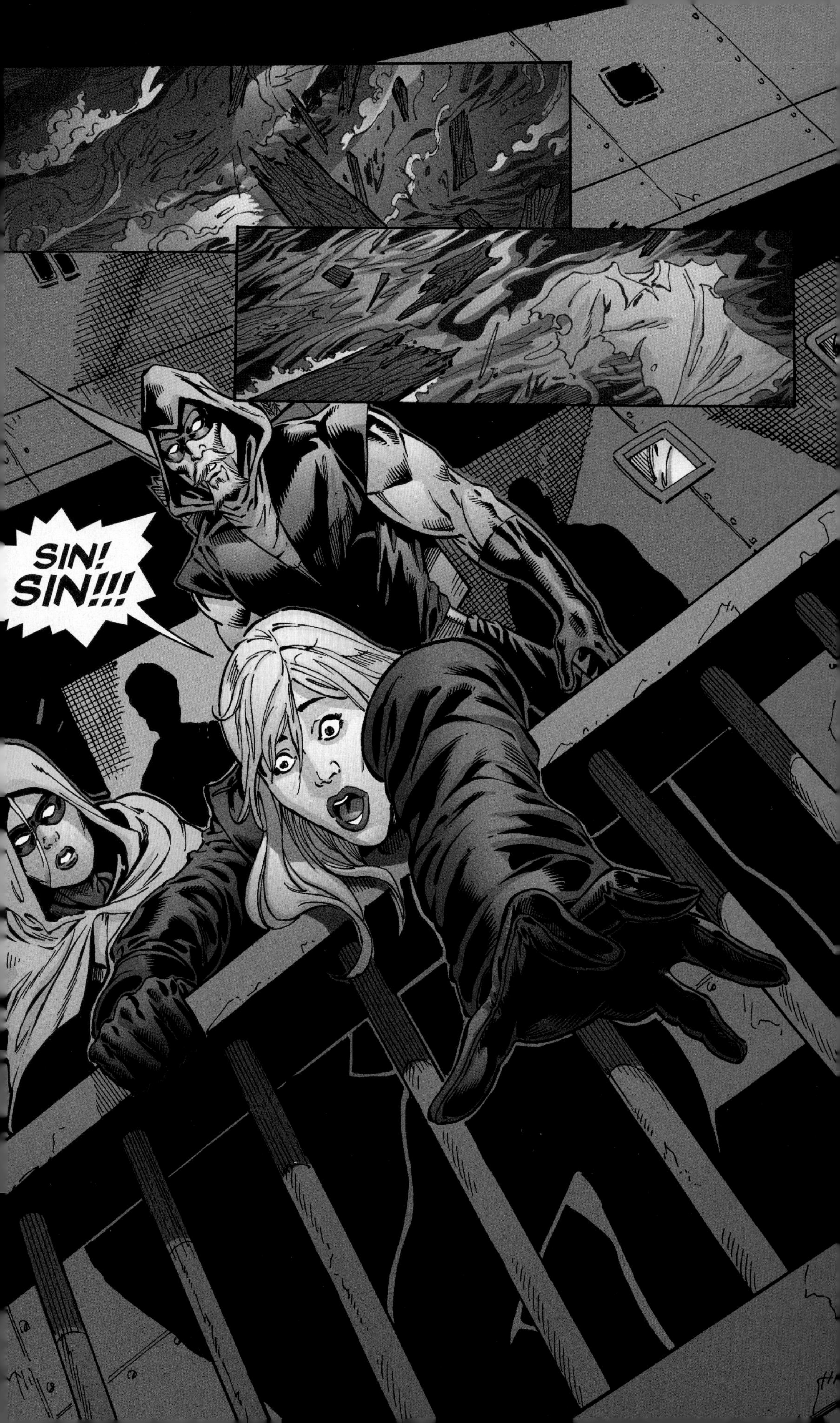
SIN!
SIN!!!

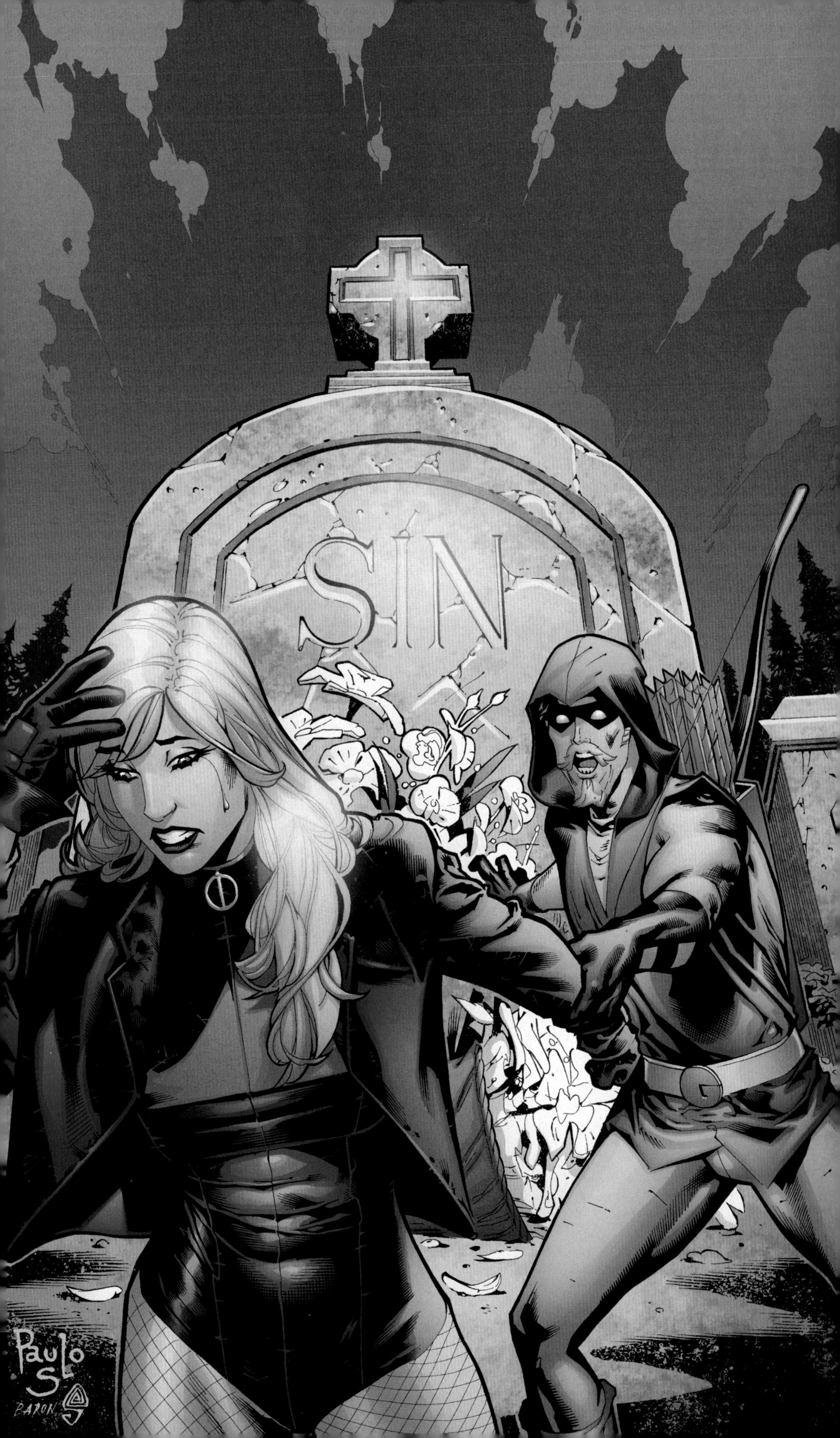
SIN
Paulo S
BARON

BLACK CANARY #4

TONY BEDARD
WRITER

MIKE NORTON
LAYOUTS

PAULO SIQUEIRA
JOE PRADO
PENCILLERS

AMILTON SANTOS
JOE PRADO
INKERS

I.L.L.
COLORIST

PAT BROSSEAU
LETTERER

PAULO SIQUEIRA & AMILTON SANTOS
WITH DAVID BARON
COVER

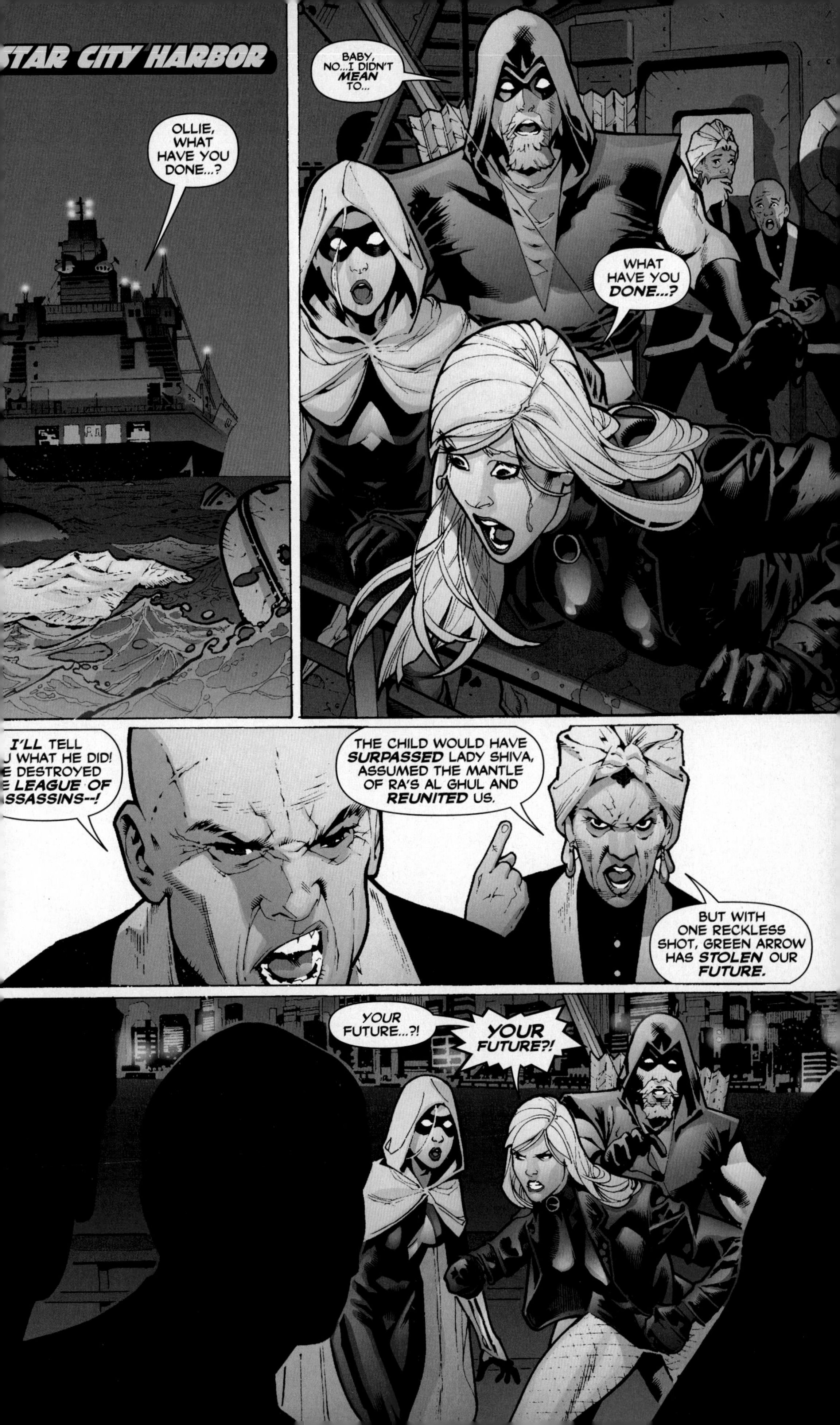
STAR CITY HARBOR
OLLIE, WHAT HAVE YOU DONE...?
BABY, NO...I DIDN'T MEAN TO...
WHAT HAVE YOU DONE...?
I'LL TELL U WHAT HE DID! E DESTROYED E LEAGUE OF SSASSINS--!
THE CHILD WOULD HAVE SURPASSED LADY SHIVA, ASSUMED THE MANTLE OF RA'S AL GHUL AND REUNITED US.
BUT WITH ONE RECKLESS SHOT, GREEN ARROW HAS STOLEN OUR FUTURE.
YOUR FUTURE...?!
YOUR FUTURE?!

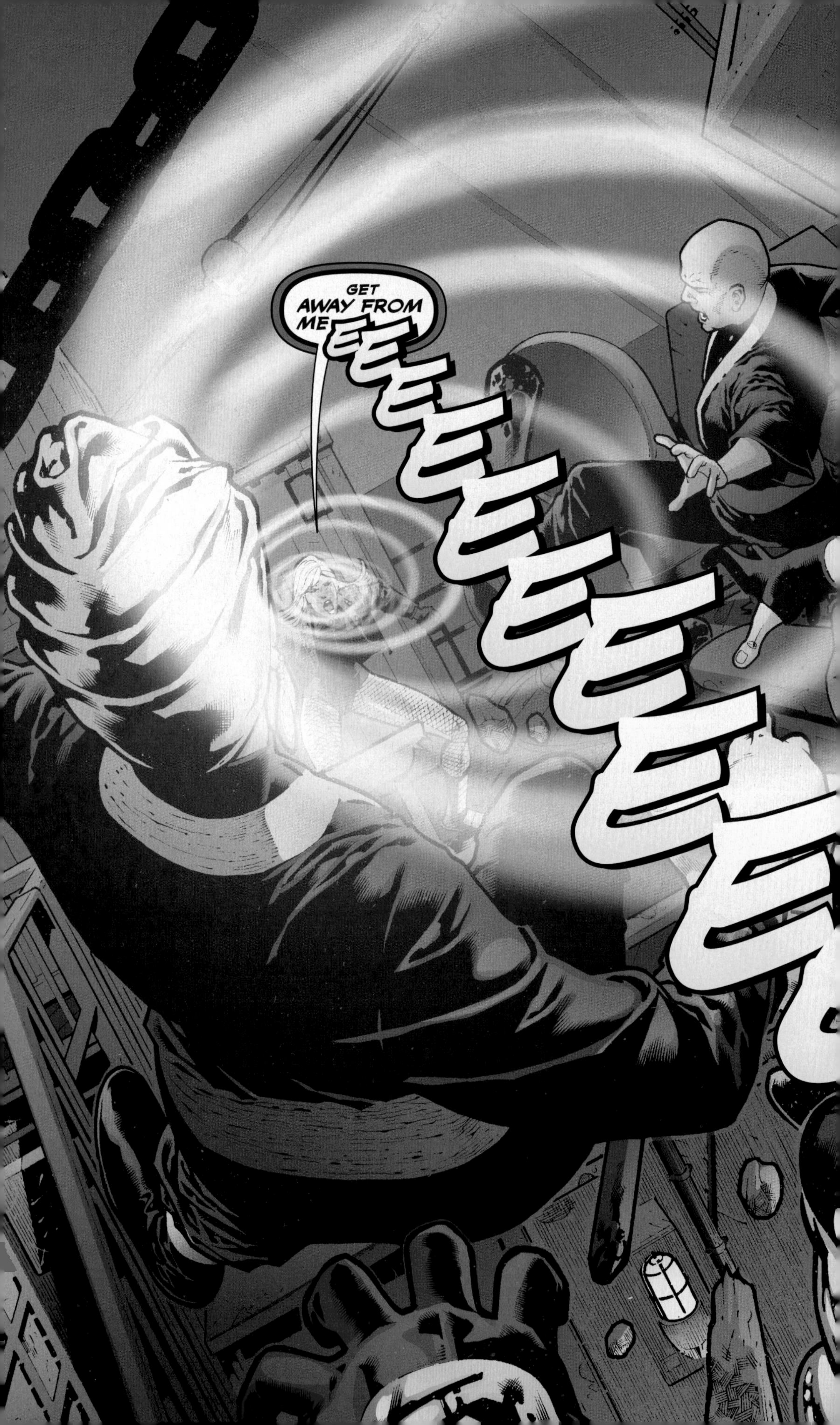
GET AWAY FROM MEEEEEEEEEEEEE

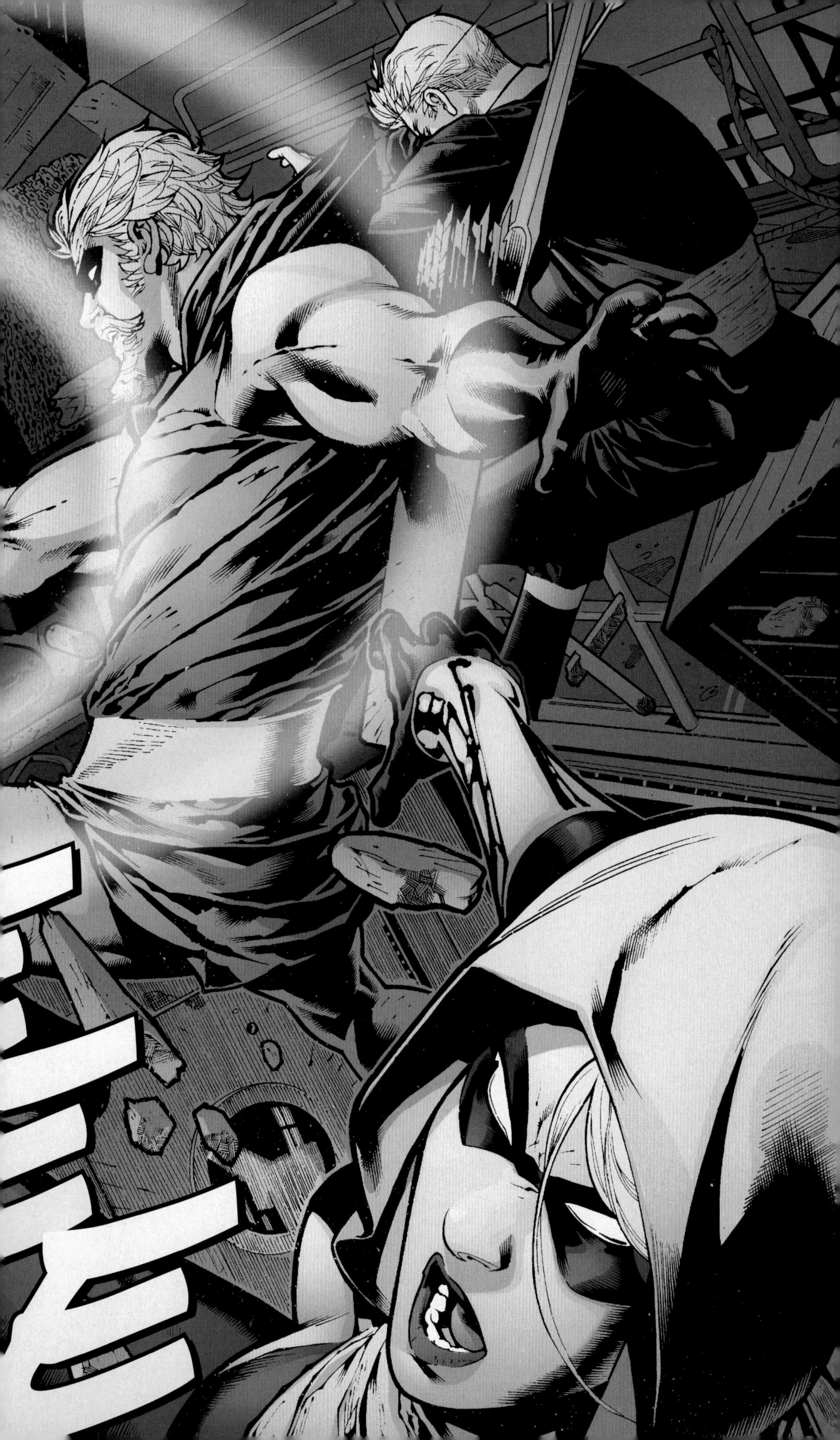

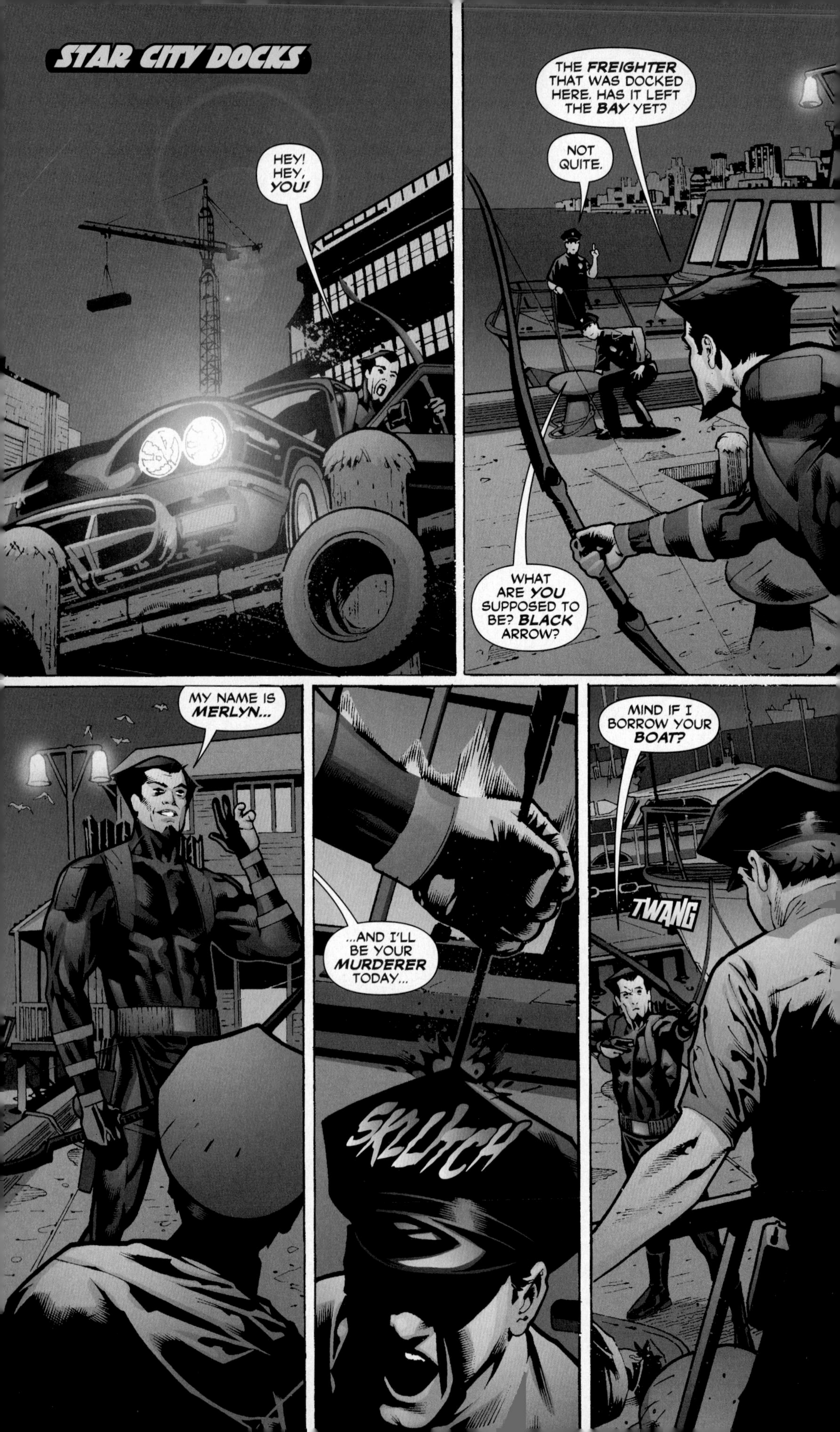
STAR CITY DOCKS
HEY! HEY, YOU!
THE FREIGHTER THAT WAS DOCKED HERE. HAS IT LEFT THE BAY YET?
NOT QUITE.
WHAT ARE YOU SUPPOSED TO BE? BLACK ARROW?
MY NAME IS MERLYN...
...AND I'LL BE YOUR MURDERER TODAY...
SKLITCH
MIND IF I BORROW YOUR BOAT?
TWANG

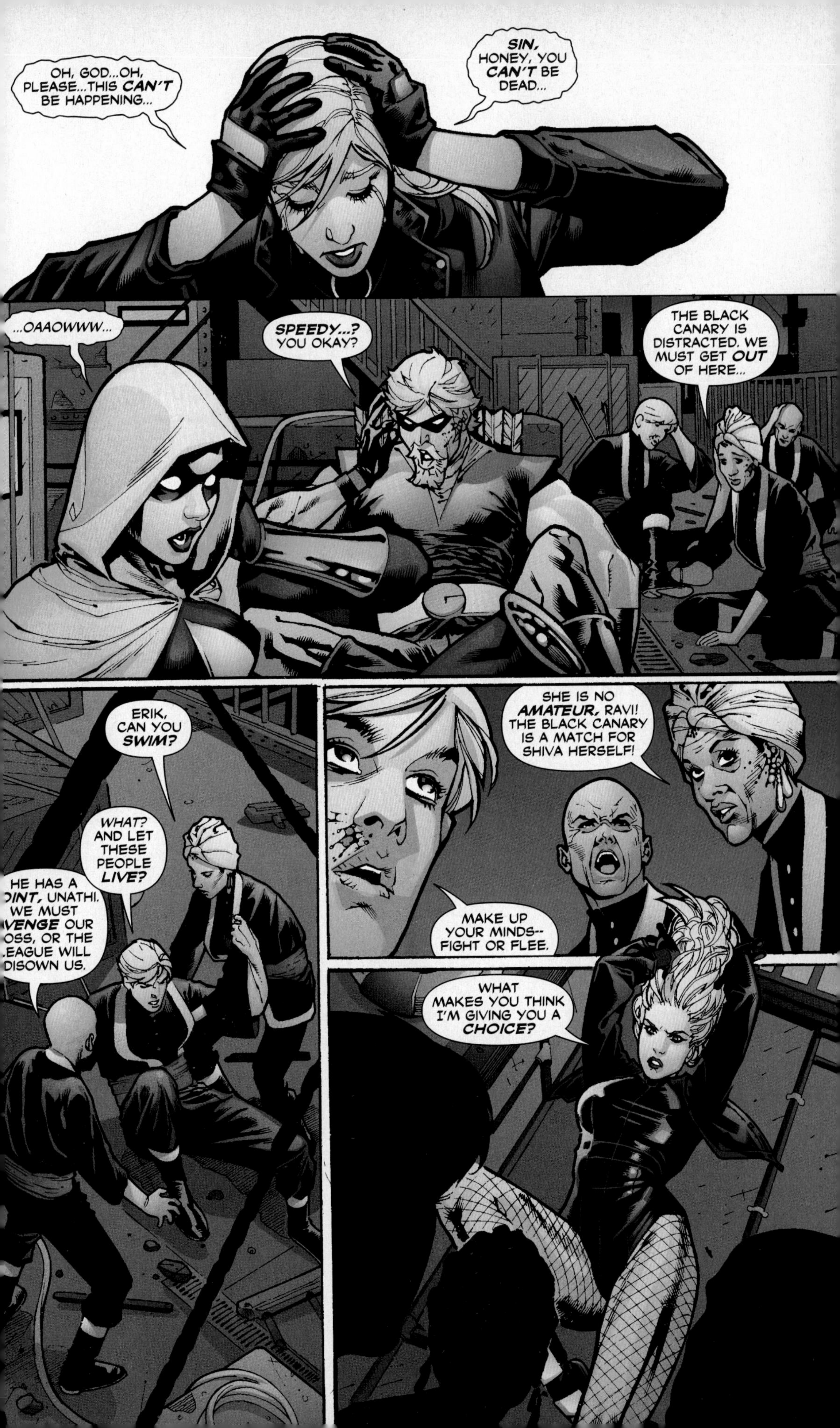

OH, GOD...OH, PLEASE...THIS CAN'T BE HAPPENING...
SIN, HONEY, YOU CAN'T BE DEAD...
...OAAOWWW...
SPEEDY...? YOU OKAY?
THE BLACK CANARY IS DISTRACTED. WE MUST GET OUT OF HERE...
ERIK, CAN YOU SWIM?
WHAT? AND LET THESE PEOPLE LIVE?
HE HAS A OINT, UNATHI. WE MUST VENGE OUR OSS, OR THE EAGUE WILL DISOWN US.
SHE IS NO AMATEUR, RAVI! THE BLACK CANARY IS A MATCH FOR SHIVA HERSELF!
MAKE UP YOUR MINDS--FIGHT OR FLEE.
WHAT MAKES YOU THINK I'M GIVING YOU A CHOICE?

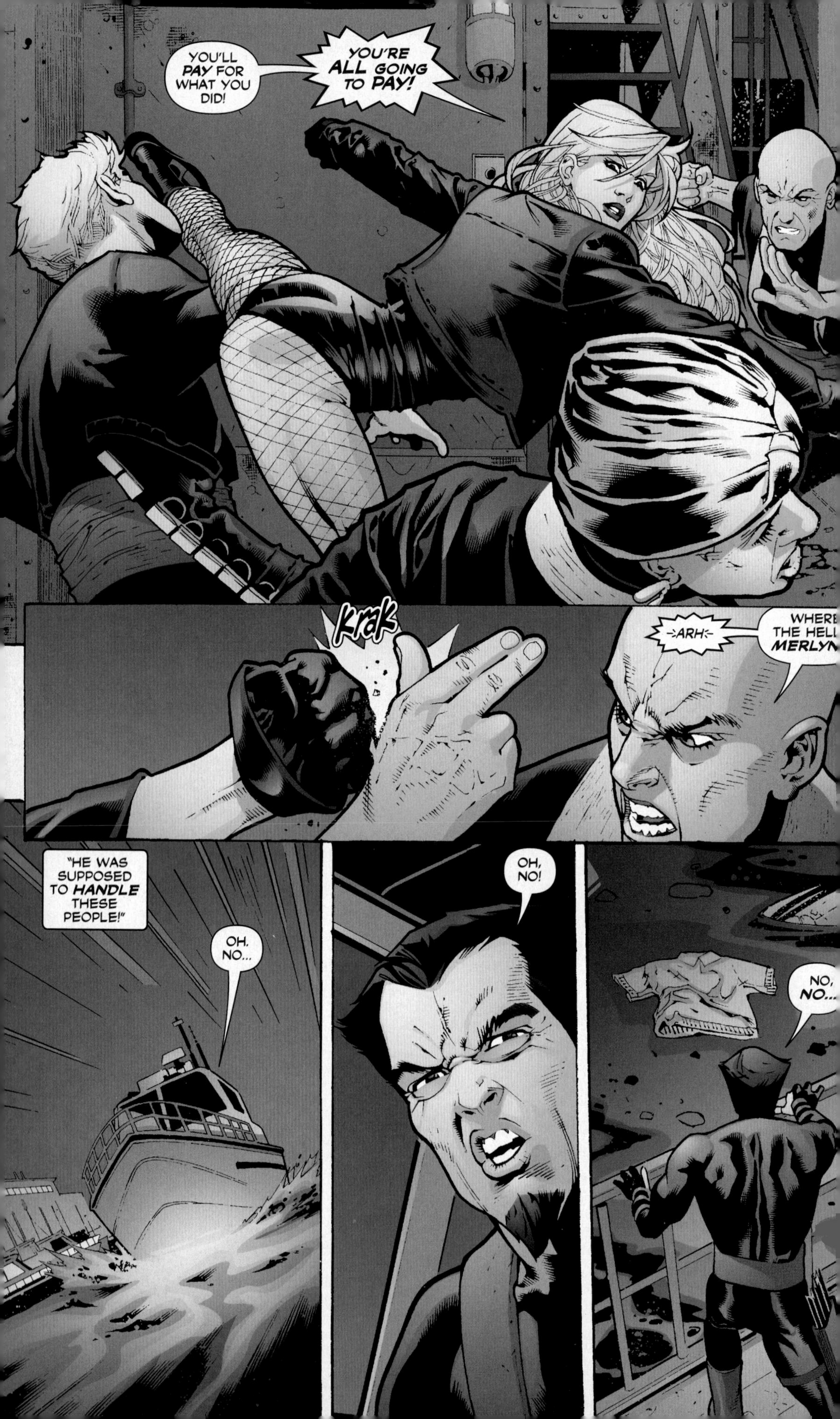
YOU'LL PAY FOR WHAT YOU DID!
YOU'RE ALL GOING TO PAY!
KRAK
ARH
WHERE THE HELL MERLYN
"HE WAS SUPPOSED TO HANDLE THESE PEOPLE!"
OH. NO...
OH, NO!
NO, NO...

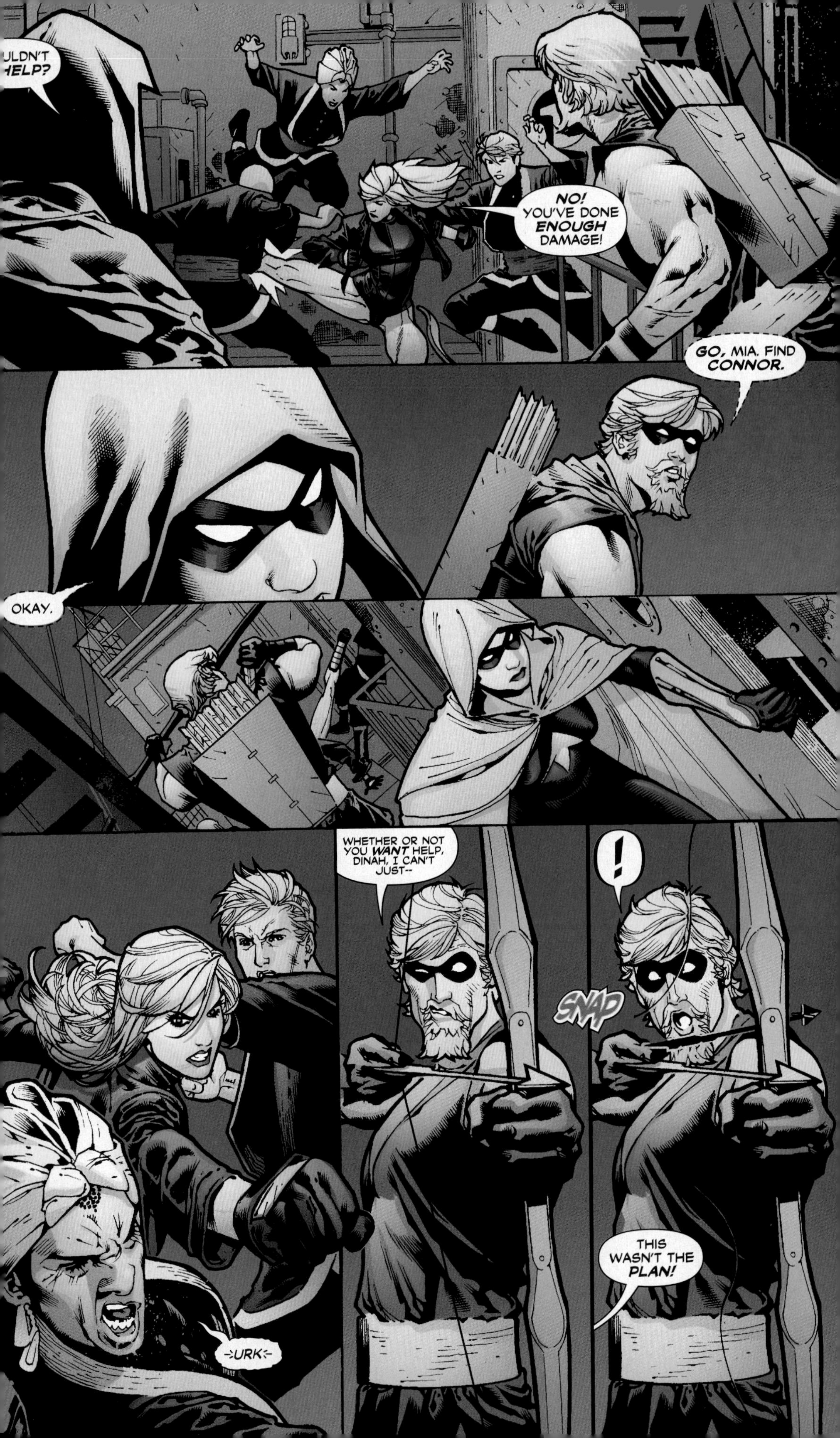
ULDN'T
HELP?
NO! YOU'VE DONE ENOUGH DAMAGE!
GO, MIA. FIND CONNOR.
OKAY.
WHETHER OR NOT YOU WANT HELP, DINAH, I CAN'T JUST--
!
SNAP
-URK-
THIS WASN'T THE PLAN!

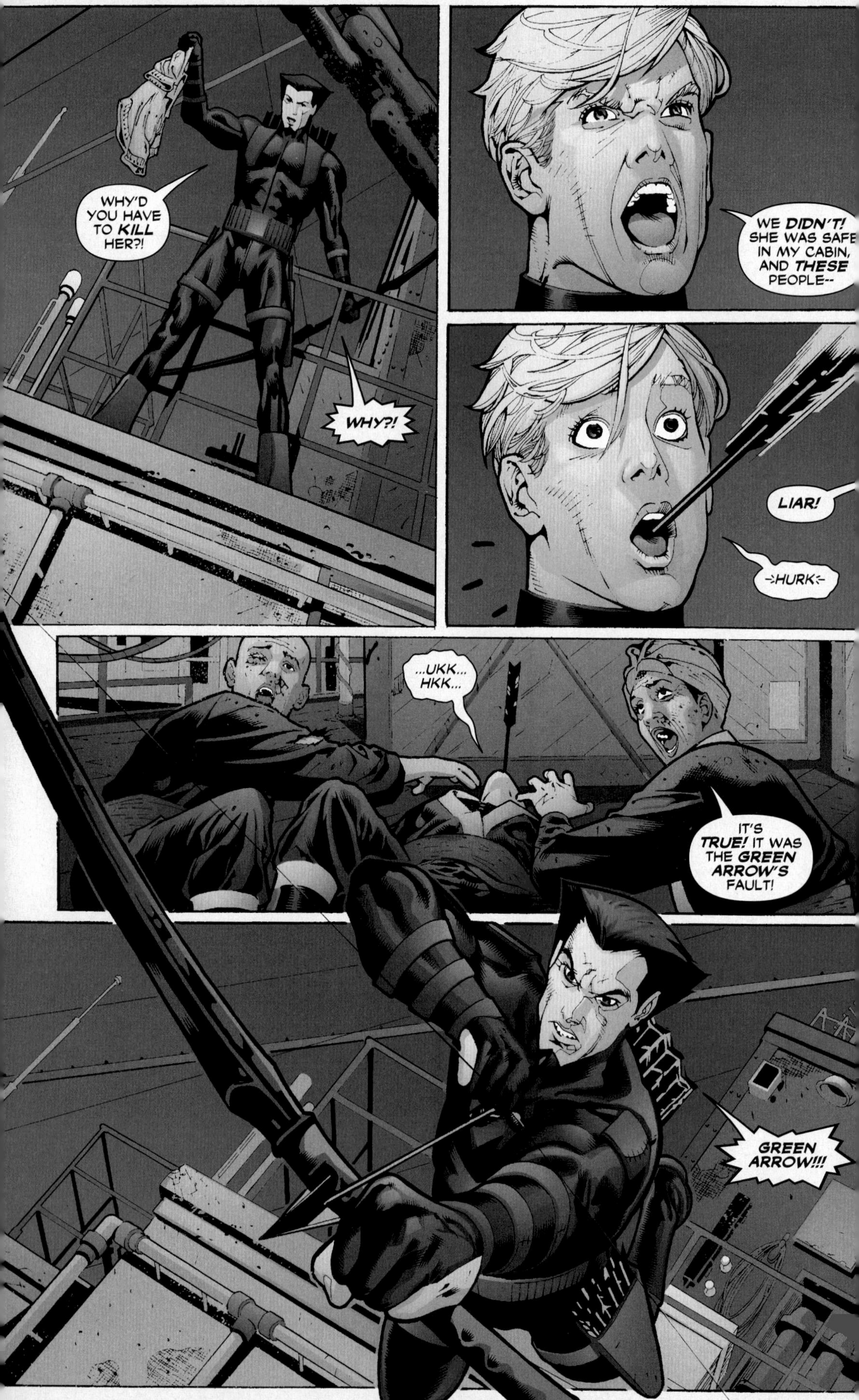
WHY'D YOU HAVE TO KILL HER?!
WHY?!
WE DIDN'T! SHE WAS SAFE IN MY CABIN, AND THESE PEOPLE--
LIAR!
HURK
...UKK... HKK...
IT'S TRUE! IT WAS THE GREEN ARROW'S FAULT!
GREEN ARROW!!!

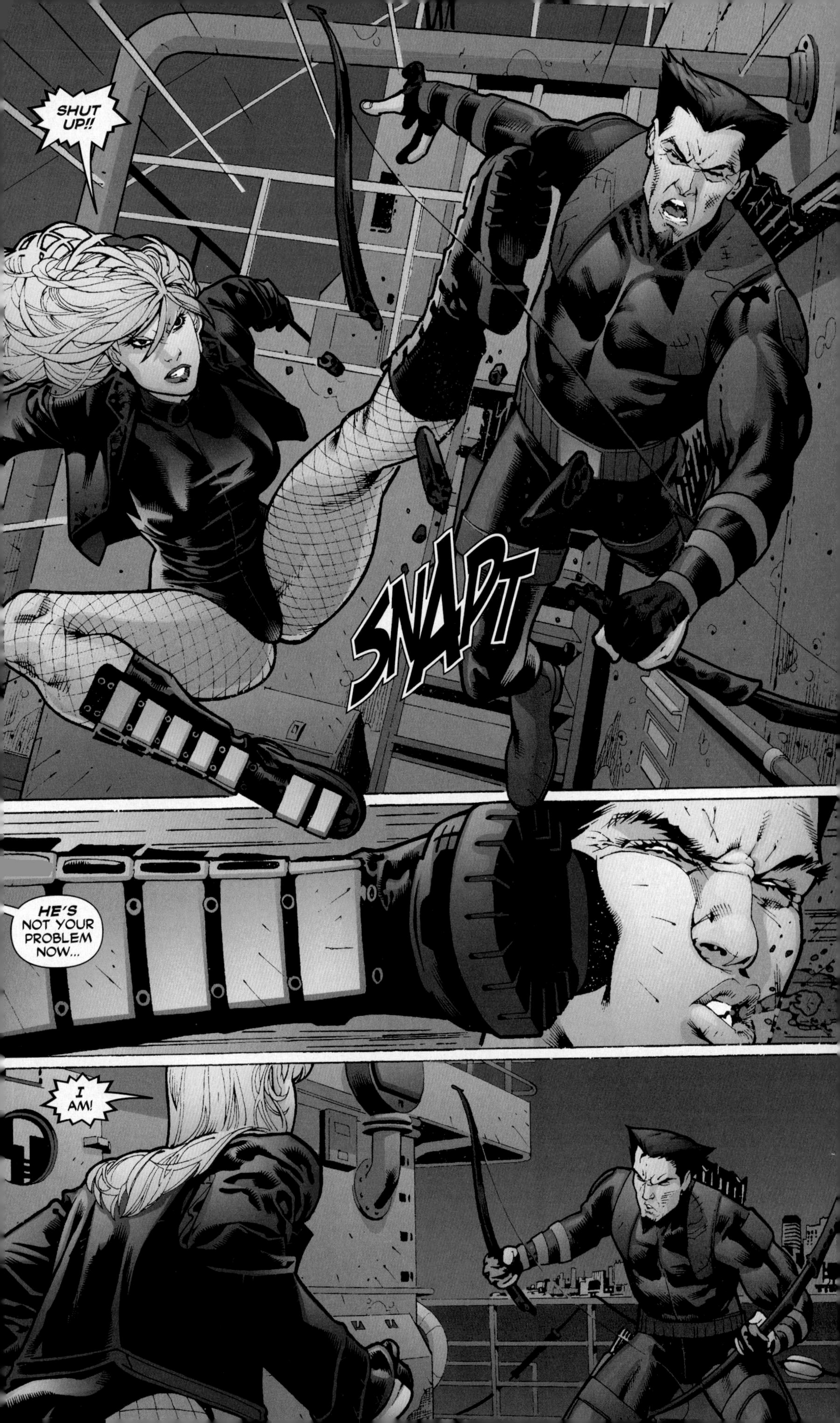
SHUT UP!!
SNAPT
HE'S NOT YOUR PROBLEM NOW...
I AM!

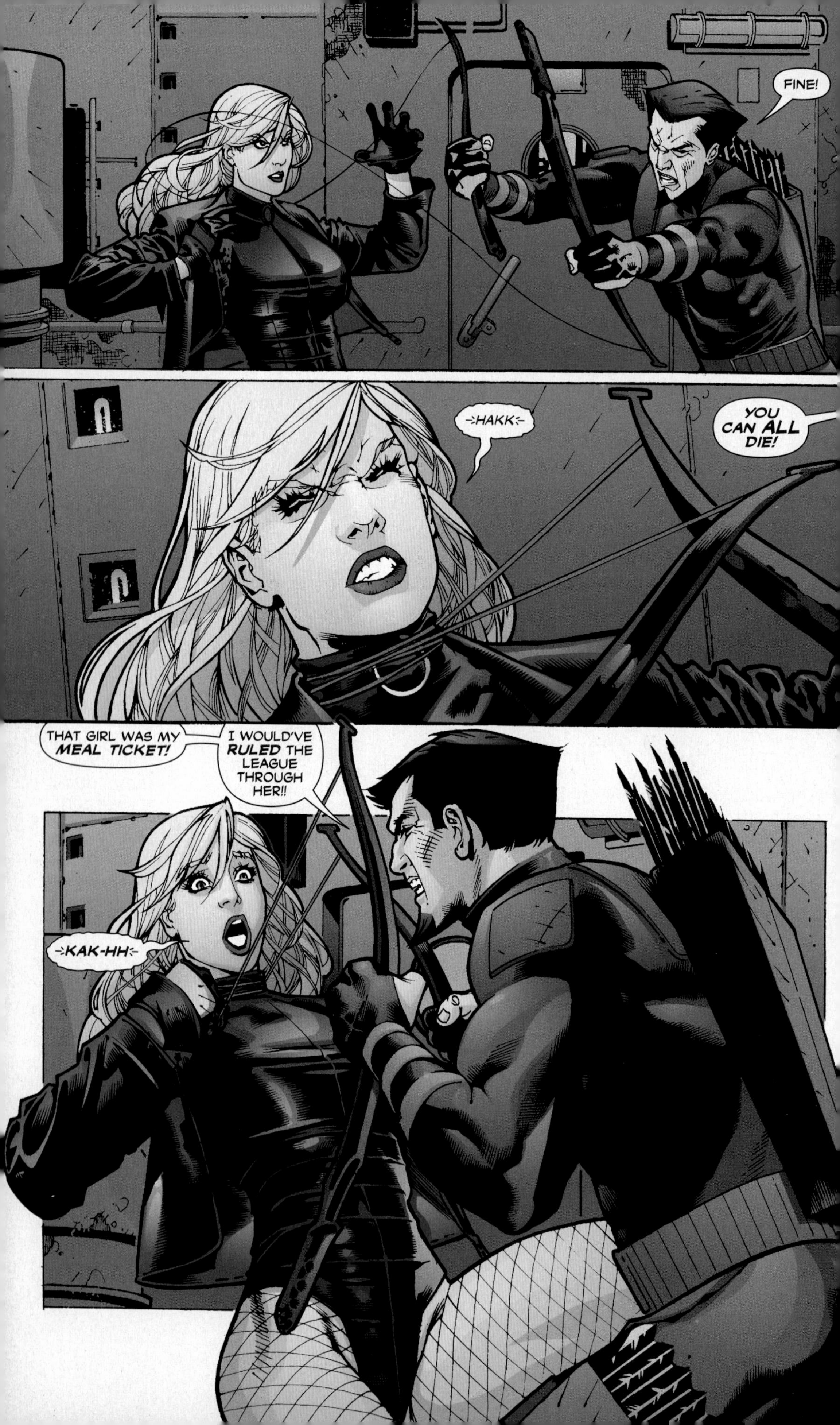
FINE!
-HAKK-
YOU CAN ALL DIE!
THAT GIRL WAS MY MEAL TICKET!
I WOULD'VE RULED THE LEAGUE THROUGH HER!!
-KAK-HH-

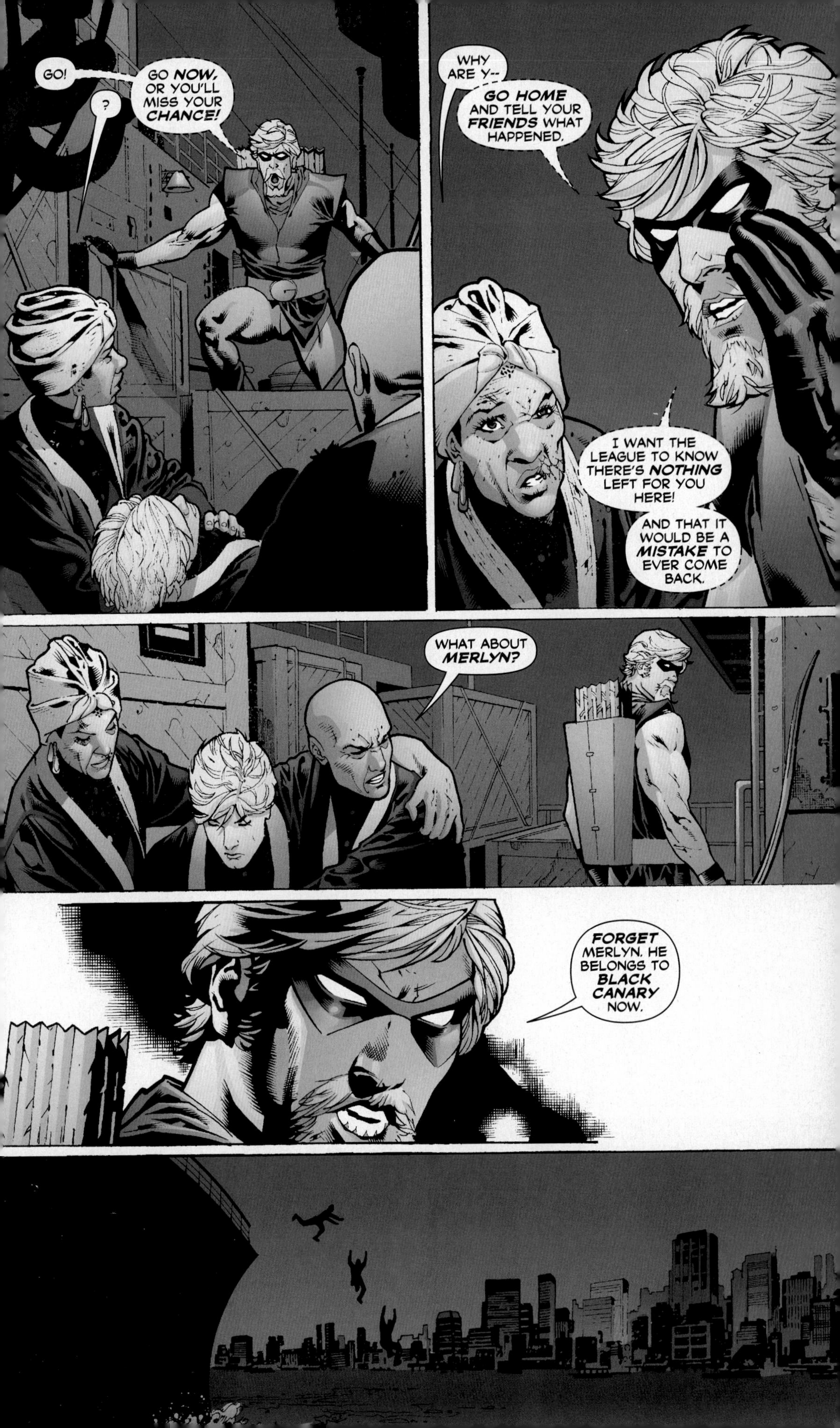
GO!
?
GO NOW, OR YOU'LL MISS YOUR CHANCE!
WHY ARE Y--
GO HOME AND TELL YOUR FRIENDS WHAT HAPPENED.
I WANT THE LEAGUE TO KNOW THERE'S NOTHING LEFT FOR YOU HERE!
AND THAT IT WOULD BE A MISTAKE TO EVER COME BACK.
WHAT ABOUT MERLYN?
FORGET MERLYN. HE BELONGS TO BLACK CANARY NOW.

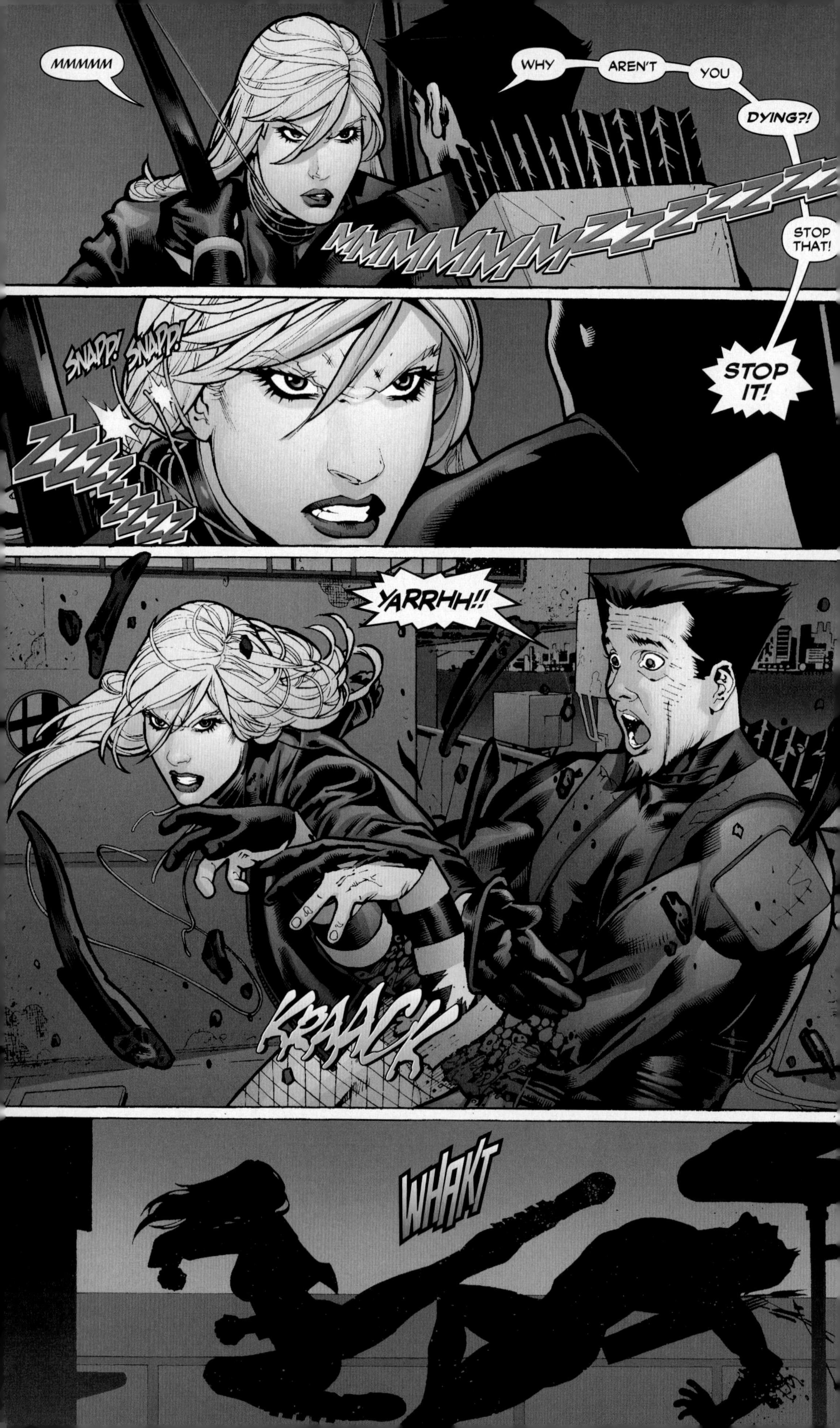
MMMMM
WHY
AREN'T
YOU
DYING?!
MMMMMMZZZZZZ
STOP THAT!
SNAPP! SNAPP!
STOP IT!
ZZZZZZZ
YARRHH!!
KRAACK
WHAKT

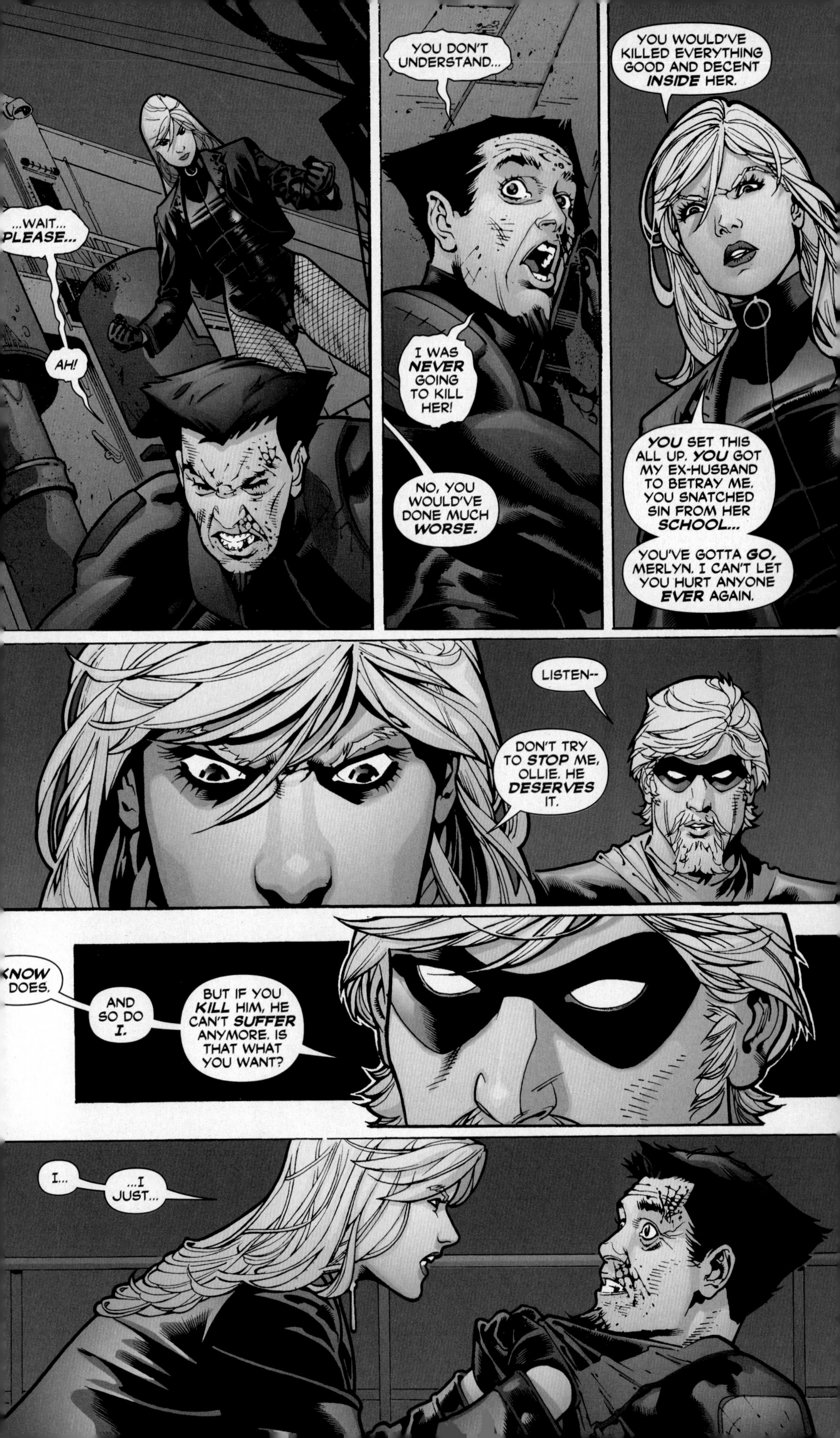
...WAIT... PLEASE...
AH!
YOU DON'T UNDERSTAND...
I WAS NEVER GOING TO KILL HER!
NO, YOU WOULD'VE DONE MUCH WORSE.
YOU WOULD'VE KILLED EVERYTHING GOOD AND DECENT INSIDE HER.
YOU SET THIS ALL UP. YOU GOT MY EX-HUSBAND TO BETRAY ME. YOU SNATCHED SIN FROM HER SCHOOL...
YOU'VE GOTTA GO, MERLYN. I CAN'T LET YOU HURT ANYONE EVER AGAIN.
LISTEN--
DON'T TRY TO STOP ME, OLLIE. HE DESERVES IT.
KNOW DOES.
AND SO DO I.
BUT IF YOU KILL HIM, HE CAN'T SUFFER ANYMORE. IS THAT WHAT YOU WANT?
I...
...I JUST...

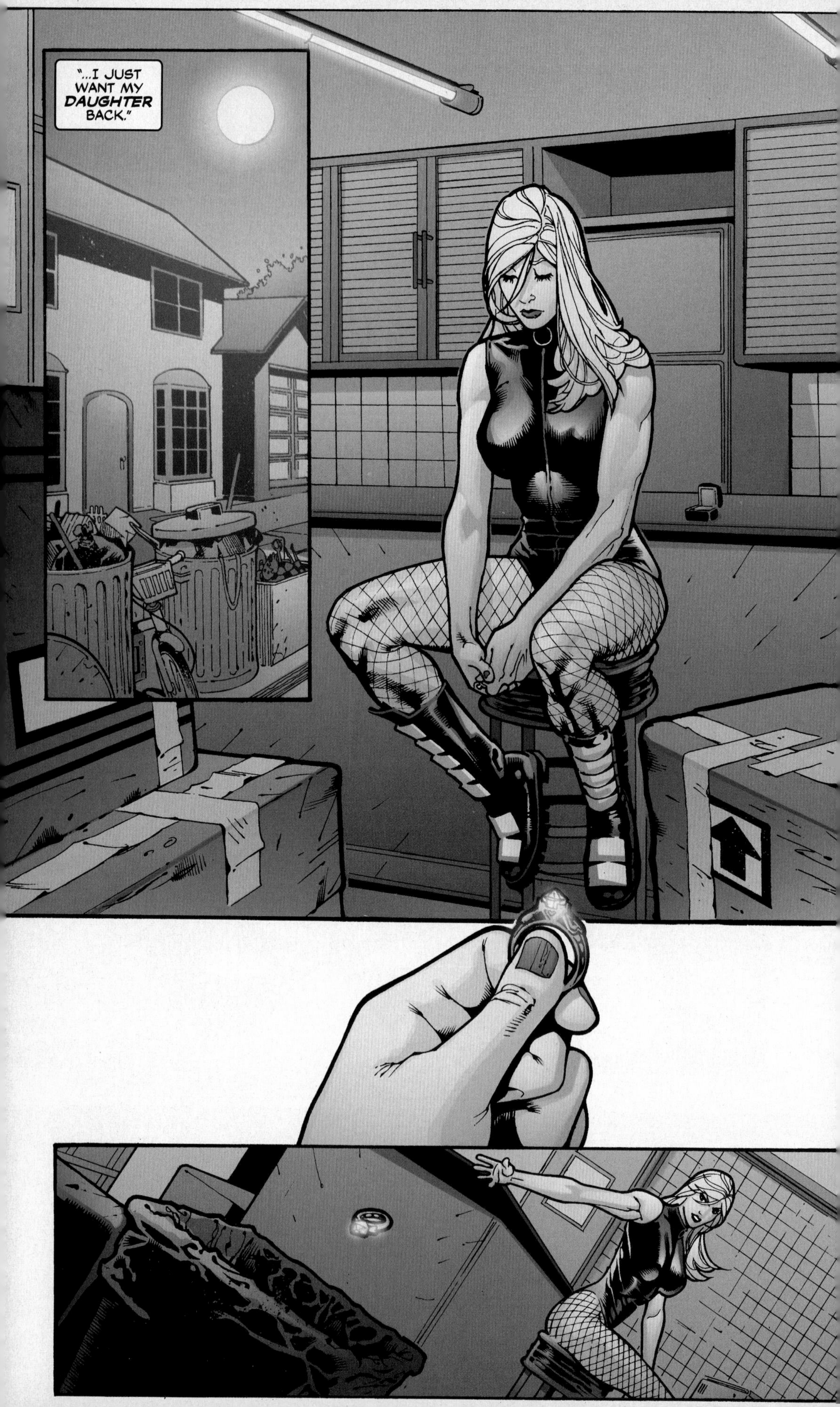
"...I JUST WANT MY DAUGHTER BACK."

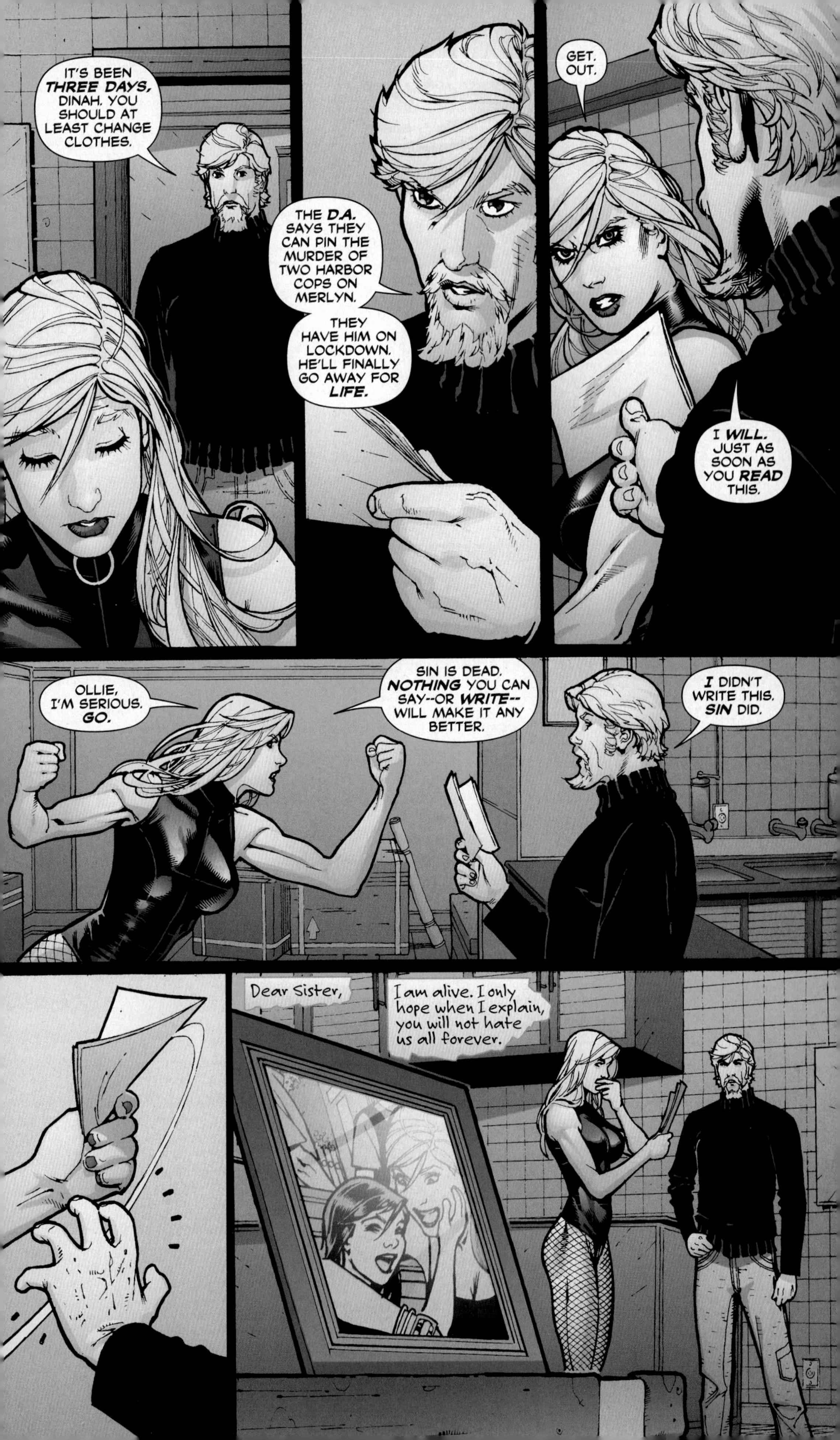
IT'S BEEN THREE DAYS, DINAH. YOU SHOULD AT LEAST CHANGE CLOTHES.
THE D.A. SAYS THEY CAN PIN THE MURDER OF TWO HARBOR COPS ON MERLYN.
THEY HAVE HIM ON LOCKDOWN. HE'LL FINALLY GO AWAY FOR LIFE.
GET. OUT.
I WILL. JUST AS SOON AS YOU READ THIS.
OLLIE, I'M SERIOUS. GO.
SIN IS DEAD. NOTHING YOU CAN SAY--OR WRITE--WILL MAKE IT ANY BETTER.
I DIDN'T WRITE THIS. SIN DID.
Dear Sister,
I am alive. I only hope when I explain, you will not hate us all forever.

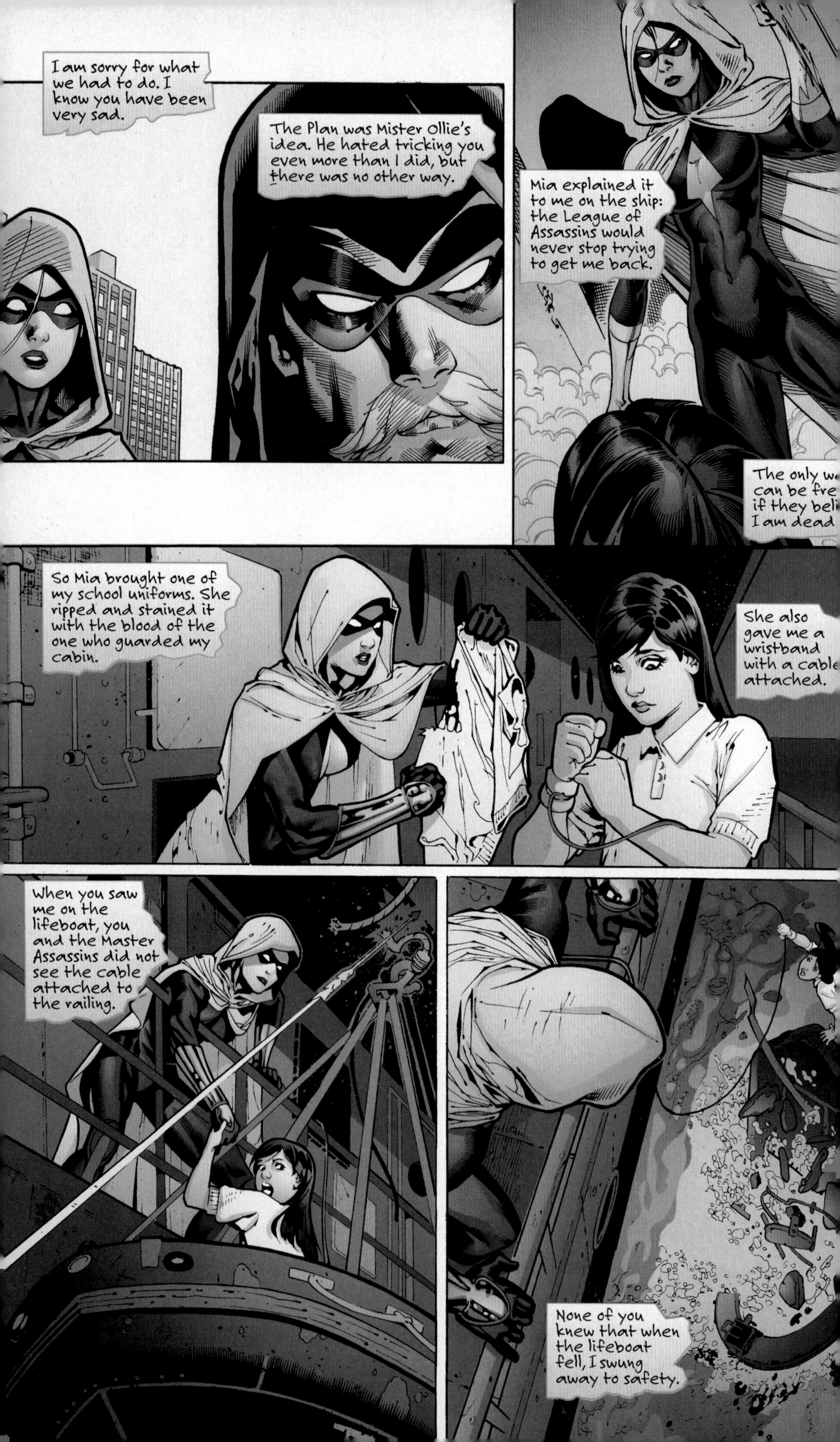
I am sorry for what we had to do. I know you have been very sad.
The Plan was Mister Ollie's idea. He hated tricking you even more than I did, but there was no other way.
Mia explained it to me on the ship: the League of Assassins would never stop trying to get me back.
The only w can be fre if they beli I am dead
So Mia brought one of my school uniforms. She ripped and stained it with the blood of the one who guarded my cabin.
She also gave me a wristband with a cable attached.
When you saw me on the lifeboat, you and the Master Assassins did not see the cable attached to the railing.
None of you knew that when the lifeboat fell, I swung away to safety.

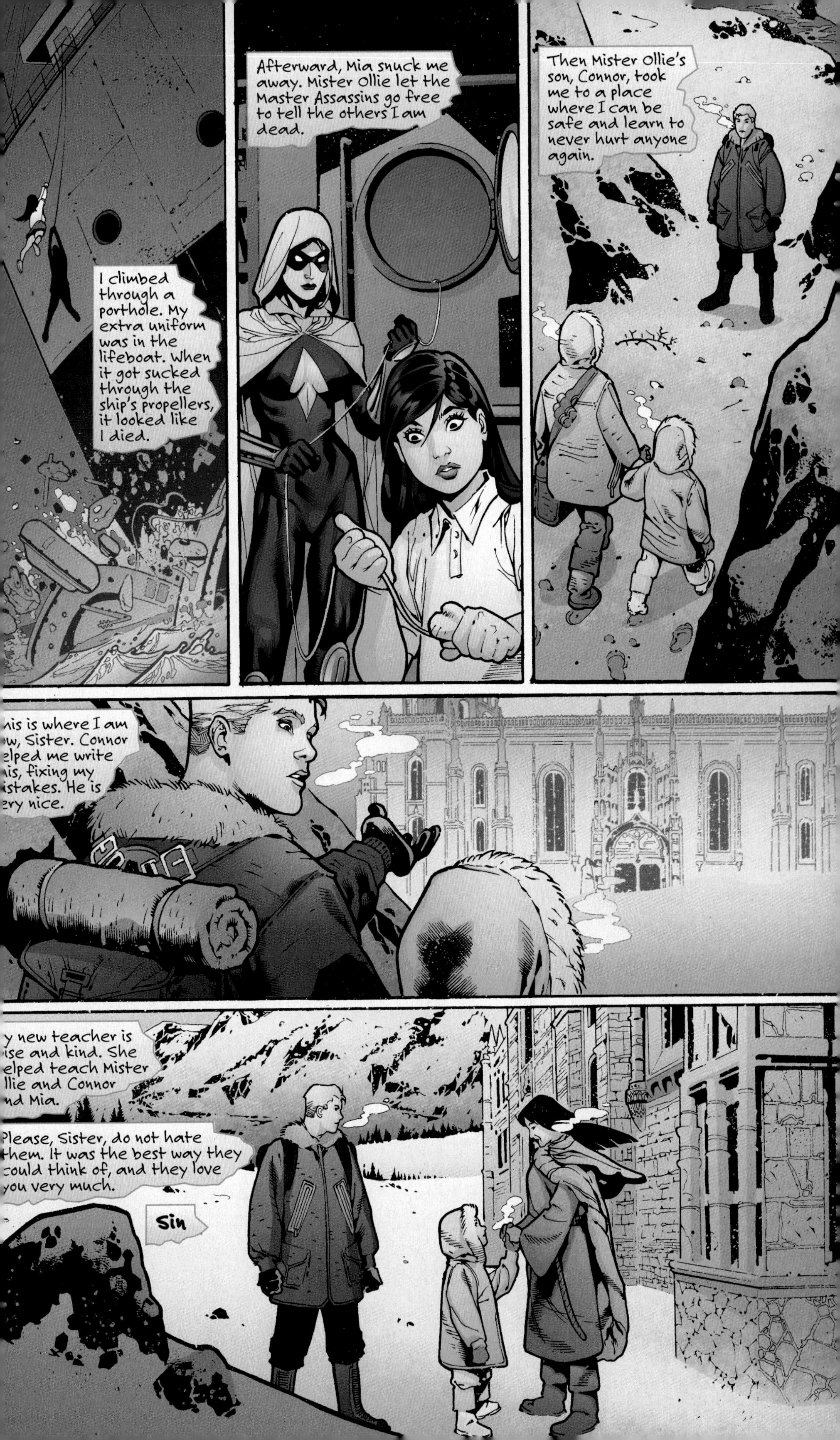
I climbed through a porthole. My extra uniform was in the lifeboat. When it got sucked through the ship's propellers, it looked like I died.
Afterward, Mia snuck me away. Mister Ollie let the Master Assassins go free to tell the others I am dead.
Then Mister Ollie's son, Connor, took me to a place where I can be safe and learn to never hurt anyone again.
his is where I am w, Sister. Connor elped me write his, fixing my istakes. He is ery nice.
y new teacher is ise and kind. She elped teach Mister llie and Connor nd Mia.
Please, Sister, do not hate them. It was the best way they could think of, and they love you very much.
Sin

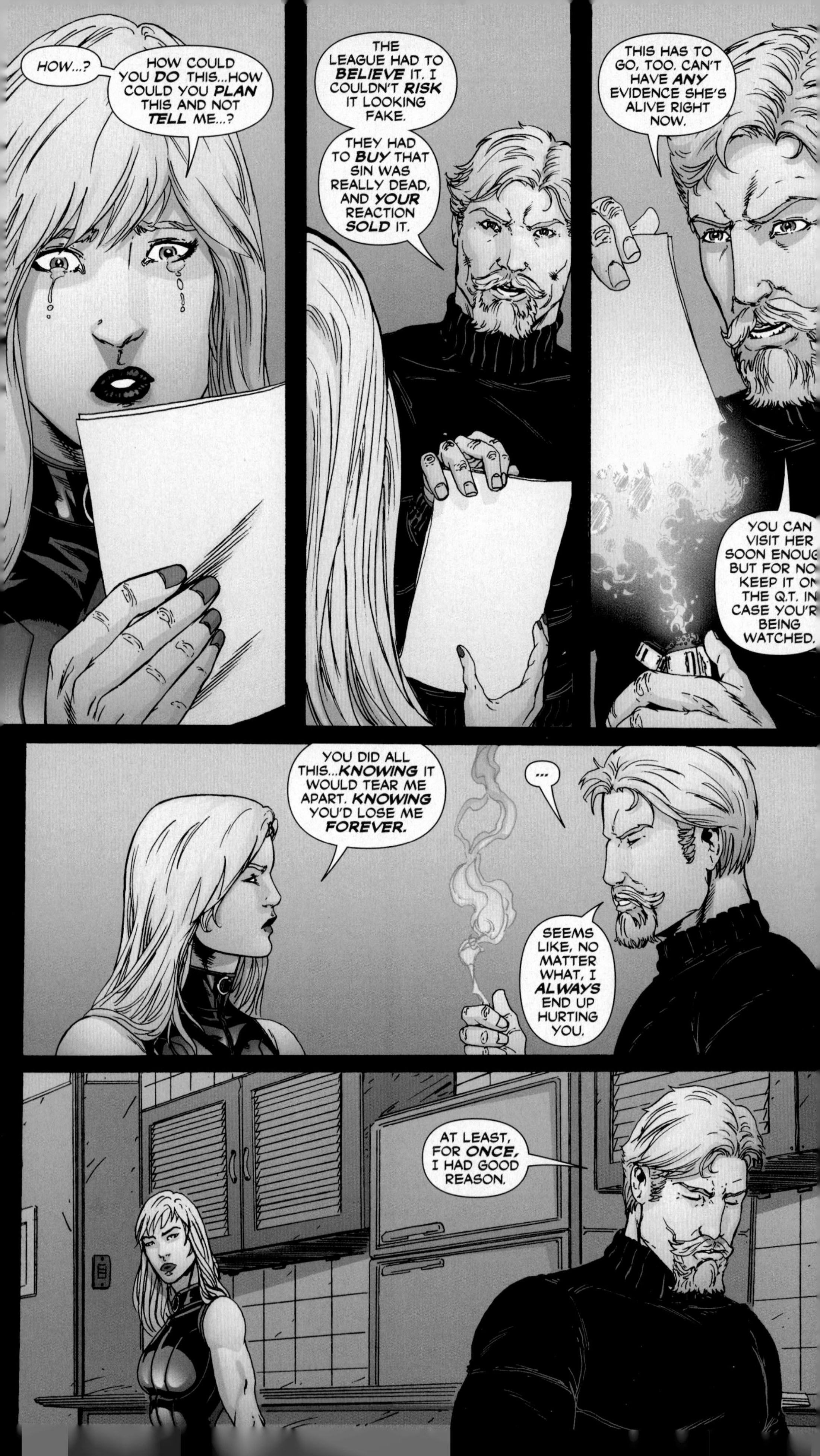
HOW...?
HOW COULD YOU DO THIS...HOW COULD YOU PLAN THIS AND NOT TELL ME...?
THE LEAGUE HAD TO BELIEVE IT. I COULDN'T RISK IT LOOKING FAKE.
THEY HAD TO BUY THAT SIN WAS REALLY DEAD, AND YOUR REACTION SOLD IT.
THIS HAS TO GO, TOO. CAN'T HAVE ANY EVIDENCE SHE'S ALIVE RIGHT NOW.
YOU CAN VISIT HER SOON ENOUG BUT FOR NO KEEP IT ON THE Q.T. IN CASE YOU'R BEING WATCHED.
YOU DID ALL THIS...KNOWING IT WOULD TEAR ME APART. KNOWING YOU'D LOSE ME FOREVER.
...
SEEMS LIKE, NO MATTER WHAT, I ALWAYS END UP HURTING YOU.
AT LEAST, FOR ONCE, I HAD GOOD REASON.

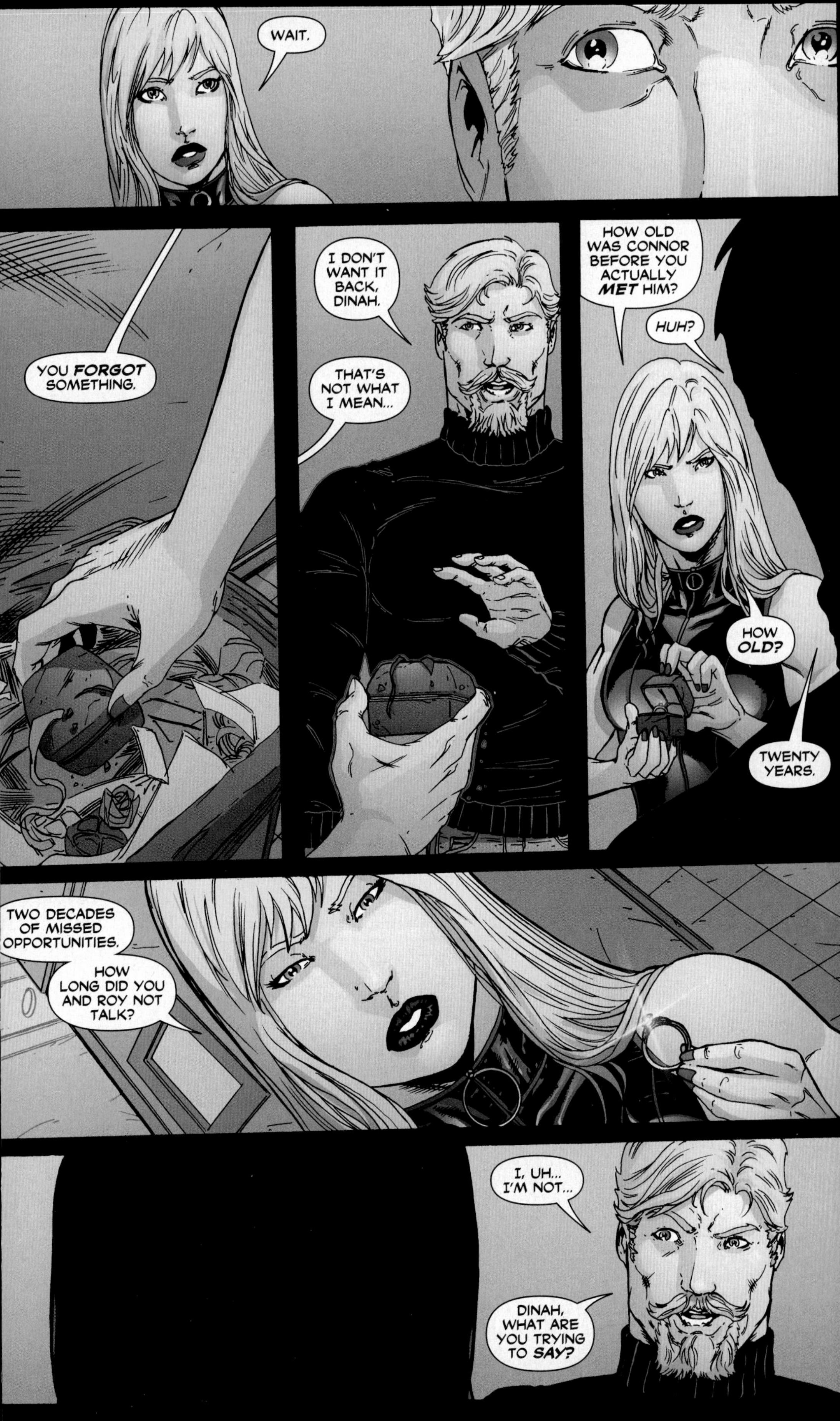
WAIT.
YOU FORGOT SOMETHING.
I DON'T WANT IT BACK, DINAH.
THAT'S NOT WHAT I MEAN...
HOW OLD WAS CONNOR BEFORE YOU ACTUALLY MET HIM?
HUH?
HOW OLD?
TWENTY YEARS.
TWO DECADES OF MISSED OPPORTUNITIES.
HOW LONG DID YOU AND ROY NOT TALK?
I, UH... I'M NOT...
DINAH, WHAT ARE YOU TRYING TO SAY?

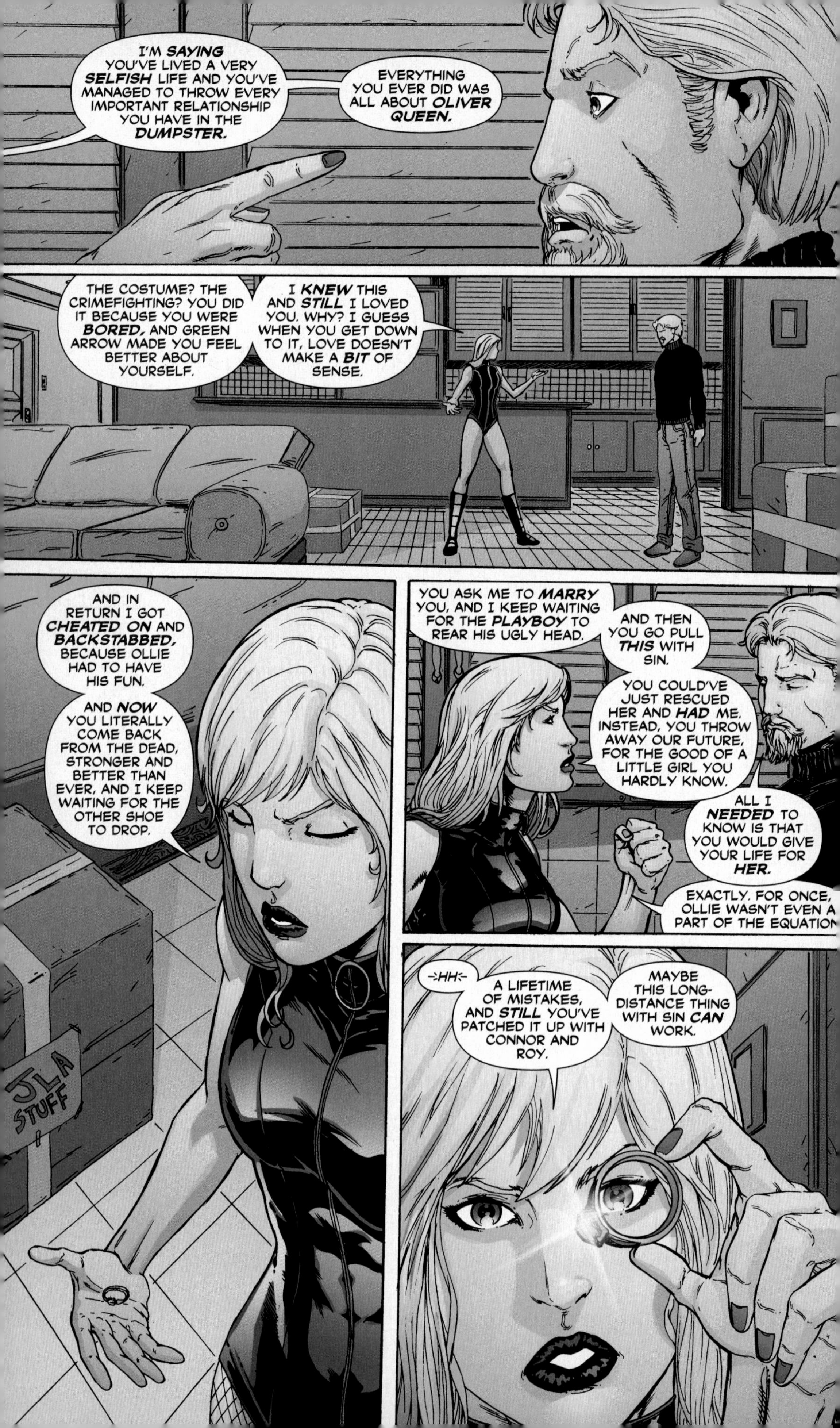

I'M SAYING YOU'VE LIVED A VERY SELFISH LIFE AND YOU'VE MANAGED TO THROW EVERY IMPORTANT RELATIONSHIP YOU HAVE IN THE DUMPSTER.
EVERYTHING YOU EVER DID WAS ALL ABOUT OLIVER QUEEN.
THE COSTUME? THE CRIMEFIGHTING? YOU DID IT BECAUSE YOU WERE BORED, AND GREEN ARROW MADE YOU FEEL BETTER ABOUT YOURSELF.
I KNEW THIS AND STILL I LOVED YOU. WHY? I GUESS WHEN YOU GET DOWN TO IT, LOVE DOESN'T MAKE A BIT OF SENSE.
AND IN RETURN I GOT CHEATED ON AND BACKSTABBED, BECAUSE OLLIE HAD TO HAVE HIS FUN.
AND NOW YOU LITERALLY COME BACK FROM THE DEAD, STRONGER AND BETTER THAN EVER, AND I KEEP WAITING FOR THE OTHER SHOE TO DROP.
JLA STUFF
YOU ASK ME TO MARRY YOU, AND I KEEP WAITING FOR THE PLAYBOY TO REAR HIS UGLY HEAD.
AND THEN YOU GO PULL THIS WITH SIN.
YOU COULD'VE JUST RESCUED HER AND HAD ME. INSTEAD, YOU THROW AWAY OUR FUTURE, FOR THE GOOD OF A LITTLE GIRL YOU HARDLY KNOW.
ALL I NEEDED TO KNOW IS THAT YOU WOULD GIVE YOUR LIFE FOR HER.
EXACTLY. FOR ONCE, OLLIE WASN'T EVEN A PART OF THE EQUATION
HH
A LIFETIME OF MISTAKES, AND STILL YOU'VE PATCHED IT UP WITH CONNOR AND ROY.
MAYBE THIS LONG-DISTANCE THING WITH SIN CAN WORK.

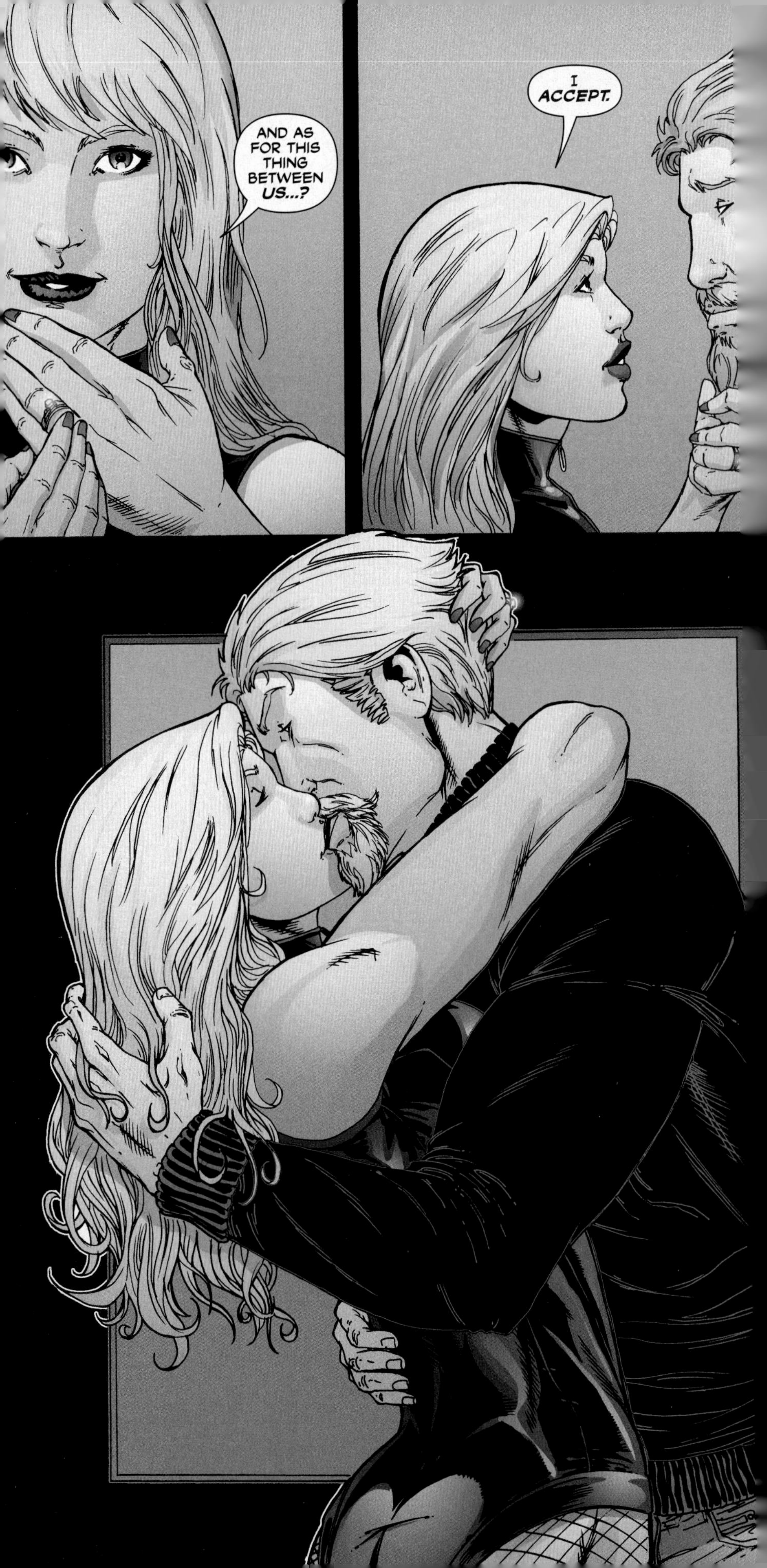
AND AS FOR THIS THING BETWEEN US...?
I ACCEPT.

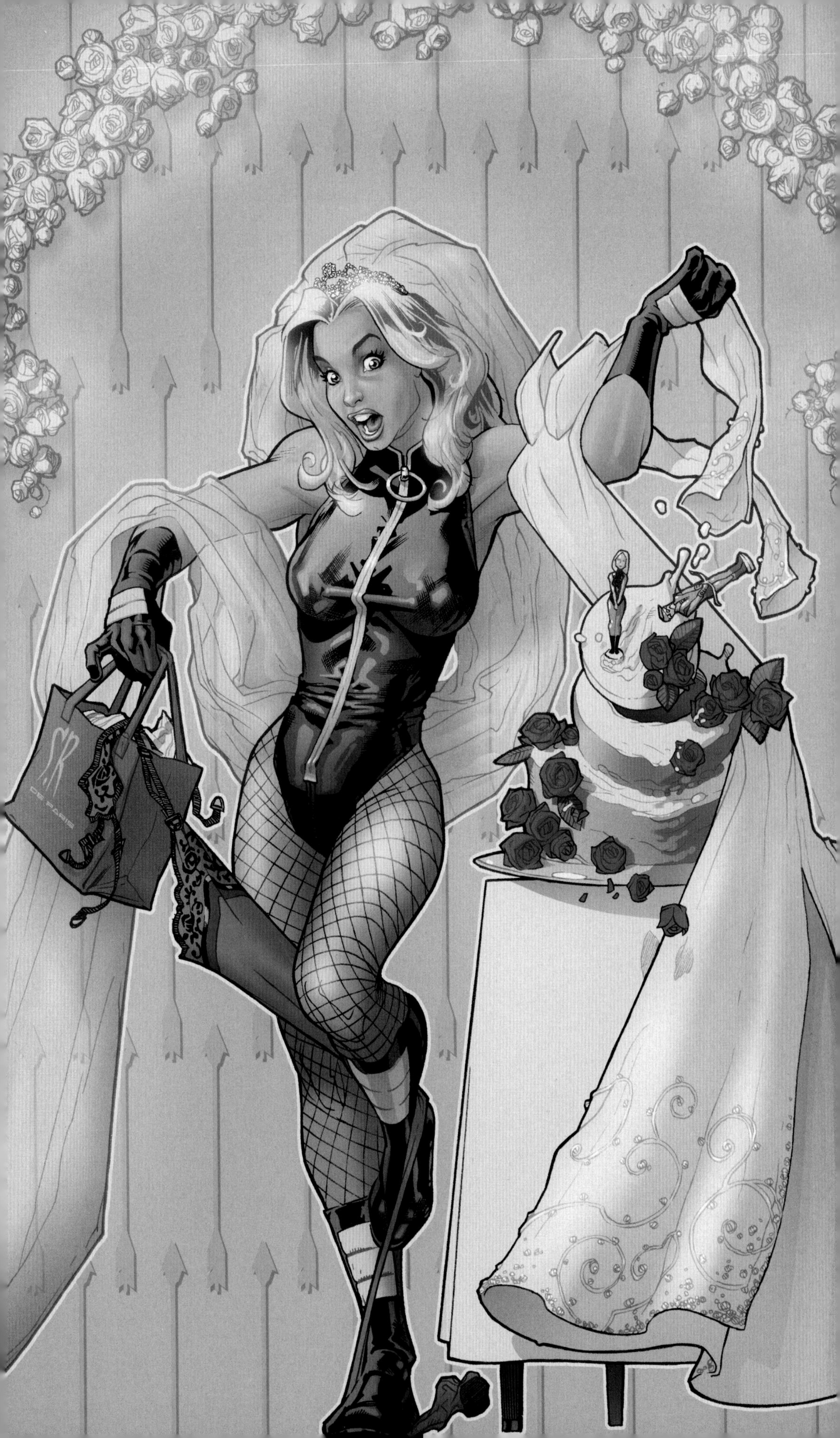
DE PARIS

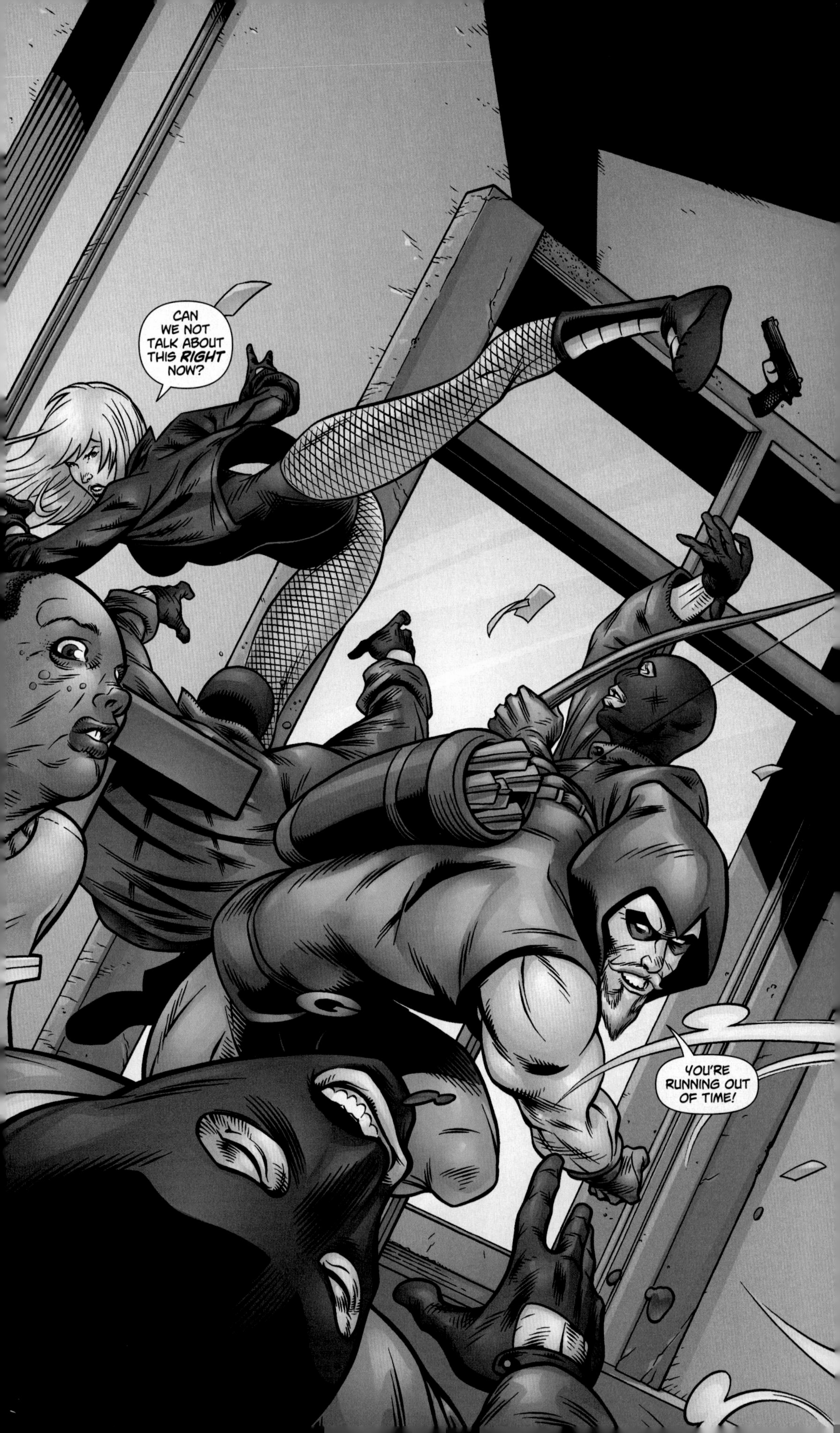
CAN WE NOT TALK ABOUT THIS RIGHT NOW?
YOU'RE RUNNING OUT OF TIME!

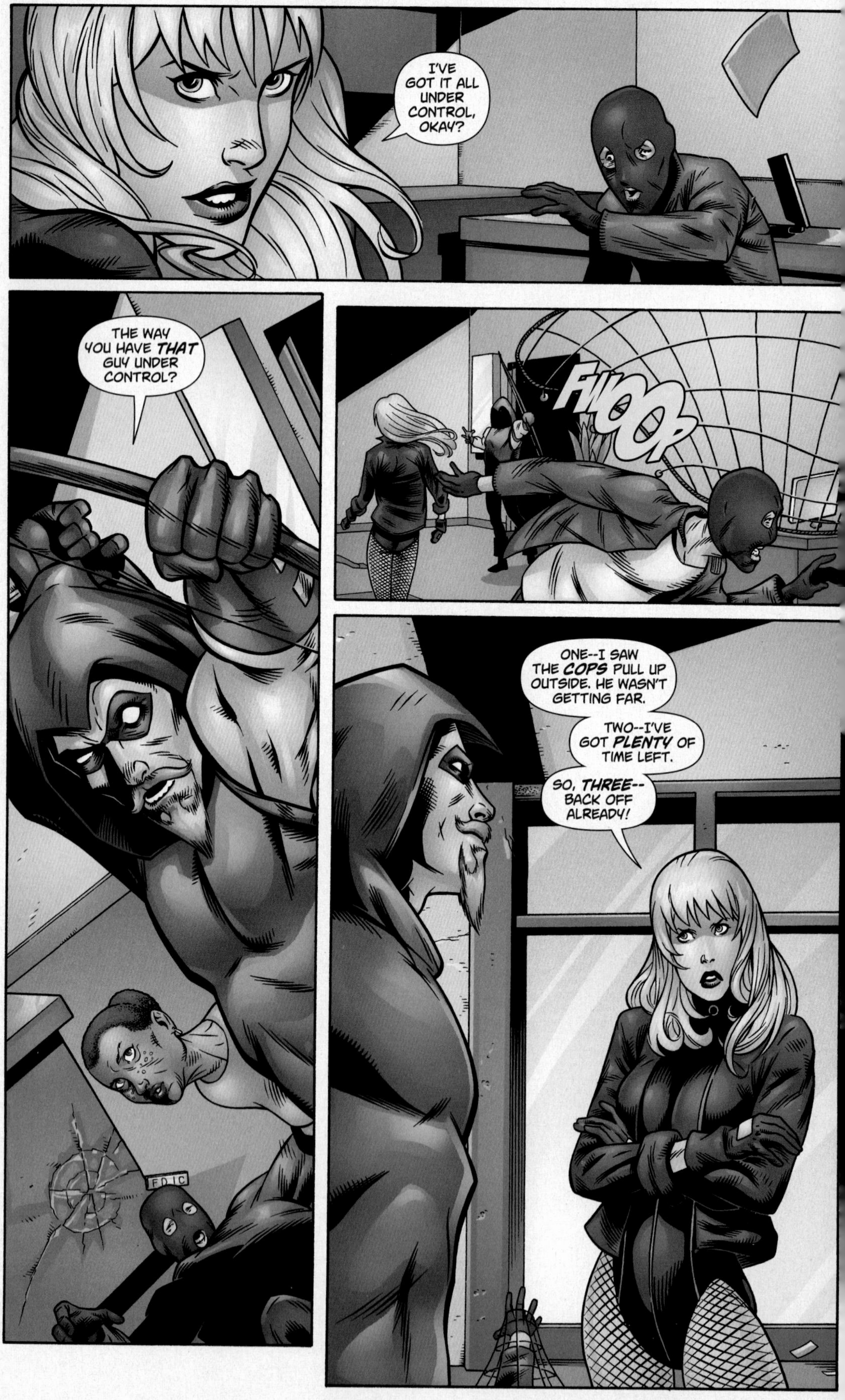

I'VE GOT IT ALL UNDER CONTROL, OKAY?
THE WAY YOU HAVE *THAT* GUY UNDER CONTROL?
FWOOP
ONE--I SAW THE *COPS* PULL UP OUTSIDE. HE WASN'T GETTING FAR.
TWO--I'VE GOT *PLENTY* OF TIME LEFT.
SO, *THREE*-- BACK OFF ALREADY!

Checklist

12 Months Before Your Wedding: *HA!*

- Announce your engagement.

- Decide if you want to hire a wedding planner or coordinator.

- Set a budget for the wedding and reception.
"MONEY IS NO OBJECT."
– OLIVER "DADDY WARBUCKS" QUEEN

- Decide the size of your wedding party. Select attendants. *BABS ROY* *MIA HAL* *SHV CONNOR*

- Decide what kind of wedding you want to have. Indoor? Outdoor? Formal? Casual?
"COME AS YOU ARE"?

- Select the date for your ceremony.

- Select the location for your ceremony. *SAINT SEBASTIAN? BOTANICAL GARDENS? OLLIE'S BACKYARD? ASK CONNOR!*

- Select a location for your reception.
DRAGONFLY INN? THE GRAND? THE HALL? THE SATELLITE?

- Shop for a wedding dress and accessories.
BOUTIQUE MARIÉE WEDNESDAY 2:30

- Shop for vendors: photographer/videographer, musicians/DJ, florists, and caterer.

- Determine who will officiate your ceremony.

- Register for a bridal gift registry. *REQUEST DONATIONS TO CHARITY?*

- Order wedding invitations and stationery.

OLLIE'S CHECKLIST:
-TALK TO CONNOR
-TALK TO ROY
-TALK TO HAL

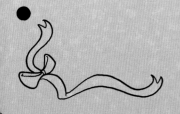

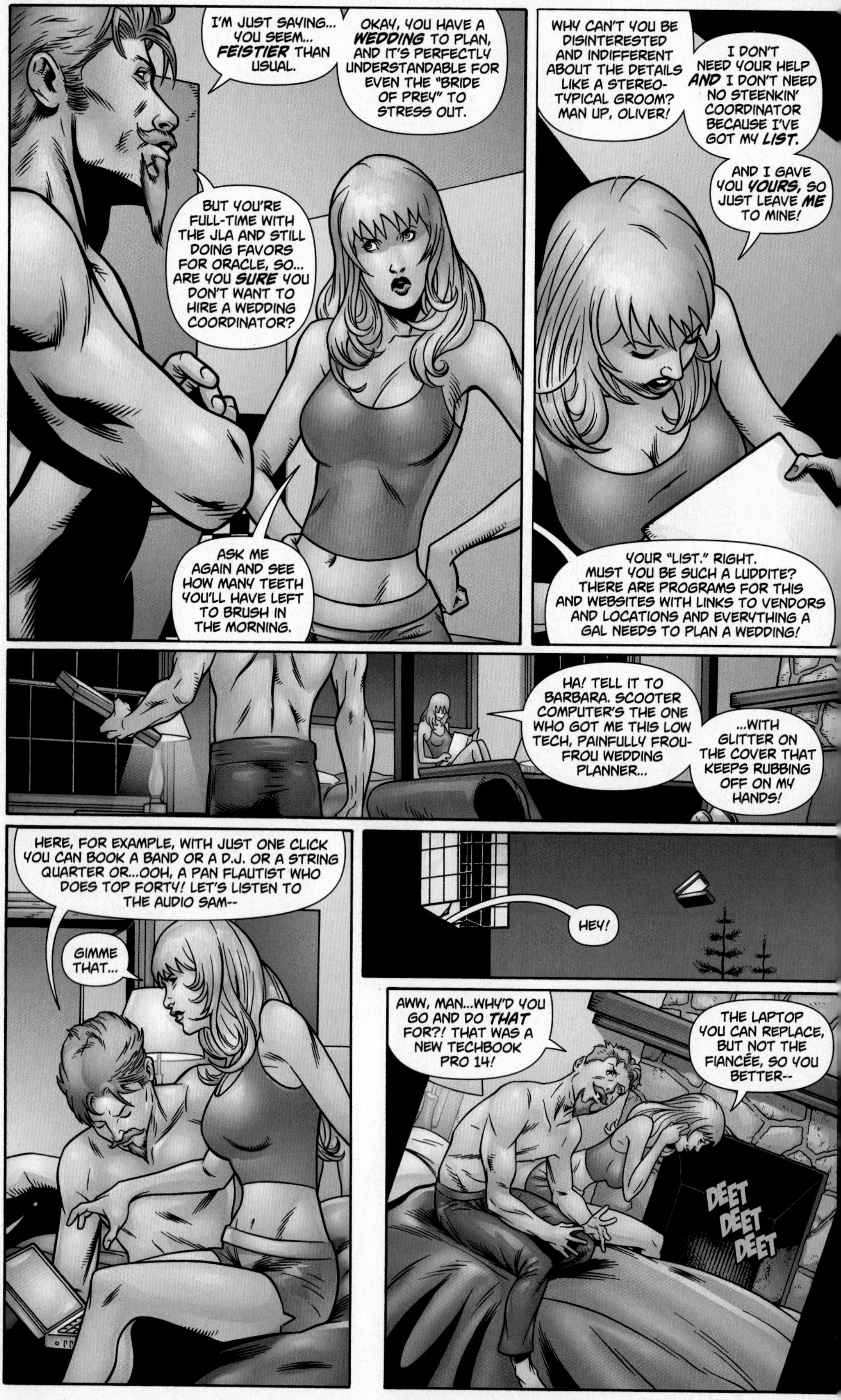
I'M JUST SAYING... YOU SEEM... FEISTIER THAN USUAL.
OKAY, YOU HAVE A WEDDING TO PLAN, AND IT'S PERFECTLY UNDERSTANDABLE FOR EVEN THE "BRIDE OF PREY" TO STRESS OUT.
BUT YOU'RE FULL-TIME WITH THE JLA AND STILL DOING FAVORS FOR ORACLE, SO... ARE YOU SURE YOU DON'T WANT TO HIRE A WEDDING COORDINATOR?
ASK ME AGAIN AND SEE HOW MANY TEETH YOU'LL HAVE LEFT TO BRUSH IN THE MORNING.
WHY CAN'T YOU BE DISINTERESTED AND INDIFFERENT ABOUT THE DETAILS LIKE A STEREO-TYPICAL GROOM? MAN UP, OLIVER!
I DON'T NEED YOUR HELP AND I DON'T NEED NO STEENKIN' COORDINATOR BECAUSE I'VE GOT MY LIST.
AND I GAVE YOU YOURS, SO JUST LEAVE ME TO MINE!
YOUR "LIST." RIGHT. MUST YOU BE SUCH A LUDDITE? THERE ARE PROGRAMS FOR THIS AND WEBSITES WITH LINKS TO VENDORS AND LOCATIONS AND EVERYTHING A GAL NEEDS TO PLAN A WEDDING!
HA! TELL IT TO BARBARA. SCOOTER COMPUTER'S THE ONE WHO GOT ME THIS LOW TECH, PAINFULLY FROU-FROU WEDDING PLANNER...
...WITH GLITTER ON THE COVER THAT KEEPS RUBBING OFF ON MY HANDS!
HERE, FOR EXAMPLE, WITH JUST ONE CLICK YOU CAN BOOK A BAND OR A D.J. OR A STRING QUARTER OR...OOH, A PAN FLAUTIST WHO DOES TOP FORTY! LET'S LISTEN TO THE AUDIO SAM--
GIMME THAT...
HEY!
AWW, MAN...WHY'D YOU GO AND DO THAT FOR?! THAT WAS A NEW TECHBOOK PRO 14!
THE LAPTOP YOU CAN REPLACE, BUT NOT THE FIANCÉE, SO YOU BETTER--
DEET DEET DEET DEET

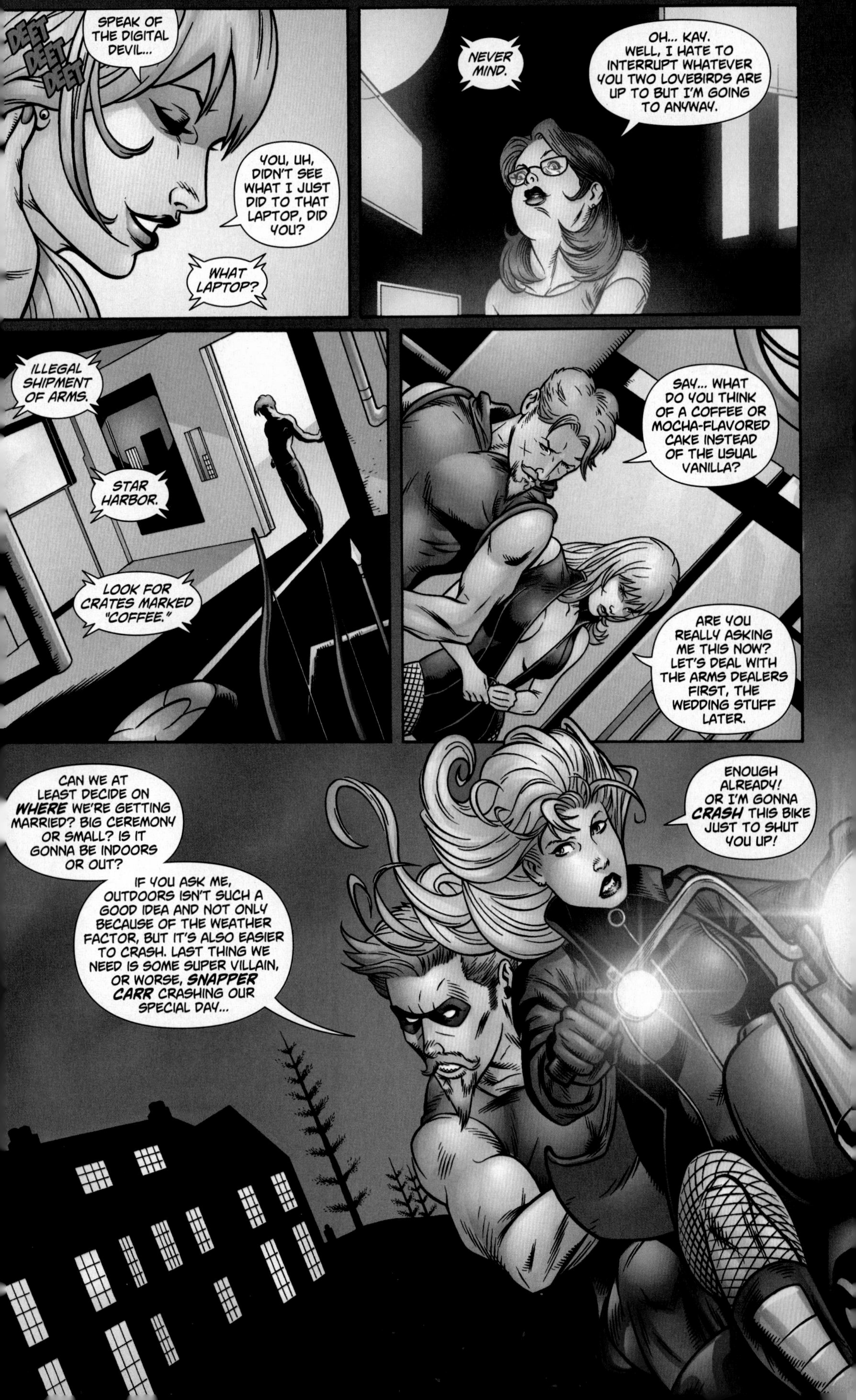

DEET DEET DEET
SPEAK OF THE DIGITAL DEVIL...
YOU, UH, DIDN'T SEE WHAT I JUST DID TO THAT LAPTOP, DID YOU?
WHAT LAPTOP?
NEVER MIND.
OH... KAY. WELL, I HATE TO INTERRUPT WHATEVER YOU TWO LOVEBIRDS ARE UP TO BUT I'M GOING TO ANYWAY.
ILLEGAL SHIPMENT OF ARMS.
STAR HARBOR.
LOOK FOR CRATES MARKED "COFFEE."
SAY... WHAT DO YOU THINK OF A COFFEE OR MOCHA-FLAVORED CAKE INSTEAD OF THE USUAL VANILLA?
ARE YOU REALLY ASKING ME THIS NOW? LET'S DEAL WITH THE ARMS DEALERS FIRST, THE WEDDING STUFF LATER.
CAN WE AT LEAST DECIDE ON WHERE WE'RE GETTING MARRIED? BIG CEREMONY OR SMALL? IS IT GONNA BE INDOORS OR OUT?
IF YOU ASK ME, OUTDOORS ISN'T SUCH A GOOD IDEA AND NOT ONLY BECAUSE OF THE WEATHER FACTOR, BUT IT'S ALSO EASIER TO CRASH. LAST THING WE NEED IS SOME SUPER VILLAIN, OR WORSE, SNAPPER CARR CRASHING OUR SPECIAL DAY...
ENOUGH ALREADY! OR I'M GONNA CRASH THIS BIKE JUST TO SHUT YOU UP!

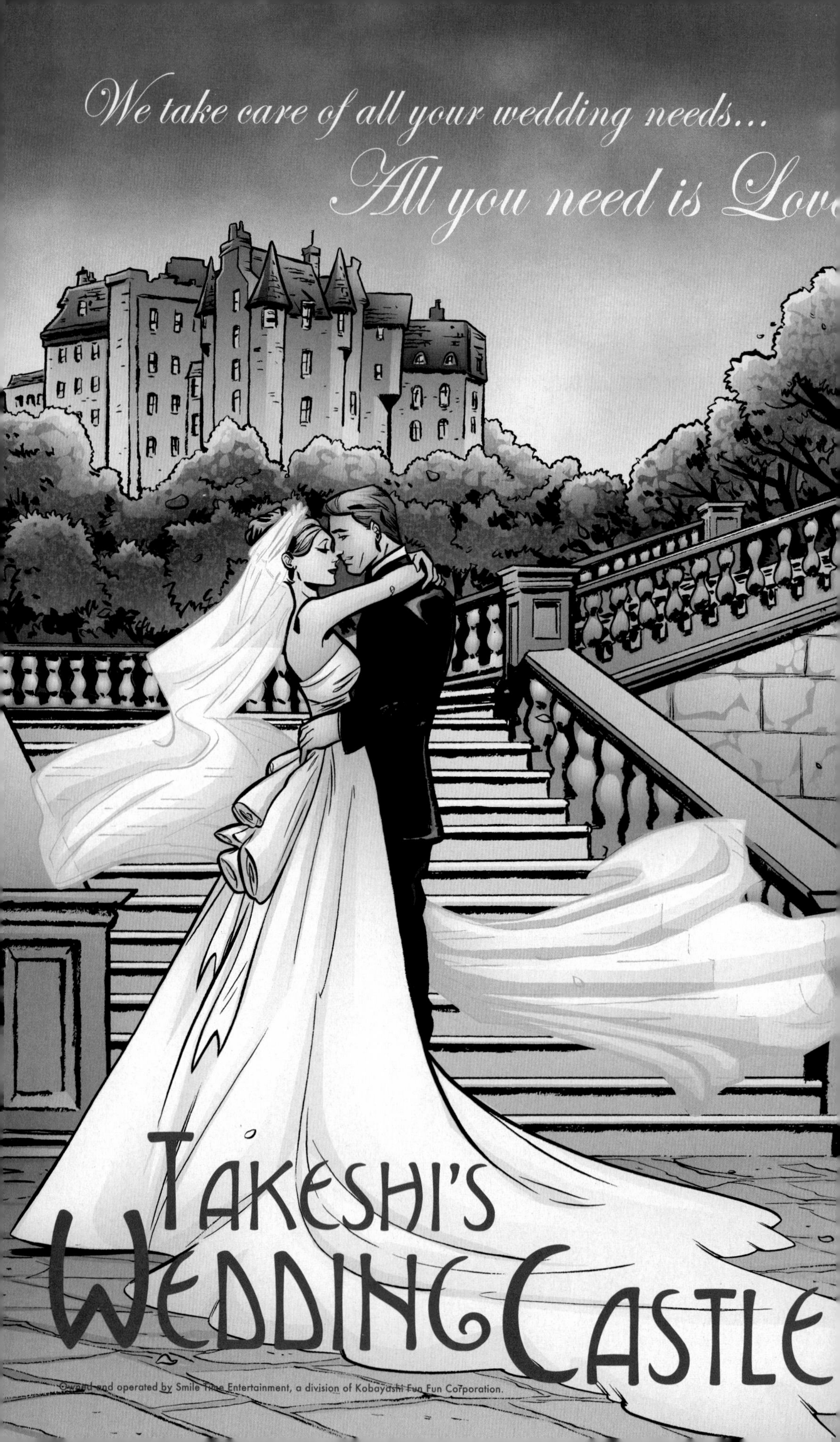
We take care of all your wedding needs...
All you need is Love
Takeshi's Wedding Castle
Owned and operated by Smile Time Entertainment, a division of Kobayashi Fun Fun Corporation.

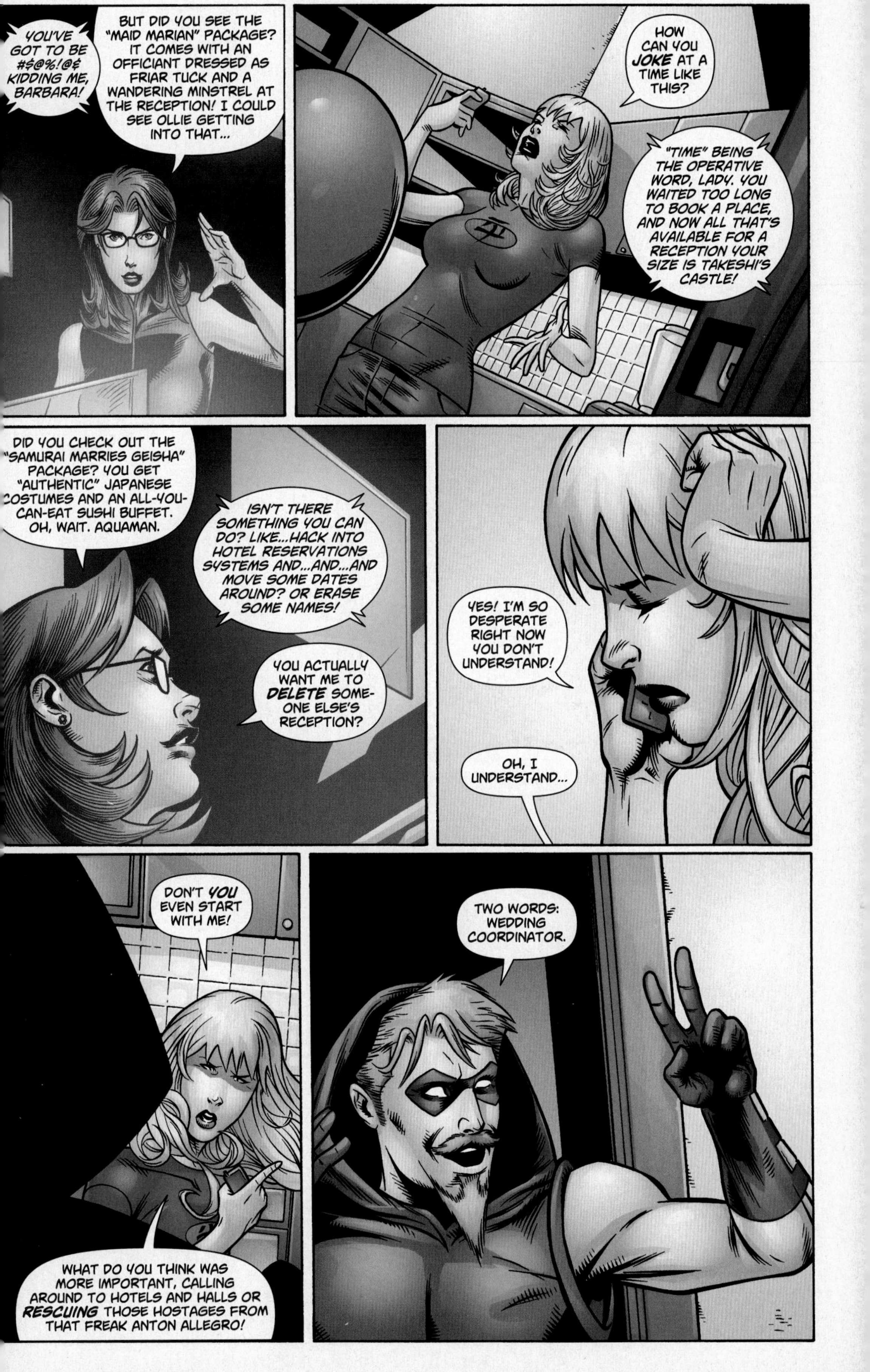

YOU'VE GOT TO BE #$@%!@$ KIDDING ME, BARBARA!
BUT DID YOU SEE THE "MAID MARIAN" PACKAGE? IT COMES WITH AN OFFICIANT DRESSED AS FRIAR TUCK AND A WANDERING MINSTREL AT THE RECEPTION! I COULD SEE OLLIE GETTING INTO THAT...
HOW CAN YOU JOKE AT A TIME LIKE THIS?
"TIME" BEING THE OPERATIVE WORD, LADY. YOU WAITED TOO LONG TO BOOK A PLACE, AND NOW ALL THAT'S AVAILABLE FOR A RECEPTION YOUR SIZE IS TAKESHI'S CASTLE!
DID YOU CHECK OUT THE "SAMURAI MARRIES GEISHA" PACKAGE? YOU GET "AUTHENTIC" JAPANESE COSTUMES AND AN ALL-YOU-CAN-EAT SUSHI BUFFET. OH, WAIT. AQUAMAN.
ISN'T THERE SOMETHING YOU CAN DO? LIKE...HACK INTO HOTEL RESERVATIONS SYSTEMS AND...AND...AND MOVE SOME DATES AROUND? OR ERASE SOME NAMES!
YOU ACTUALLY WANT ME TO DELETE SOME-ONE ELSE'S RECEPTION?
YES! I'M SO DESPERATE RIGHT NOW YOU DON'T UNDERSTAND!
OH, I UNDERSTAND...
DON'T YOU EVEN START WITH ME!
WHAT DO YOU THINK WAS MORE IMPORTANT, CALLING AROUND TO HOTELS AND HALLS OR RESCUING THOSE HOSTAGES FROM THAT FREAK ANTON ALLEGRO!
TWO WORDS: WEDDING COORDINATOR.

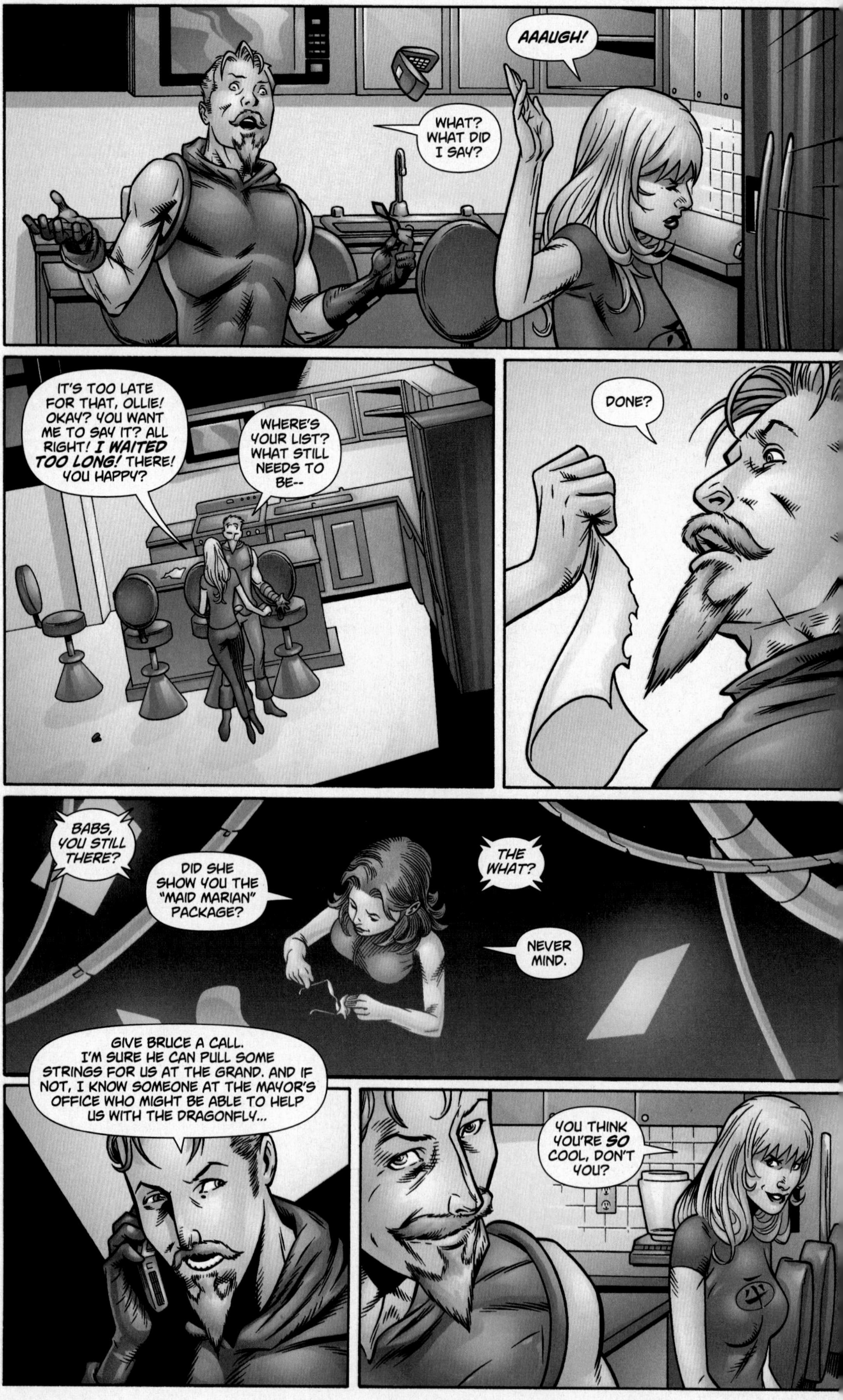
AAAUGH!
WHAT? WHAT DID I SAY?
IT'S TOO LATE FOR THAT, OLLIE! OKAY? YOU WANT ME TO SAY IT? ALL RIGHT! I WAITED TOO LONG! THERE! YOU HAPPY?
WHERE'S YOUR LIST? WHAT STILL NEEDS TO BE--
DONE?
BABS, YOU STILL THERE?
DID SHE SHOW YOU THE "MAID MARIAN" PACKAGE?
THE WHAT?
NEVER MIND.
GIVE BRUCE A CALL. I'M SURE HE CAN PULL SOME STRINGS FOR US AT THE GRAND. AND IF NOT, I KNOW SOMEONE AT THE MAYOR'S OFFICE WHO MIGHT BE ABLE TO HELP US WITH THE DRAGONFLY...
YOU THINK YOU'RE SO COOL, DON'T YOU?

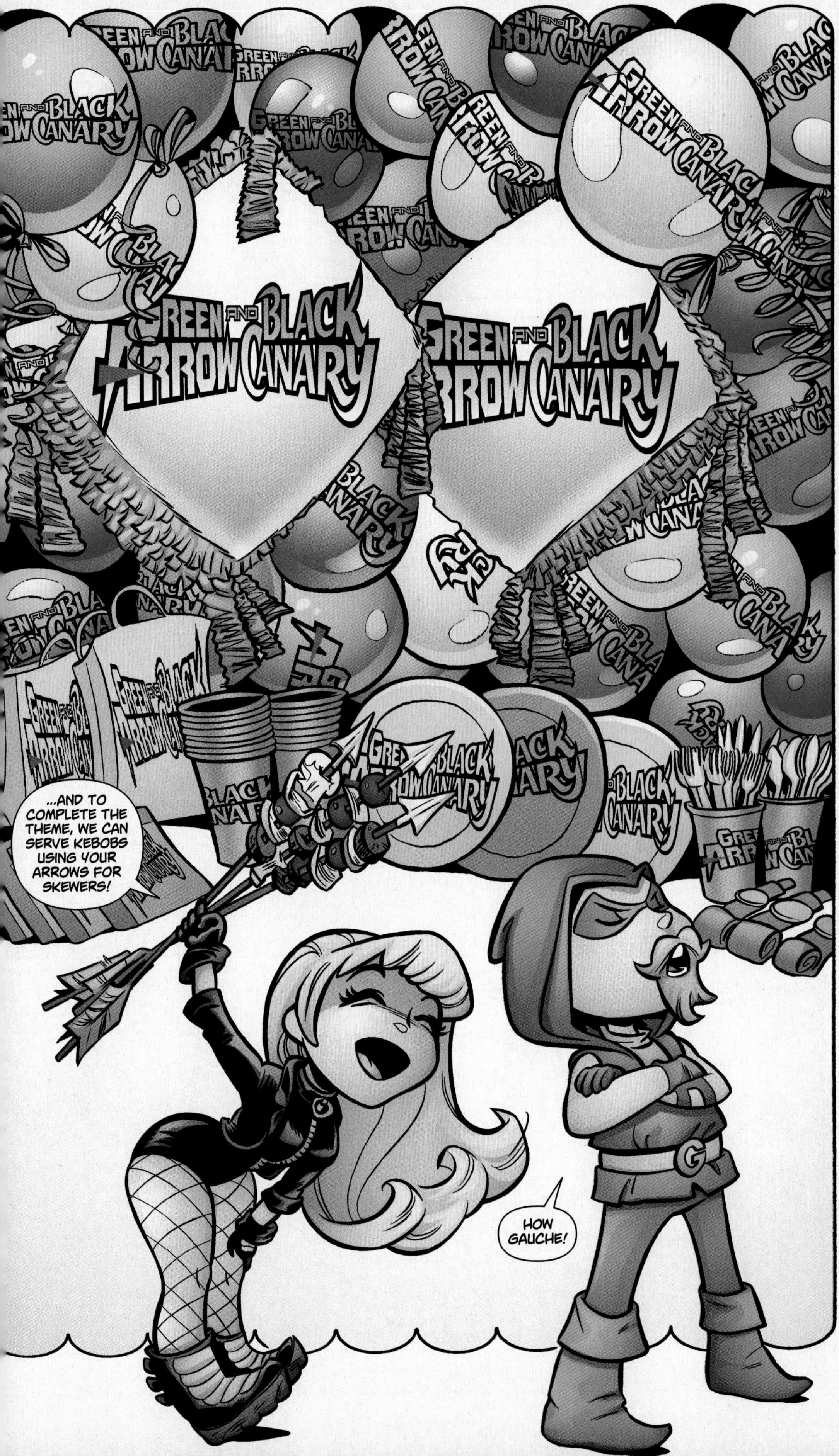
...AND TO COMPLETE THE THEME, WE CAN SERVE KEBOBS USING YOUR ARROWS FOR SKEWERS!
HOW GAUCHE!

MR. QUEEN, MS. LANCE...

CHEF DENNIS! NICE TO SEE YOU AGAIN!

...THIS IS AN APPETIZER OF ROAST QUAIL WITH A LIME GASTRIQUE AND ORGANIC GREENS ON A RISOTTO CAKE.

I'M SO HONORED TO BE CATERING YOUR WEDDING. I KNOW YOU'RE SHORT ON TIME SO SHALL WE GET RIGHT TO THE TASTING?

QUAIL...?

SORRY, CHEF. WE SHOULD'VE MENTIONED. NO FOWL PLEASE.

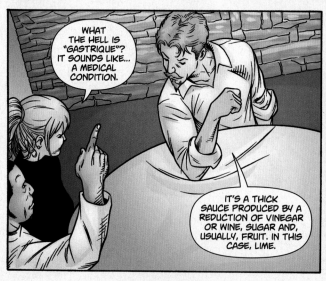

WHAT THE HELL IS "GASTRIQUE"? IT SOUNDS LIKE... A MEDICAL CONDITION.

IT'S A THICK SAUCE PRODUCED BY A REDUCTION OF VINEGAR OR WINE, SUGAR AND, USUALLY, FRUIT. IN THIS CASE, LIME.

THIS MIGHT BE MORE TO YOUR LIKING...

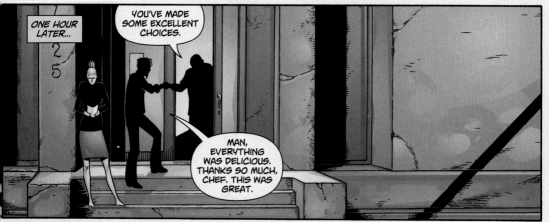

ONE HOUR LATER...

YOU'VE MADE SOME EXCELLENT CHOICES.

MAN, EVERYTHING WAS DELICIOUS. THANKS SO MUCH, CHEF. THIS WAS GREAT.

"TENDERLOIN ROULADE, SALSIFY PUREE, ROSTI STACK WITH SPICY MANGO COULIS."

THAT'S WHAT WE CHOSE FOR THE MAIN COURSE?

YES.

I ONLY UNDERSTAND EVERY OTHER WORD...

...BUT I LIKED HOW IT ALL TASTED?

YES.

OH, VEGAN MEALS FOR ANIMAL MAN AND--

WE TOOK CARE OF THAT, BABE.

WE DID? I'M SORRY...I WAS JUST...SO CONFUSED...IT WAS LIKE YOU TWO WERE SPEAKING ANOTHER LANGUAGE...

IT'S OKAY, WE CAN NOW CROSS "EATS" OFF THE LIST.

BUT... SOMETHING I WANTED TO TALK TO YOU ABOUT... THIS WHOLE "COSTUMES" IDEA?

LETTING EVERYONE SHOW UP IN THEIR CAPES AND TIGHTS IS ONE THING, BUT ARE YOU *SURE* YOU DON'T WANT A WHITE WEDDING WITH THE VEIL AND THE TRAIN AND ALL OF THAT?

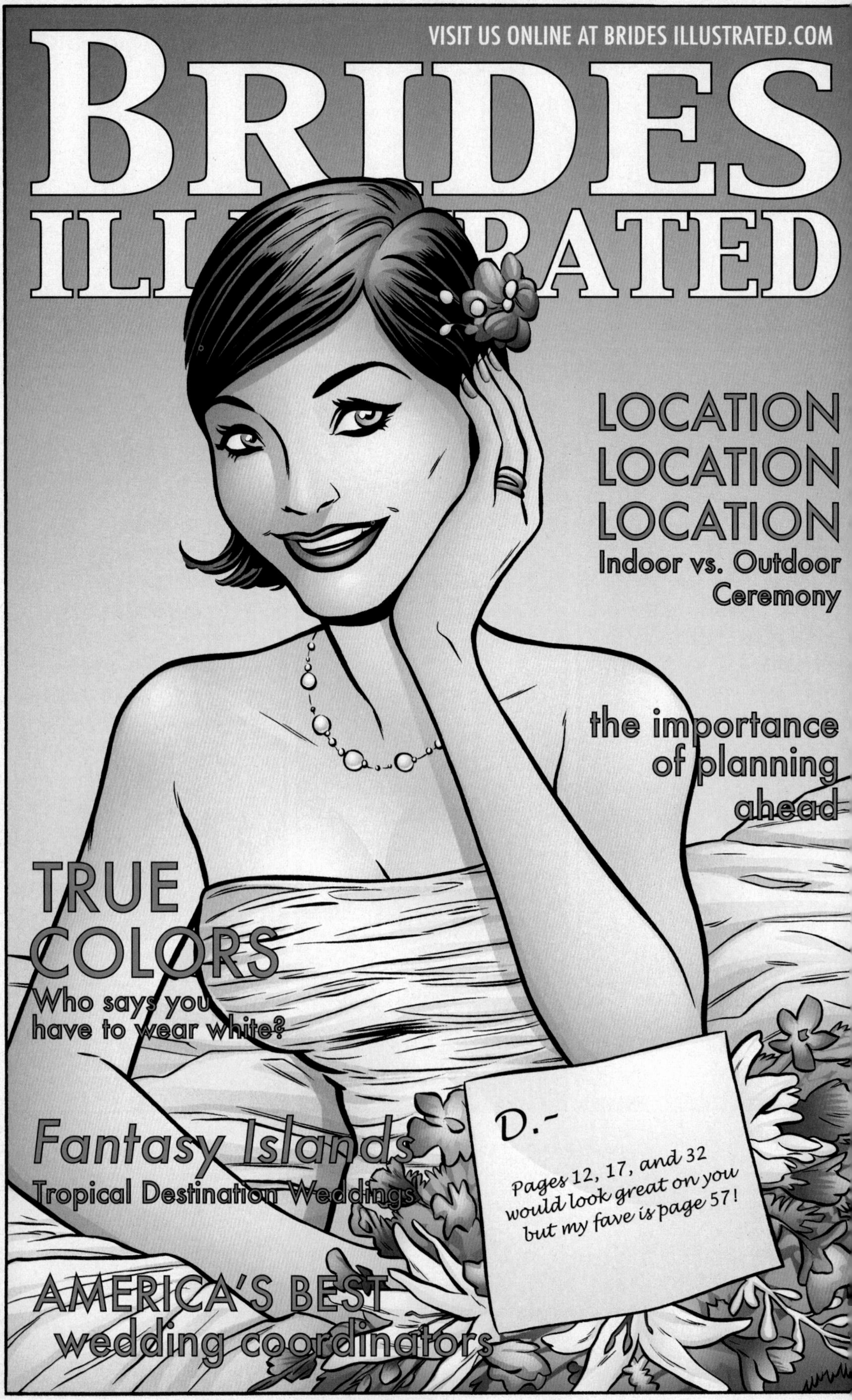
VISIT US ONLINE AT BRIDES ILLUSTRATED.COM
BRIDES ILLUSTRATED
LOCATION LOCATION LOCATION
Indoor vs. Outdoor Ceremony
the importance of planning ahead
TRUE COLORS
Who says you have to wear white?
Fantasy Islands
Tropical Destination Weddings
AMERICA'S BEST wedding coordinators
D.-
Pages 12, 17, and 32 would look great on you but my fave is page 57!

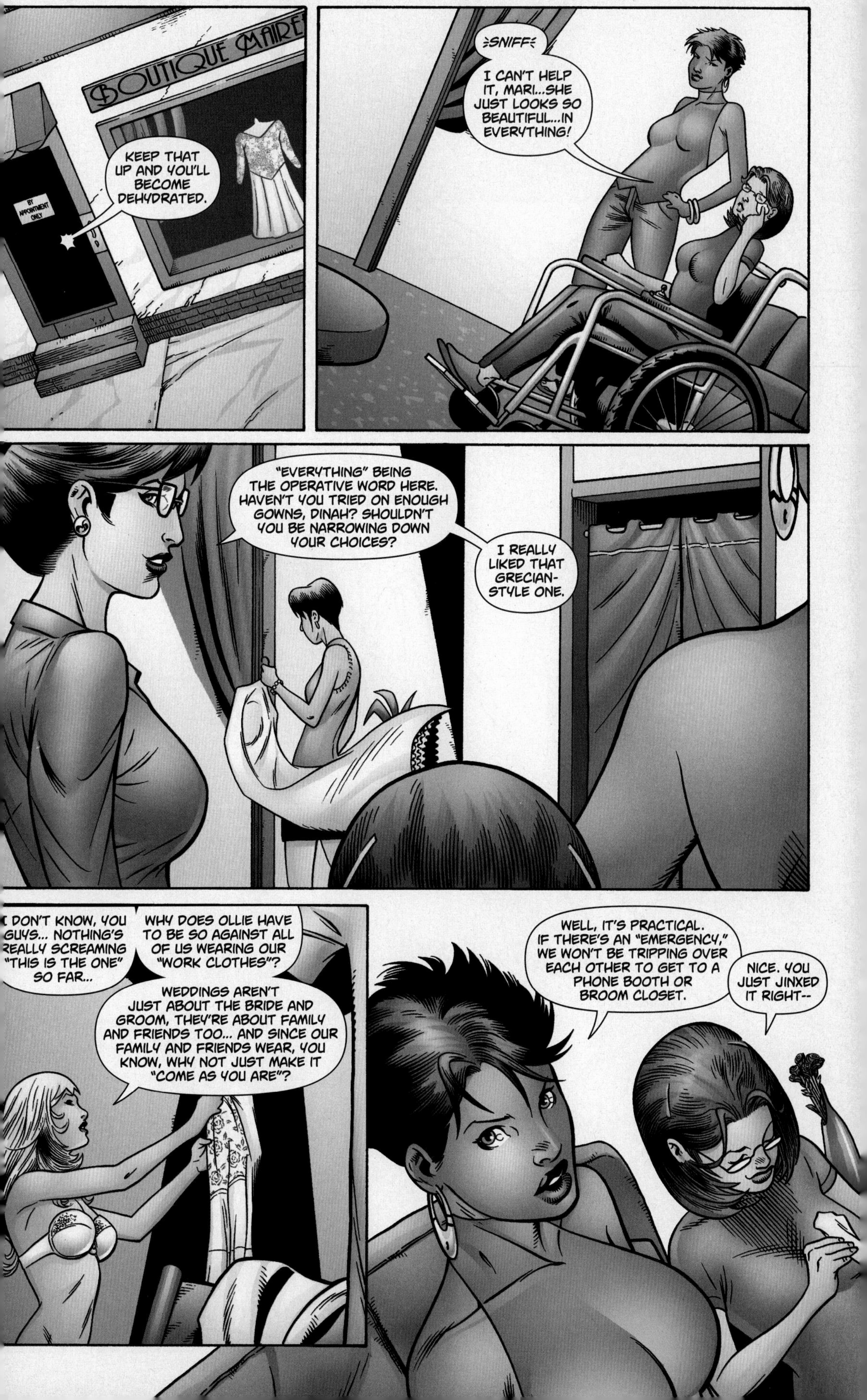
BOUTIQUE MAIRE
BY APPOINTMENT ONLY
KEEP THAT UP AND YOU'LL BECOME DEHYDRATED.
SNIFF
I CAN'T HELP IT, MARI...SHE JUST LOOKS SO BEAUTIFUL...IN EVERYTHING!
"EVERYTHING" BEING THE OPERATIVE WORD HERE. HAVEN'T YOU TRIED ON ENOUGH GOWNS, DINAH? SHOULDN'T YOU BE NARROWING DOWN YOUR CHOICES?
I REALLY LIKED THAT GRECIAN-STYLE ONE.
I DON'T KNOW, YOU GUYS... NOTHING'S REALLY SCREAMING "THIS IS THE ONE" SO FAR...
WHY DOES OLLIE HAVE TO BE SO AGAINST ALL OF US WEARING OUR "WORK CLOTHES"?
WEDDINGS AREN'T JUST ABOUT THE BRIDE AND GROOM, THEY'RE ABOUT FAMILY AND FRIENDS TOO... AND SINCE OUR FAMILY AND FRIENDS WEAR, YOU KNOW, WHY NOT JUST MAKE IT "COME AS YOU ARE"?
WELL, IT'S PRACTICAL. IF THERE'S AN "EMERGENCY," WE WON'T BE TRIPPING OVER EACH OTHER TO GET TO A PHONE BOOTH OR BROOM CLOSET.
NICE. YOU JUST JINXED IT RIGHT--

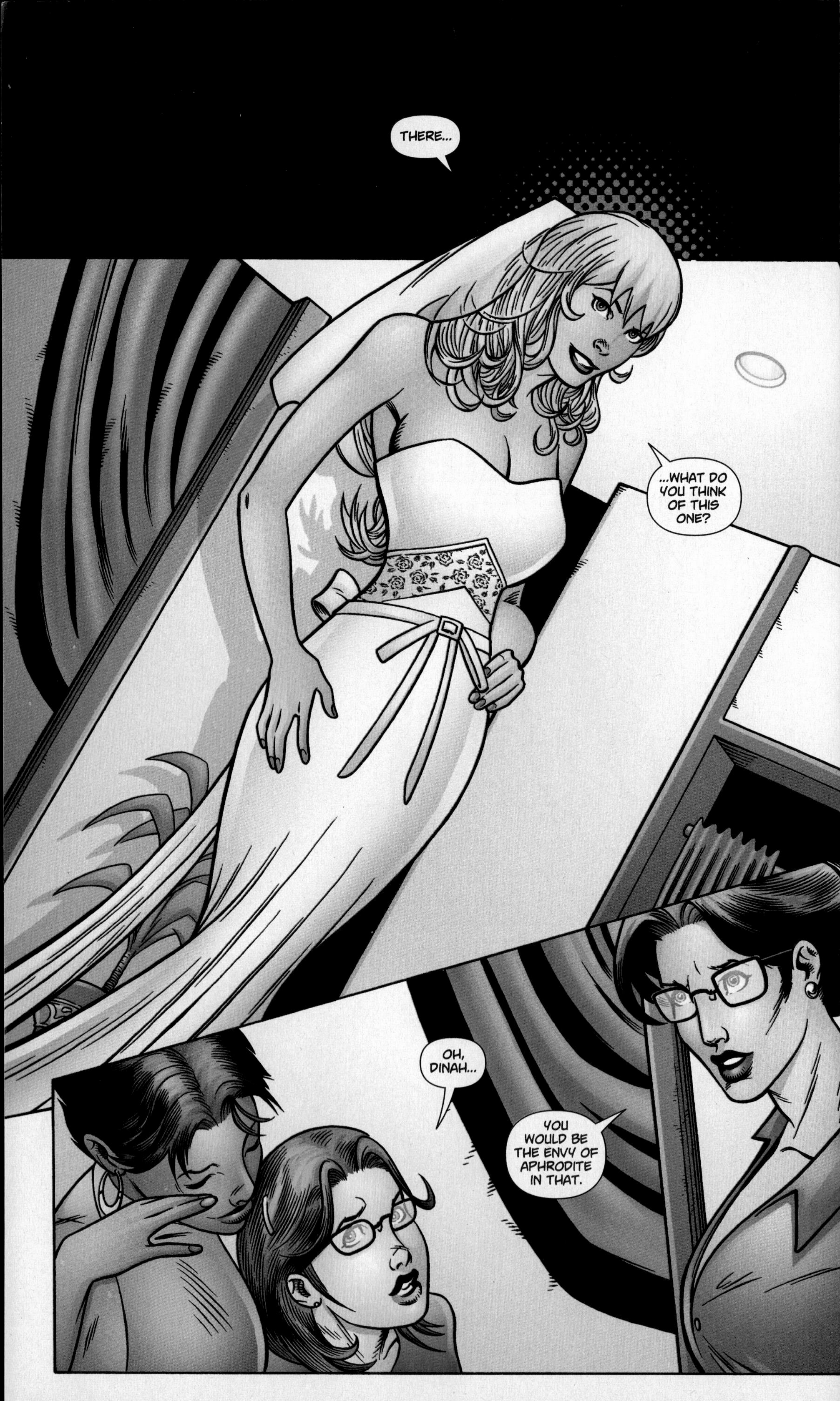
THERE...
...WHAT DO YOU THINK OF THIS ONE?
OH, DINAH...
YOU WOULD BE THE ENVY OF APHRODITE IN THAT.

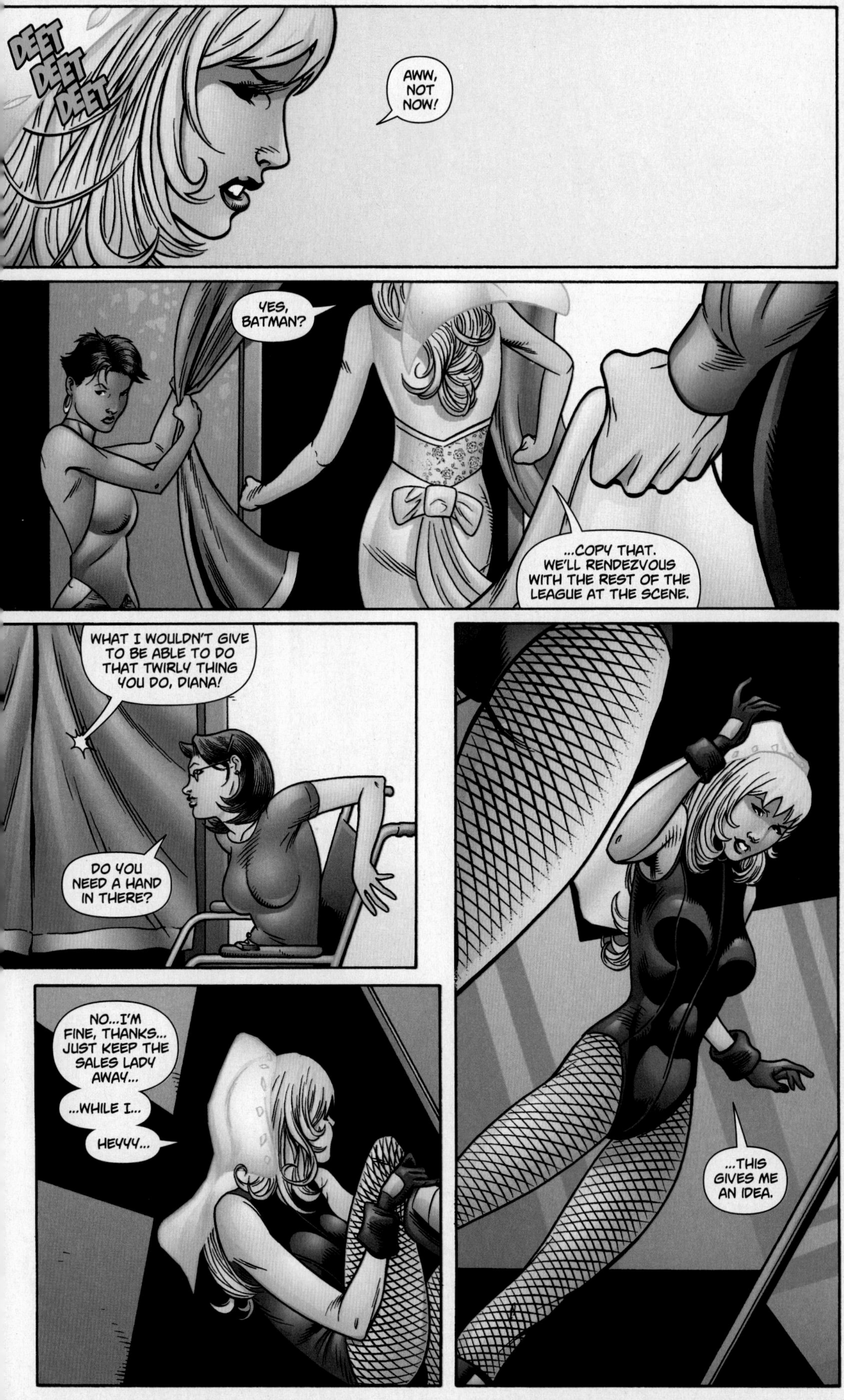
DEET DEET DEET
AWW, NOT NOW!
YES, BATMAN?
...COPY THAT. WE'LL RENDEZVOUS WITH THE REST OF THE LEAGUE AT THE SCENE.
WHAT I WOULDN'T GIVE TO BE ABLE TO DO THAT TWIRLY THING YOU DO, DIANA!
DO YOU NEED A HAND IN THERE?
NO...I'M FINE, THANKS... JUST KEEP THE SALES LADY AWAY...
...WHILE I...
HEYYY...
...THIS GIVES ME AN IDEA.

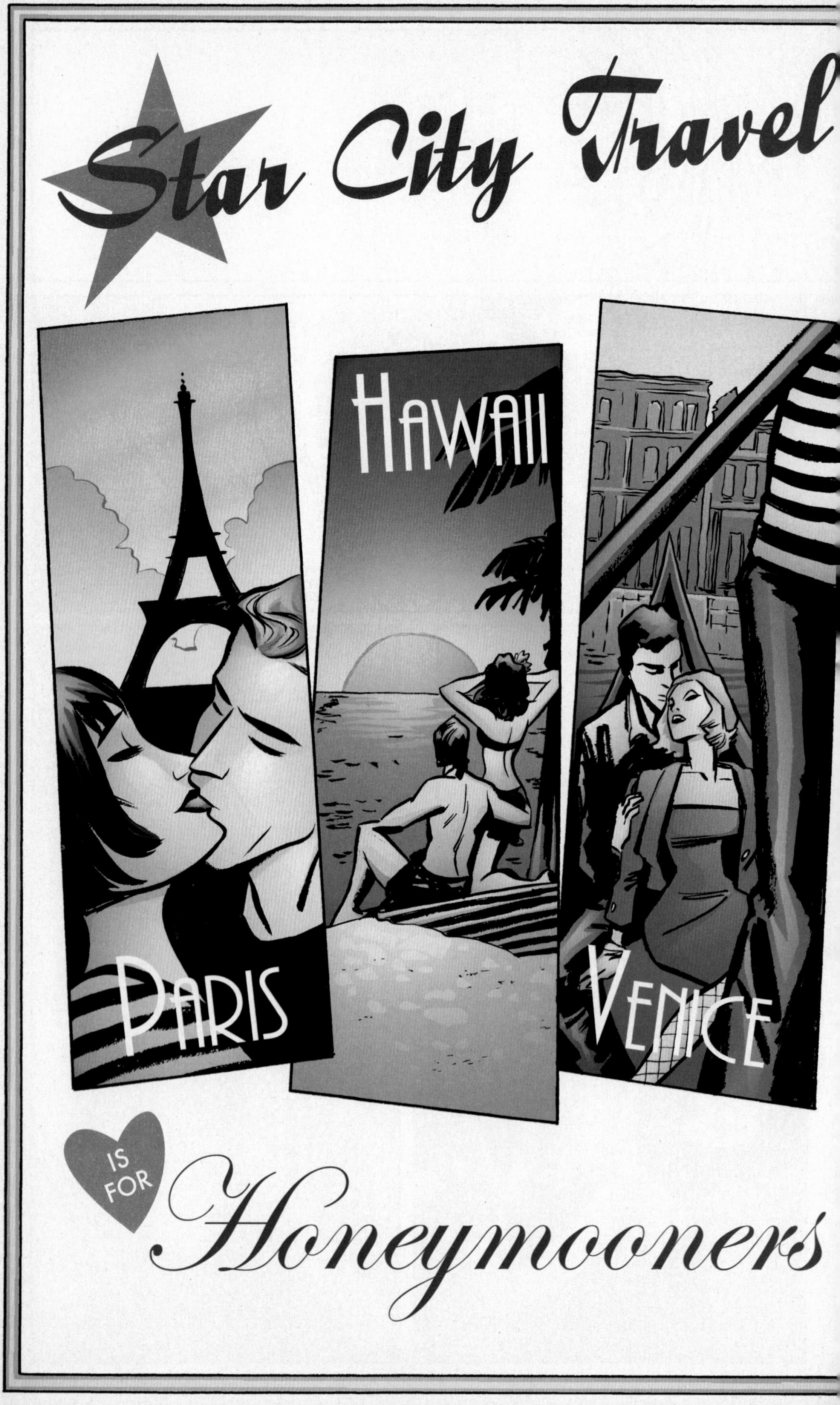
Star City Travel
HAWAII
PARIS
VENICE
IS FOR
Honeymooners

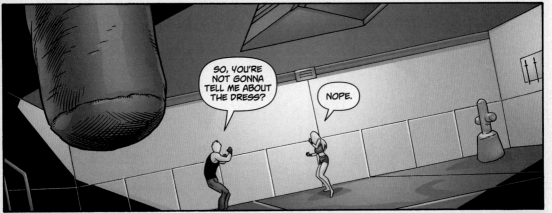

SO, YOU'RE NOT GONNA TELL ME ABOUT THE DRESS?

NOPE.

FINE. KEEP YOUR SECRETS. SURPRISE ME.

YOU BET YOUR WHISKERS I WILL!

DID YOU GET A CHANCE TO ASK DIANA ABOUT THE CEREMONY?

SHE SAID SHE'D BE HONORED.

AND EVERYONE'S COOL ABOUT THE CAVE?

YUP!

SEE WHAT A LITTLE COOPERATION AND COMPROMISE WILL GET YOU?

WE COULD'VE FINISHED ALL THIS PLANNING MUCH EARLIER IF YOU JUST LET ME SHARE SOME IDEAS AND GIVE YOU...

...A HAND!

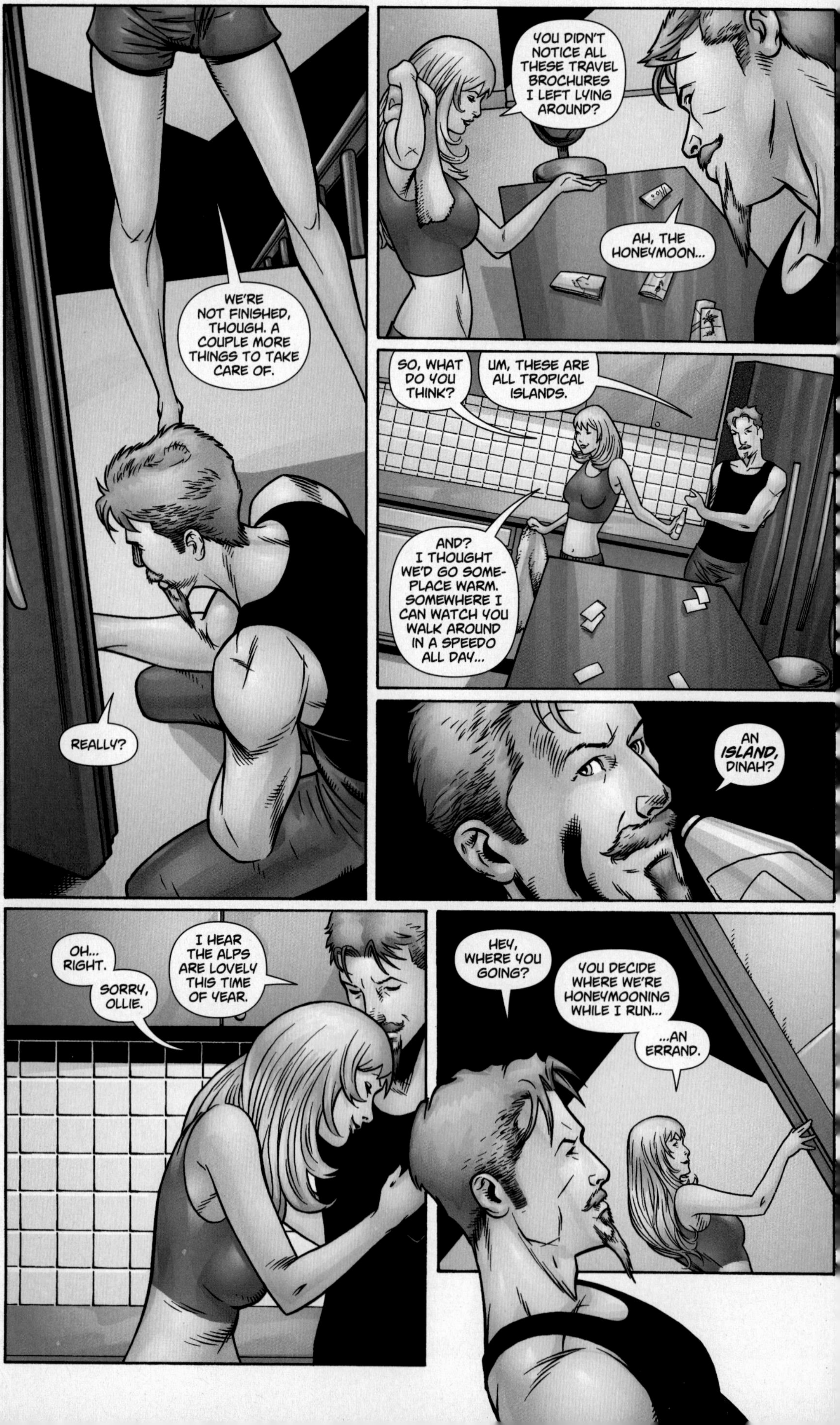
WE'RE NOT FINISHED, THOUGH. A COUPLE MORE THINGS TO TAKE CARE OF.
REALLY?
YOU DIDN'T NOTICE ALL THESE TRAVEL BROCHURES I LEFT LYING AROUND?
AH, THE HONEYMOON...
SO, WHAT DO YOU THINK?
UM, THESE ARE ALL TROPICAL ISLANDS.
AND? I THOUGHT WE'D GO SOME-PLACE WARM. SOMEWHERE I CAN WATCH YOU WALK AROUND IN A SPEEDO ALL DAY...
AN *ISLAND*, DINAH?
OH... RIGHT.
SORRY, OLLIE.
I HEAR THE ALPS ARE LOVELY THIS TIME OF YEAR.
HEY, WHERE YOU GOING?
YOU DECIDE WHERE WE'RE HONEYMOONING WHILE I RUN...
...AN ERRAND.

HER SECRET
FREE SHIPPING on any purchase of $100 or more
OFFER CODE: BC2798
SEE PAGE 2 FOR DETAILS
AMAZING LACE
BLACK IS THE NEW BLACK
BE MY BABY DOLL
heat up your honeymoon
I'd like this back when you're done, please.
Roy

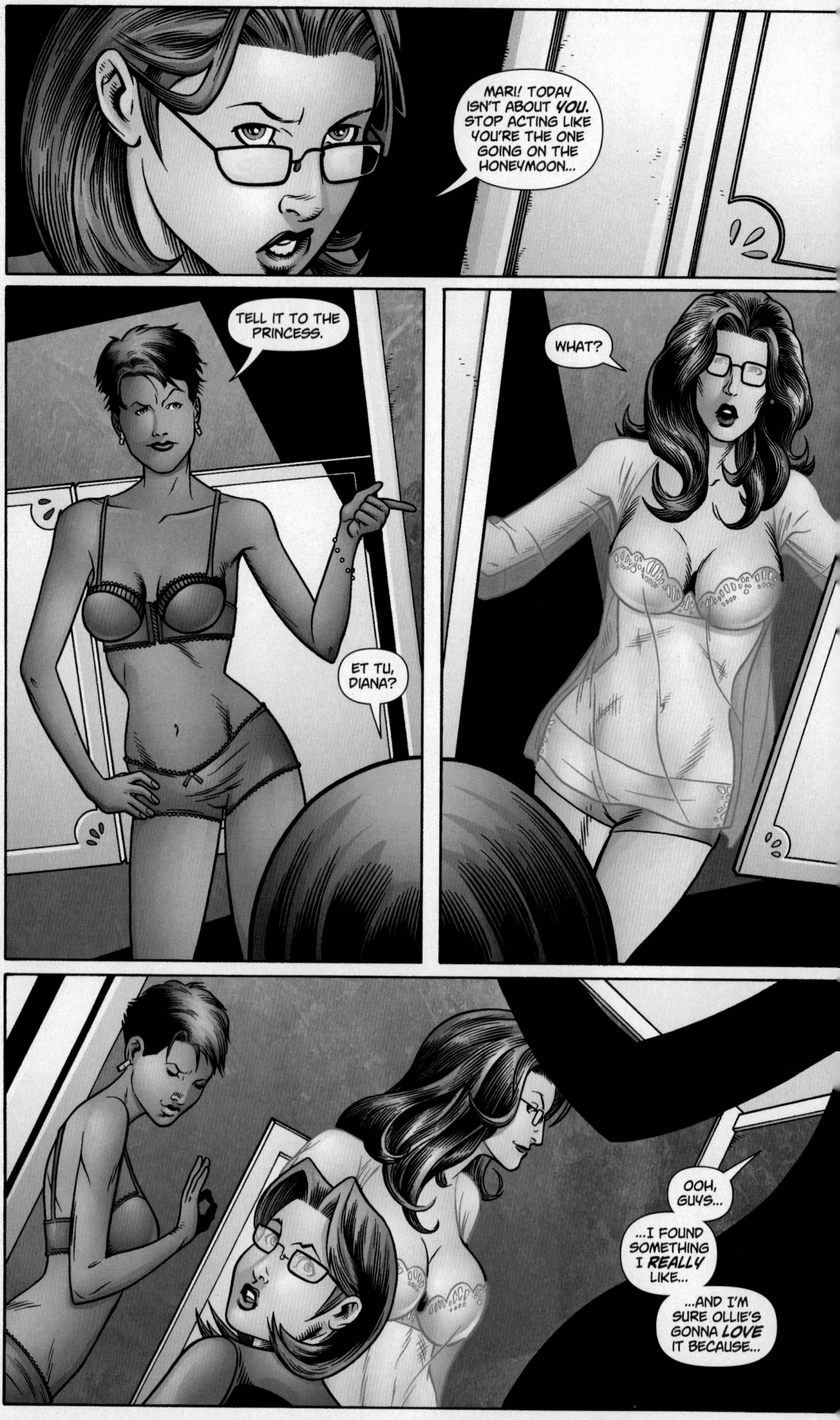
MARI! TODAY ISN'T ABOUT *YOU.* STOP ACTING LIKE YOU'RE THE ONE GOING ON THE HONEYMOON...
TELL IT TO THE PRINCESS.
WHAT?
ET TU, DIANA?
OOH, GUYS...
...I FOUND SOMETHING I *REALLY* LIKE...
...AND I'M SURE OLLIE'S GONNA *LOVE* IT BECAUSE...

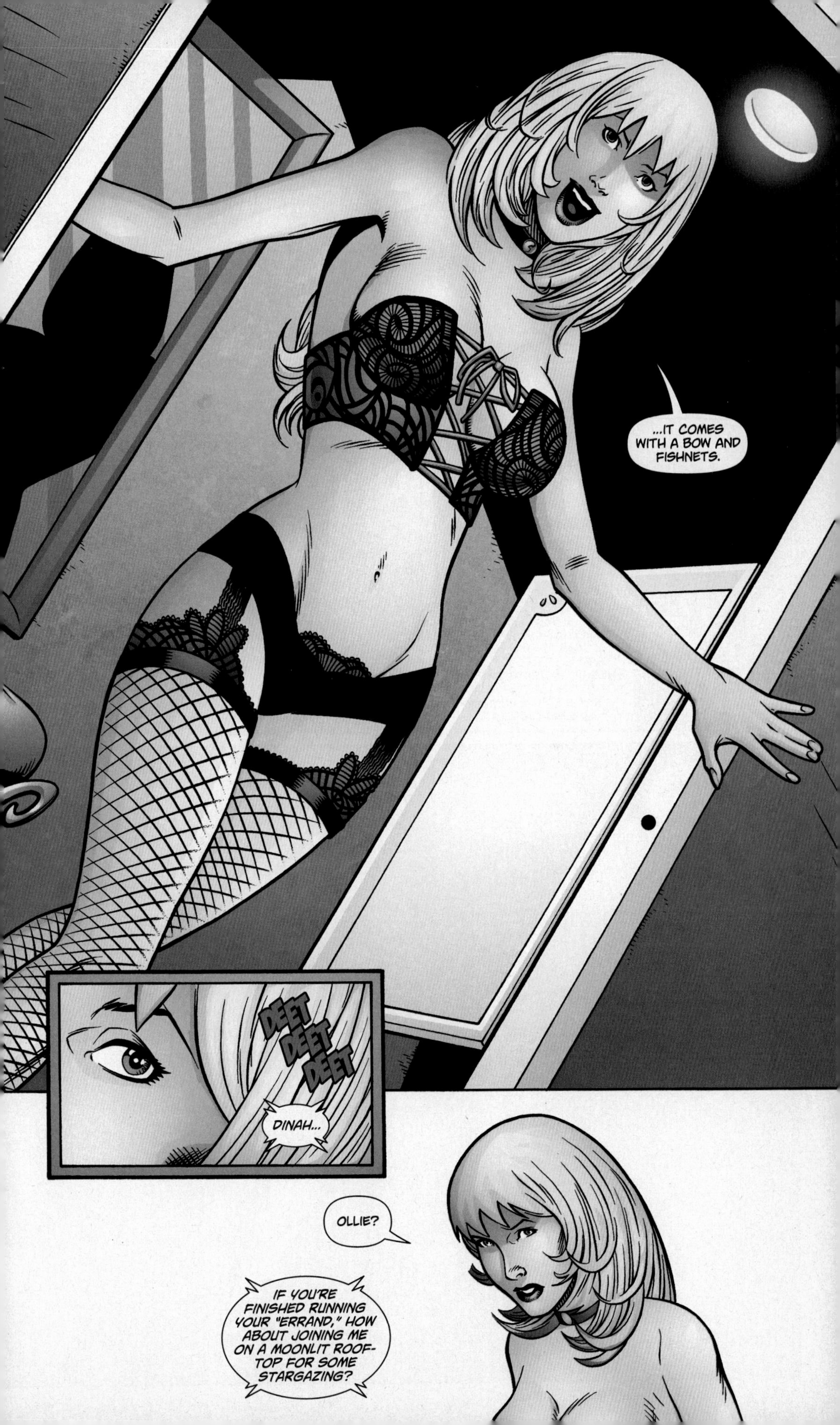
...IT COMES WITH A BOW AND FISHNETS.
DEET DEET DEET
DINAH...
OLLIE?
IF YOU'RE FINISHED RUNNING YOUR "ERRAND," HOW ABOUT JOINING ME ON A MOONLIT ROOF-TOP FOR SOME STARGAZING?

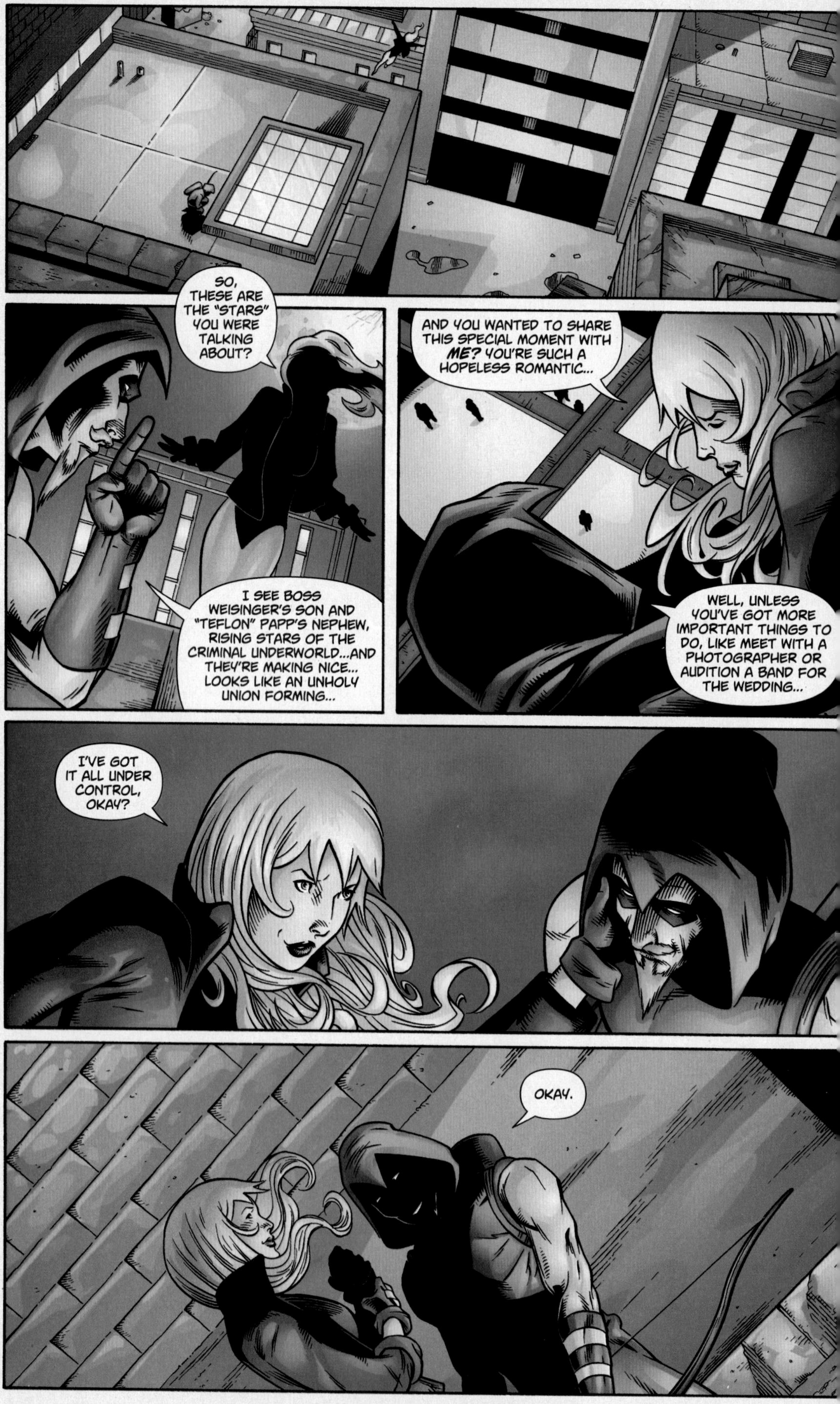
SO, THESE ARE THE "STARS" YOU WERE TALKING ABOUT?
I SEE BOSS WEISINGER'S SON AND "TEFLON" PAPP'S NEPHEW, RISING STARS OF THE CRIMINAL UNDERWORLD...AND THEY'RE MAKING NICE... LOOKS LIKE AN UNHOLY UNION FORMING...
AND YOU WANTED TO SHARE THIS SPECIAL MOMENT WITH ME? YOU'RE SUCH A HOPELESS ROMANTIC...
WELL, UNLESS YOU'VE GOT MORE IMPORTANT THINGS TO DO, LIKE MEET WITH A PHOTOGRAPHER OR AUDITION A BAND FOR THE WEDDING...
I'VE GOT IT ALL UNDER CONTROL, OKAY?
OKAY.

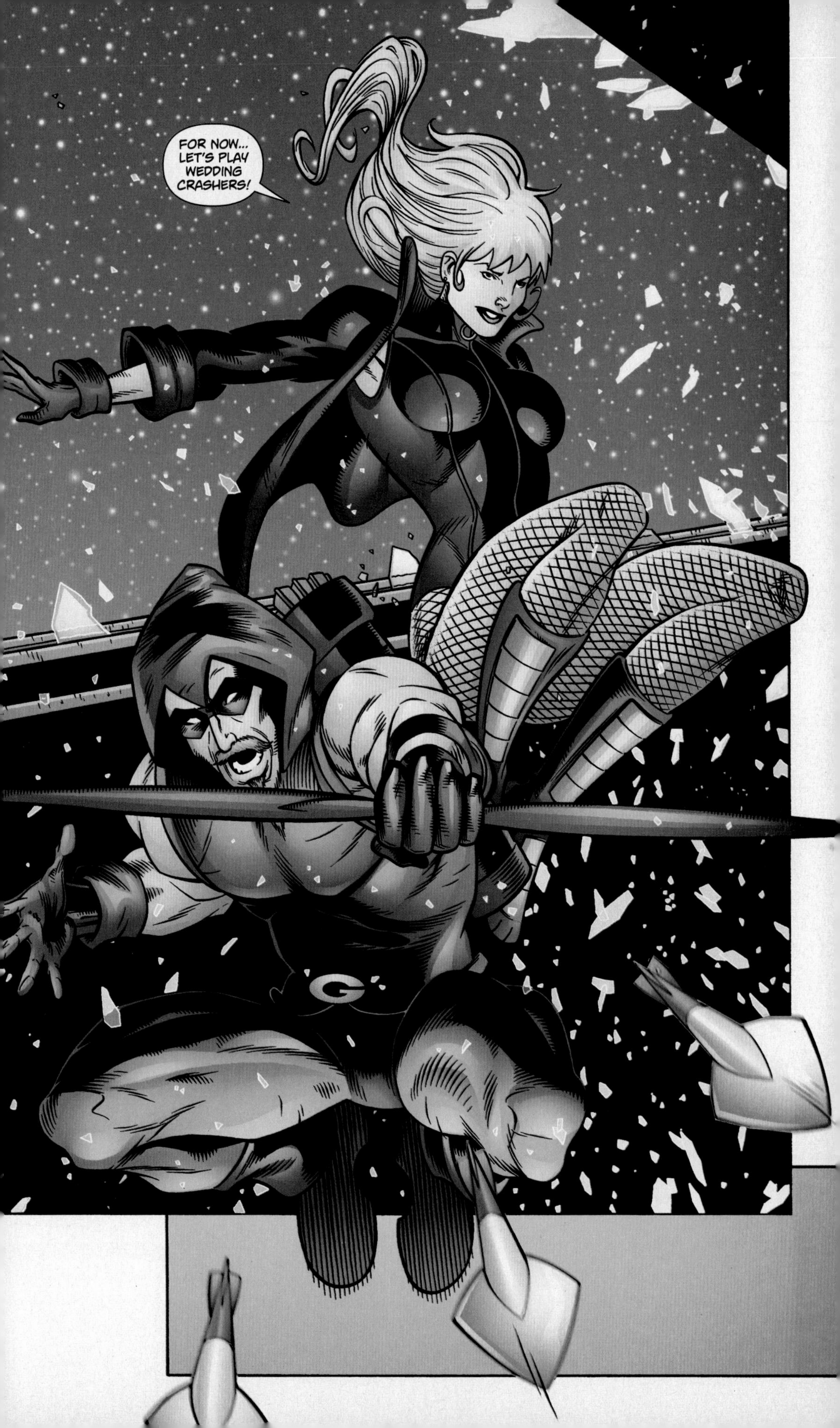
FOR NOW... LET'S PLAY WEDDING CRASHERS!

READ MORE ADVENTURES OF YOUR
FAVORITE HEROES IN THESE
COLLECTIONS FROM DC COMICS:

KINGDOM COME

Mark Waid and **Alex Ross** deliver a grim tale of youth versus experience, tradition versus change and what defines a hero. KINGDOM COME is a riveting story pitting the old guard — Superman, Batman, Wonder Woman and their peers — against a new uncompromising generation.

WINNER OF FIVE EISNER AND HARVEY AWARDS, INCLUDING BEST LIMITED SERIES AND BEST ARTIST

THE GREATEST SUPER HERO EPIC OF TOMORROW!

KINGDOM COME

Mark WAID   Alex ROSS

IDENTITY CRISIS

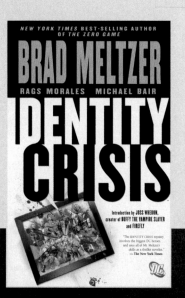

CRISIS ON INFINITE EARTHS

DC: THE NEW FRONTIER VOLUME 1

DARWYN
DAVE ST

DON'T MISS THESE OTHER GREAT TITLES FROM AROUND THE **DCU!**

SUPERMAN: BIRTHRIGHT

**MARK WAID
LEINIL FRANCIS YU
GERRY ALANGUILAN**

BATMAN: DARK VICTORY

**JEPH LOEB
TIM SALE**

WONDER WOMAN: GODS AND MORTALS

**GEORGE PÉREZ
LEN WEIN/GREG POTTER
BRUCE PATTERSON**

GREEN LANTERN: NO FEAR

**GEOFF JOHNS
CARLOS PACHECO
ETHAN VAN SCIVER**

GREEN ARROW: QUIVER

**KEVIN SMITH
PHIL HESTER
ANDE PARKS**

TEEN TITANS: A KID'S GAME

**GEOFF JOHNS
MIKE McKONE**

SEARCH THE GRAPHIC NOVELS SECTION OF

WWW.**DCCOMICS**.COM

FOR ART AND INFORMATION ON ALL OF OUR BOOKS!

DETECTIVE'S ADVENTURES
IN THESE COLLECTIONS
FROM DC COMICS:

BATMAN

BATMAN: HUSH VOLUME 1

Jeph Loeb, Jim Lee and **Scott Williams** tell an epic tale of friendship, trust and betrayal, in the first volume of a tale that spans a lifetime of the Dark Knight.

"THE ACTION IS EXCITING AND THE DETAIL IS METICULOUS."
— CRITIQUES ON INFINITE EARTHS

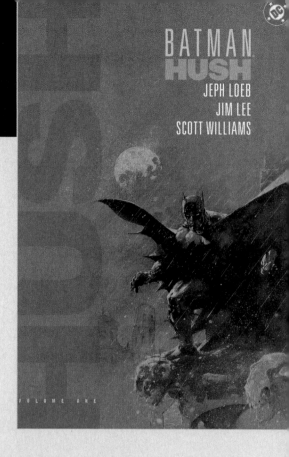

BATMAN HUSH
JEPH LOEB
JIM LEE
SCOTT WILLIAMS

VOLUME ONE

BATMAN:
THE DARK KNIGHT RETURNS

FRANK MILLER
KLAUS JANSON
LYNN VARLEY

BATMAN:
THE LONG HALLOWEEN

JEPH LOEB
TIM SALE

BATMAN:
YEAR ONE

FRANK MILLER
DAVID MAZZUCCHELLI

SEARCH THE GRAPHIC NOVELS SECTION OF
www.DCCOMICS.com
FOR ART AND INFORMATION ON ALL OF OUR BOOK